KU-577-021

# THE WOLF CUB'S HANDBOOK

BADEN-POWELL'S

# WOLF CUB'S HANDBOOK

*Published by arrangement with*
*The Boy Scouts Association*
*by*

C. ARTHUR PEARSON LTD.
TOWER HOUSE, SOUTHAMPTON STREET
STRAND, LONDON, W.C.2

| | | |
|---|---|---|
| *First published* . . | *December* | 1916 |
| *Second Edition* . . | *January* | 1918 |
| *Third Edition* . . | *October* | 1919 |
| *Fourth Edition* . . | *January* | 1921 |
| *Fifth Edition* . . | *March* | 1923 |
| *Sixth Edition* . . | *January* | 1925 |
| *Seventh Edition* . . | *June* | 1926 |
| *Reprinted* . . . | *October* | 1929 |
| *Reprinted* . . . | *May* | 1930 |
| *Eighth Edition* . . | *July* | 1931 |
| *Reprinted* . . . | *January* | 1934 |
| *Ninth Edition* . . | *December* | 1938 |
| *Tenth Edition* . . | *April* | 1941 |
| *Reprinted* . . . | *August* | 1943 |
| *Reprinted* . . . | *November* | 1944 |
| *Reprinted* . . . | *December* | 1945 |
| *Eleventh Edition* . . | *January* | 1949 |
| *Reprinted* . . . | *November* | 1949 |
| *Twelfth Edition* . . | *July* | 1952 |
| *Reprinted* . . . | *March* | 1954 |
| *Reprinted* . . . | *October* | 1955 |
| *Thirteenth Edition* . . | *April* | 1957 |
| *Fourteenth Edition* . | *July* | 1958 |
| *Fifteenth Edition* . . | *March* | 1960 |
| *Reprinted* . . . | *February* | 1961 |
| *Reprinted* . . . | *October* | 1962 |

*Printed for the Publishers, C. Arthur Pearson, Ltd., Tower House, Southampton Street, London, W.C.2, by C. Tinling & Co., Ltd., Liverpool, London and Prescot.*

# INTRODUCTION

EVERY boy, like every young Wolf, has a hearty appetite. This book is a meal offered by an old Wolf to the young Cubs.

There is juicy meat in it to be eaten, and there are tough bones to be gnawed.

But if every Cub who devours it will tackle the bone as well as the meat, and will eat up the fat with the lean, I hope that he will get good strength, as well as some enjoyment, out of every bite.

B.-P.

*To Rudyard Kipling, who has done so much to put the right spirit into our rising manhood, I am very grateful for the permission to quote as my text his inimitable "Jungle Book."*

*My thanks are also due to his publishers, Messrs. Macmillan and Co., Ltd., for their courtesy in allowing these extracts to be made.*

## THE LAW OF THE WOLF CUB PACK

1. The Cub gives in to the Old Wolf;
2. The Cub does not give in to himself.

## THE WOLF CUB'S PROMISE

I promise to DO MY BEST—

To do my duty to God, and the Queen,
To keep the Law of the Wolf Cub Pack, and to do a good turn to somebody every day.

# CONTENTS

## PART II

## PROFICIENCY BADGES

### AND HOW TO QUALIFY FOR THEM

## PART III

## OBJECTS AND METHODS OF WOLF CUB TRAINING

# THE WOLF CUB'S HANDBOOK

## PART I

## FIRST BITE

MOWGLI—THE WOLF CUBS—THE TEST OF THE ZULU BOY—BRITISH SCOUTS—THE COUNCIL ROCK AND CIRCLES—THE ALERT—THE GRAND HOWL—GAME: *Shere Khan and Mowgli.*

### NOTE TO THE CUBMASTER

*"The Jungle Books," by Rudyard Kipling, are the basis of the Wolf story which is our theme in the first few "bites." If you can read the books to the Cubs after giving the outline as above they will enjoy and appreciate its meaning all the more.*

ONCE upon a time, far away in India, a great big tiger was prowling about in the jungle trying to find food. Presently he came to a place where a wood-cutter and his family were camped, and he thought it would be a grand thing to get hold of a sleeping man or, better still, a fat child for his supper.

Although he was a great strong animal he was not very brave, and he did not want to face an armed man in the open.

So he crept up close to the camp fire, but in gazing at his prey he did not look carefully where he was putting his feet, and in crawling forward he trod on some hot embers.

The pain made him howl, which roused the camp, and he had to go limping away hungry.

One small boy ran off into the bushes to hide, and there he met a great grey Wolf. But the Wolf was a brave and kindly animal, and seeing that the child was not afraid of him he picked him up gently in his mouth as a dog does a puppy, and carried him into its cave close by.

Here the Mother Wolf took care of the child and put it among her family of cubs.

Shortly afterwards Tabaqui, that is the jackal, came to the tiger whose name was Shere Khan and said to him, " Mr. Tiger, I know where that small boy has gone to, and if you will kill him you might give me a nice little bit of him to eat as a reward for my telling you where to find him. He is in that little cave under the rock."

A jackal is a nasty sneaking kind of animal, who lets other animals do the hunting and killing, while he loafs about picking up the scraps.

So Shere Khan went to the mouth of the cave, and though he could put his head inside, the opening was too small for his body to get through, and the grey Wolf inside knew this and defied him.

The Wolf told him to go away and hunt for his food, and not to go trying to steal what other folk had captured; he must not break the Law of the Jungle which says that no animal shall kill a human being because it causes more men to come to the place to hunt out the murderer, and this brings trouble on all the animals in that jungle.

Shere Khan roared with anger, and wanted to bully the Wolf with threats of what he would do to him, when Mother Wolf suddenly joined in and told him to go about his business; that she would take care of the boy, and that some day the boy would grow up and kill Shere Khan if he was not careful.

So the boy remained with the Wolves and grew up as one of the family. They called him Mowgli—and they taught him all the tricks of the Jungle; how to run and how to hunt his game.

In this way he became brave and strong. Then they also took him to the Council meeting of the Pack of all the Wolves which was held at a certain rock.

As a young wolf he had lots to learn.

The first lessons are to make him quick and active, and for this he is allowed to hunt grasshoppers—to leap and snap, and twist and pounce after them. Then he is not given any food, but is shown that if he wants it he must go and hunt it for himself.

He tries his pouncing and rushing dodges on birds, but very soon finds that these do not pay. If he wants to kill, he must creep and crawl and stalk, and lie in wait. If he does not learn to do the business properly, he will starve to death. His dinner depends on himself.

It is just the same with a boy who wants to be a Scout. He must first of all learn all the scouting dodges and duties from old Scouts, who can teach him.

He, too, must make himself active and strong by games and exercises; he, too, must make his own way in life, but games will not do this for him. If he wants to succeed he must go about it carefully, learning all he can that will help him in whatever profession he takes up. His success will depend on himself, not on his masters or parents.

So make up your mind to be like the real Wolf Cub, and win your own success for yourself. Later on when you are a Scout you will learn how to do it when you are grown up.

### The Wolf Cubs

Young Scouts who are not quite old enough to join the Boy Scouts are called "Wolf Cubs." Why? For this reason: a Wolf Cub is a young Wolf. Scouts are called "Wolves," and young Scouts are therefore called "Wolf Cubs."

In the far Western prairies of America the Red Indians were a nation of scouts. Every man in the tribe was a pretty good scout. Nobody thought anything of him if he wasn't.

So there was great rivalry among the young braves as to who could be the best scout. And those who proved themselves best got the nickname of "Wolf."

There would be "Grey Wolf," or "Black Wolf," "Red Wolf," "Lean Wolf," and so on; but "Wolf" was the title of honour, meaning a real good scout.

If you went across the world to South Africa, though the people were entirely different (they were negro savages instead of Red Indians), you would find that they, too, were good scouts, and they, too, called their best scouts "Wolf."

A scout, as you know, is a man who is brave and strong, who willingly risks death in order to carry out his duty, who knows how to find his way over strange country by day or night, who can look after himself, light his fire, cook his own food; he can follow the tracks of animals or men, can see without being seen; at the same time he is helpful and kind to women and children, and, above all, he obeys the orders of his chief to the death.

In South Africa the finest of the tribes were the Zulus, with their offshoots the Matabele, the Swazis, and the Masai.

These were, every man of them, good warriors and scouts, because they learnt scouting while they were yet boys.

The boys of the tribe always went on the warpath when the men went, in order to carry the sleeping-mats and food for the warriors.

They did not fight themselves; they only looked on at a distance at the battles, and learnt how to behave when it should come to their turn. The smartest and best of the boys were the "Wolf Cubs," the future Wolf Scouts of the tribe.

### The Test of the Zulu Boy

But before they were allowed to become scouts and warriors they had to pass a pretty tough examination. This is what they had to do.

When a boy was becoming old enough to be a warrior he was taken and stripped of his clothing, and was painted white all over. He was given a shield with which to protect himself, and an assegai or small spear with which to kill animals or enemies. And he was then turned loose into the "bush."

If anyone saw him while he was still white they would hunt him and kill him; and that white paint took about a month to wear off—it would not wash off.

So for a month the boy had to hide away in the jungle, and live as best he could.

He had to follow the tracks of the deer, and to creep up near enough to spear the animal in order to get food and clothing for himself. He had to make fire to cook his food by rubbing two sticks together—he had no matches with him. Nor had he any pockets to put them in if he had them. He had to be careful not to let his fire smoke too much, or it would catch the eye of scouts on the look-out to hunt him.

He had to be able to run long distances, to climb trees, and to swim rivers in order to escape from his pursuers. He had to be brave, and stand up to a lion or any other wild animal that attacked him.

He had to know which plants were good to eat and which were poisonous, and how to cook them. He had, of course, to make his own cooking pots out of the bark of trees or of clay. He had to build himself a hut to live in, but well hidden.

He had to take care that wherever he went he left no foot tracks by which he could be followed up. If he snored when he was asleep, it would give him away to a keen-eared enemy. So he learnt to keep his mouth shut, and to breathe quietly through his nose.

For a month he had to live this life, sometimes in burning heat, sometimes in cold and rain.

When at last the white stain had worn off, he was able to return to his village, and then he was received with great joy, and was allowed to take his place among the young warriors of the tribe.

*From left to right you see an Um-fan (mat-boy), a young warrior, and a Ring-Kop veteran. These correspond to our Wolf Cubs, Boy Scouts and Scouters*

He could go on, and by his bravery get to be a " Ring-Kop " —that is, a real proved warrior, who was allowed to wear a ring on his head. Then he could possibly go on, and in the end earn the honourable title of " Wolf."

But you can magine that a good many boys who went out did not get through their white period at all; some got killed by wild animals, some got killed by the men, and numbers of them died of starvation or of cold, or got drowned. It was only the good ones among them who got through successfully—and thereby proved that they really were good men.

It was a pretty stiff exam.—wasn't it ?

### British Scouts

In our own country hundreds of years ago our scouts were the Knights—men who were ready to die for their duty, and who were sworn to be polite to old people, and generous and kind to women and children.

They, like the Zulus, first learnt their duties while boys—that is, as pages who attended on the Knights, and helped them to put on their armour. As these grew up into young men they became Esquires and learnt to ride and to use their weapons, and to carry out the laws of the Knights, so that they would be true Knights when they had proved themselves really good at their duty and worthy of promotion, just like the young warriors of the Zulus.

That was all hundreds of years ago, and lots of boys have said they only wish that the Knights lived now and carried on their duty as of old, and they themselves would be glad to become their pages and Esquires.

Well, so they do exist to-day in a way.

The men whom I look on as our Knights and scouts of to-day are the frontiersmen in the wilder parts of our Empire. The backwoodsmen, the hunters, the explorers, the map-makers, our soldiers and sailors, the Arctic navigators, the missionaries—all those men of our race who are living out in the wild, facing difficulties and dangers because it is their duty, enduring hardships, looking after themselves, keeping up the name of Britons for bravery, kindness, and justice all over the world—those are the scouts of the nation to-day—they are the "Wolves."

But they could not do it if they had not learnt their work thoroughly while they were still boys.

So the boys of the British Empire have the chance of learning how to become its scouts by being Boy Scouts first, just as in the old days the Esquires learnt how to become Knights.

Then, too, the young Scouts, the "Wolf Cubs," like the pages of old, preparing to be Esquires, can learn how to become Boy Scouts when they get to the right age for it.

In the bites that follow I am going to show you how to pick up the different Wolf Cub duties, such as tying knots and lighting fires, how to make yourself comfortable in camp, how to build your lair, how to find your way in a strange country, how to make things and grow things, how to do good turns to people and how to help in the case of accidents.

It doesn't matter whether you are a rich boy or a poor boy, whether in the country or in a town. You can learn these things quite easily if you go about it in the way I tell you.

## The Council Rock and Circles

When the wolf pack met in the jungle, Akela, the old wolf, stood on a great rock in the middle, and the pack sat in a circle all round it.

So with our Wolf Cub Pack, we may mark out the rock by a small circle of stones, or pegs, or with chalk, like this:

*The Rock Circle*, which may be used for yarns and pow-wows, is a small circle with the Cubs standing shoulder to shoulder.

When the pack is formed up in Rock Circle, the Cubmaster gives the command " Form Parade Circle." and each Cub holds hands with the Cub on either side and pulls outwards into a big circle.

This circle is used for the Grand Howl, for Jungle Dances and for rallies.

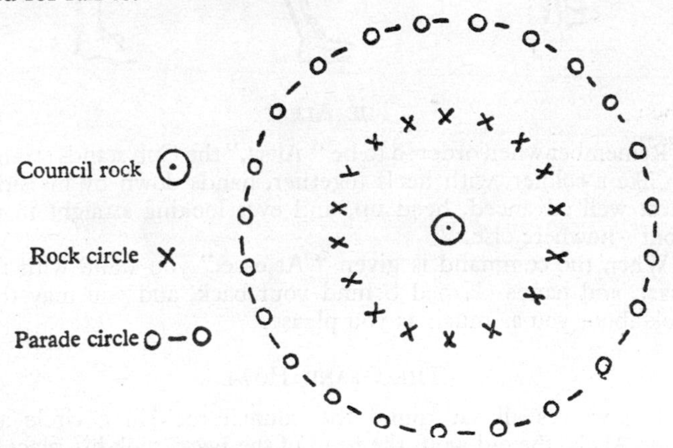


Whatever you may be doing, the moment that you hear the call of " Pack—Pack—Pack " every Cub at once answers by yelling " Pack ! " and by scampering at once to form the Parade Circle round the Cubmaster. If the Cubmaster only calls " Pack ! " once it means " Silence ! " and everyone must stop what they are doing and listen.

No one is allowed to call " Pack ! " except an Old Wolf. The Sixer may call his Six together by its Six colour.

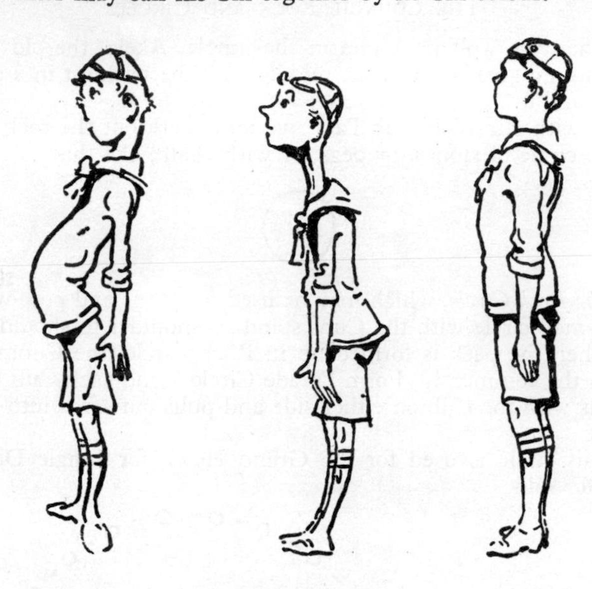

### THE ALERT

Remember when ordered to be " Alert," the Cub stands straight up like a soldier, with heels together, hands down by his sides, chest well advanced, head up, and eyes looking straight to the front—nowhere else.

When the command is given " At ease," you stand with feet apart, and hands clasped behind your back, and you may then look about you as much as you please.

### THE GRAND HOWL

The wolves all sat round the council rock in a circle and when Akela, the old wolf, the head of the pack, took his place on the rock they all threw up their heads and howled their welcome to him.

When your Old Wolf, Akela—that is your Cubmaster or other Scouter—comes to your meeting you salute him by squatting round in a circle as young wolves do, and giving him the Wolf Cub Grand Howl.

So, when Akela has called you into the Parade Circle and gives you the sign to start, you all squat down on your heels

with your two fore paws on the ground between your feet, knees out to either side like this:

Then you throw up your heads and howl. But the howl means something.

You want to welcome him, and at the same time to show that you are ready to obey his command.

The call of the Pack all over the world is " We'll do our best "; so to greet your Cubmaster you chuck up your chins and, all together, you howl out—making each syllable loud and long: " Ah—kay-la!—We-e-e-e-ll do-o-o-o o-o-u-u-r BEST." Yell the word " best " sharp and loud and short, and all together; and at the same time spring to your feet with two fingers of each hand pointing upwards at each side of your head, to look like two wolf's ears.

That's the way to do it.

Now what does it mean?

It means that you will do your best with BOTH hands—not merely with one like most boys, who only use their right hand. *Your* best will be twice as good as any ordinary boy's best. " Do your best " is the Cub's motto.

Then keep your two hands up while the leading Cub calls to the Pack, at the top of his voice: " Dyb—dyb—dyb—dyb " (meaning Do Your Best).

Then every Cub after the fourth " dyb " drops his left hand smartly to his side and keeping the right hand at the salute, with two fingers up, but now spread out making the salute (see page 26), squeals " We-e-e-ll " and barks out " Dob—dob—dob—dob " (We'll Do Our Best).

After the fourth " dob " each Cub drops his right hand smartly to his side and stands at the " Alert " and waits for orders.

Now squat down again and see how well you can do the Grand Howl to the Old Wolf.

### Game: Shere Khan and Mowgli

Father Wolf, Mother Wolf, and all the little wolves form a string one behind the other with Mowlgi, the smallest, as last in the string. Each catches hold of the waist of the one in front of him.

Then comes along Mr. Shere Khan, the tiger. He wants to catch Mowgli—but whenever he tries to get him Father Wolf put himself in the way to stop him, and all the string of wolves clinging to each other try to keep Mowgli safe behind them. Mowgli has a neckerchief hanging like a tail behind him from under his jersey, and if Shere Khan can get his tail within three minutes he wins the game, otherwise the wolves win.

# SECOND BITE

AKELA, BALOO AND BAGHEERA—THE NEW CHUM—THE SALUTE—THE TABAQUI DANCE—GAME: *Knock the Blob*—PRONUNCIATION OF JUNGLE NAMES.

Now I want to tell you some more about Mowgli and the Jungle Pack. Do you remember who the chief animals were?

*Akela* was the wise Old Wolf, the head of the Pack, who lay on the Council Rock and saw the younger Wolves all kept the Law of the Pack. He was like an older man who could teach boys what to do to make themselves strong and useful.

Akela is an Indian word, and it means "one who is alone." There can only be one Cubmaster leading the Pack, just as Akela was alone on the Council Rock. If there were several leaders in a Pack, they might all try to do different things at the same time, and some Cubs would follow one, and some another, until in the end your Pack would be like the Seeonee Pack of the Jungle Book, after the wolves set their old Akela aside and followed many leaders. After awhile, some of them were lame from the traps they had fallen into, some limped from shot wounds and some were mangy from eating bad food, and many were missing. If they had followed Akela, the one leader of the Pack, that would never have happened.

*Shere Khan* was the great bullying tiger, all stripes and teeth and claws; but, like most bullies among boys, was not very brave at heart if you only tackled him.

Then *Tabaqui* was the mean sneaking jackal who tried to make friends with everybody by flattering them; but he only wanted to get scraps from them. There are lots of boys like Tabaqui who will sneak or suck up to others hoping to get things given to them instead of working for them themselves.

So you see the animals in the jungle are very like human beings in their ways.

But there are more animals in the jungle than those I have told you about.

When Mowgli was brought to the Council Rock he had to be

made one of the Pack, which meant that he would have to be taught the laws and customs of the Pack before he could properly be made a member of it. So old *Baloo* the bear, who was a wise though fat and sleepy old beggar, was told off to teach him the laws. And *Bagheera* the great black panther, who was a strong and cunning hunter, was to teach him his hunting and jungle work.

So in your Pack I expect you will learn to call your Cubmaster "Akela," because he is your leader. If he has other grown-ups to help him, perhaps you will call them "Baloo" and "Bagheera." When you speak about all of them together, you can call them "Old Wolves."

Why not give some of the Cubs in your Pack special Jungle names! The Sixer of the Grey Six might be called "Grey Brother," for example; or the cheeriest Cub might be "Rikki-tikki-tavi" (or "Rikki," for short); or the Pack Scribe might be "Sahi' (the Porcupine).

## The New Chum

A boy who wants to be a Wolf Cub is called a "New Chum" or "Recruit" until he has learnt the Laws of the Pack, the Promise, the Salute, and the Grand Howl and their meaning. Then he is admitted to be a Tenderpad, and to wear the uniform of the Wolf Cubs.

He is called a Tenderpad because when he goes out to catch his prey or to play in the Jungle, from not knowing how to do it he runs wildly and loses his way and soon gets tired and his poor feet or "pads" get sore and tender.

But as soon as he knows a few of the dodges he becomes a full-blown Cub.

## The Salute

Now for the secret sign by which Cubs salute their Cubmasters and other Cubs, and Scouts, too.

You have learnt "the Grand Salute" which you use when doing the Grand Howl to an Old Wolf, but if you meet him or speak to him at any time you use the *ordinary salute.*

You do it in this way, with the right hand only, fore-finger touching the cap.

Why two fingers up?

Well, you know what a Wolf's head looks like with his two ears cocked up.

It is used on the Badge of the Wolf Cub.

Your two fingers in the salute are the two ears of the Wolf.

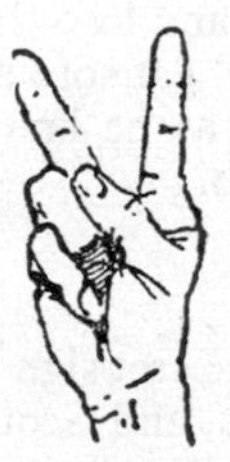

When you meet another Cub or a Scout, or anyone wearing the buttonhole badge of a Scout or Cub, give him or her the *salute*.

### The Tabaqui Dance

*Tabaqui* is the jackal, a sneaking sort of fellow. He is afraid to go about alone, so he always keeps near his fellow jackals although he tries to look like a Wolf, he never hunts or earns his food like one, but sneaks about trying to steal or beg it from others. Then when he has got it he is not a bit grateful, but runs about yapping and yelling, disturbing the game and making a regular nuisance of himself. There are lots of boys like Tabaqui who rush about yelling and making little asses of themselves and bothering people, always ready to beg for a penny or a bit of grub, but never anxious to do any work. They are quite ready to jeer or throw mud at people if they are at a safe distance away, but are awful little cowards really.

*Mowgli and Shere Khan.*

I hope no Cub will ever deserve to be called Tabaqui.

Then there is *Shere Khan*. He was the big ferocious-looking tiger. An awful bully. He was not clever enough to hunt and catch wild game, so he used to sneak about near a village and kill poor little calves and goats, and even a defenceless old man—if he could catch him asleep. Otherwise he was desperately afraid of a man.

Well, the Tabaqui thought a tremendous lot of Shere Khan. They followed him about, and though he bullied them they kept telling him he was King of the Jungle and the finest fellow on earth. Of course they did this in order that he should give them a bit of his kill when he was eating it. I have known Shere Khans among boys—big ferocious-looking boys who bullied the smaller ones in order to get what they wanted out of them, but they were arrant cowards really if the small boy would only stick up to them.

In the Tabaqui Dance the Pack is divided into two sections. Half of the Cubs—with a leader who is Shere Khan—are the Tabaqui, the others are the Wolves who, of course, have Mowgli with them.

The Tabaqui and Shere Khan do their parts first, so while the Wolves lie in wait at one end of the room (or field), the jackals form a circle round Shere Khan who prances proudly in the centre; swaggers for all he is worth; and seems to challenge any and everyone to come on and fight. " I'm Shere Khan, the Tiger King," he snarls, and the jackals, as they move around him, murmur " Jackal, Jackal."

Suddenly a Tabaqui leaves the circle, sneaks up to Shere Khan and bows most humbly to him. Shere Khan, just for the bullying fun of the thing, aims a kick at his follower. The jackal dodges the kick, bows low again as if to say " Thank you " and runs back to his place. All this time he has been where Shere Khan can see him, but when he gets behind the tiger a great change comes over him—he stops cringing (that is, bending humbly) and makes a face at Shere Khan.

They're a nice Cubby set of people, aren't they? But look! The Wolves are moving. They sweep down on the Tabaqui and each of them carries off one of these little sneaks. When the noise and scuffle has died away, and the Wolves with their captives are lying quiet again, Shere Khan, who was just a little nervous during the tumult, looks around him, sees that he is alone and thinks to himself " I'm greater than ever *I* thought I was." " I'm Shere Khan, the Tiger King," he roars, hoping that all the Jungle Folk will hear and believe him. The Jungle Folk might believe him, but Mowgli has always known the tiger to be just a cowardly bully. He comes across now, very slowly, with one arm outstretched (a finger pointing) and his eyes on those of the tiger. Shere Khan cannot look at Man. He is afraid, and though he goes on saying that he is the Tiger King, he gradually cringes down till he is flat at Mowgli's feet.

The Dance is over, and the whole Pack rushes in to form Parade Circle.

You may feel that it is rather a difficult dance, but it is well worth trying, for keen Cubs can make it very real and exciting. Others can, of course, spoil it altogether by playing about and not even trying to act. The whole success or failure rests on one thing, Cubs; you either want to show that you, for one, don't like sneaks or bullies, or you haven't worried to think!

### Game: Knock the Blob

Set up a block of wood on end, about two feet high, so as to be easily knocked over, but which a boy can skip over; or a football will do. The Cubs form a circle round it, and, hand-in-hand, they try by pulling hard to drag one or other of their number on to knock over the block. If they succeed, out he goes till the final winner is found.

### Pronunciation of Jungle Names

Some of the names in *The Jungle Book* are difficult to say. I will try to help you.

Akela. Ah-kay-lah. *Ah* and *kay* are easy, so is the *lah* you sing when you are having your singing lesson—Doh, ray, me, fah, soh, lah.

Bagheera. Bah-gheer-ah. First *Bah*, like a sheep. then *Gear* (motor cars have them), and lastly *Ah*.

Baloo. Bah-loo. First *Bah*, as in Bagheera, then *Loo*, the last part of Water-loo.

Bandarlog. Bun-der-loag. The *Ban* is pronounced *Bun* (you all know how to say Bun, I know); the *Dar* is like *Dirt* without the final T, and *Log* is like the first part of *Log*anberry.

Kaa. Pronounced like *Car*, but letting the R be scarcely sounded at all.

Mowgli. Mou-gly. The first part of *Mou*(th), and the *Gli* from glitter.

Seeonee. Say-oh-knee.

Shere Khan. Share-Kharn. Shere is said just like a *share* of anything. Khan is "*can't*" without the final *t*.

Tabaqui. Tar-bark-i. *Tar* and *Bark* are pronounced just as they are spelt, but *i* sounds like the letter *e*.

# THIRD BITE

THE WOLF LEARNS HIS WORK—THE WOLF IS OBEDIENT—THE LAW OF THE WOLF CUB PACK—THE BALOO DANCE—THE BAGHEERV DANCE—MOTHERING DAY—GAME: *Sentry-Go*—PLAYING THE GAME.

## THE WOLF LEARNS HIS WORK

HAVE you ever read the book called *White Fang*, a story by Jack London?

It is awfully good, and describes the life of a young wolf. How, as a little cub, he just tottered out of the cave where his mother lived and began to learn things.

A squirrel running round the base of a tree-trunk came suddenly upon him, and gave him a great fright. He cowered down and snarled. But the squirrel was just as badly scared, and scampered up the tree out of his reach. Then he tried to catch a ptarmigan but she pecked him on the nose and frightened him off.

Later, his mother showed him how to lie low, and to stalk his game quietly and patiently, and then to strike with lightning rapidity with his teeth. Hunting a porcupine was as good a lesson as any for a wolf cub.

*Porcupine hunting is a good lesson for a Wolf Cub.*

The porcupine, directly he is alarmed, curls up like a hedgehog, with his quills bristling in every direction, and he is able, with a flip of his tail, to jab some of these sharp darts into the face and mouth of a wolf or other animal attacking him.

The old wolf, who has been wounded in this way, is not going to be caught again. He knows that he must lie without a move—almost without breathing—perhaps for an hour, before the porcupine, thinking the coast is clear, will begin to unroll himself, and then he will do so very, very slowly and cautiously.

So Mr. Wolf will watch and wait until the animal is completely uncurled, and then he will strike on the instant, to rip its unprotected side open before it can double itself up to protect itself.

When you have a big difficulty before you, think of the wolf and the porcupine, and do not be in a hurry to settle it. Use patience. Like the native of the West Coast of Africa catching a monkey. He says: " No good try run and grab him. No, sir; softly—softly catchee monkey! "

In the story of " White Fang " the young wolf gets caught by some Indians, and becomes quite tame through living with them. But when the famine comes, and the tribes have no food to give to their many dogs about the camp, these poor animals go off into the woods to hunt for food for themselves.

The result is that, being civilised dogs, accustomed to having their food given them, they do not know how to hunt properly, and most of them die of starvation, or get killed and eaten by the wild wolves.

But " White Fang " having begun as a wolf cub, is able to hunt on his own account, and so keep himself alive and well, until one day he finds the camp with the smell of meat cooking at the fires, and he knows that the famine is over, and he returns to his old master again.

But that which happened to the dogs is very much what happens to boys when they go out into the world pioneering. If they have never learnt, while they were boys, to look after themselves, and to make their own way, they will not succeed; but those

who have, as Cubs or Scouts, been taught all the useful dodges for getting on, will go out and make a big success of it.

So try hard to pick up all the knowledge you can while you are a Wolf Cub. Try to pass all the tests, and win the badges that are given for being clever at the game. It will be useful to you afterwards, when you want to be a real Scout.

I have seen wolf families going about, the two parent wolves stalking in front, with cubs trotting along behind on their tracks. It is quite certain that the old wolves teach their cubs most carefully all the tricks and dodges which make them such splendid hunters and so difficult for a man to catch. They are the cleverest and most cunning of all the wild animals, and it is for this reason that the men who prove themselves the best scouts are very properly called "Wolves."

### The Wolf is Obedient

There are many things that wolves teach to their cubs which human Wolf Cubs might very well learn, too.

You may see several cubs playing about snapping at butterflies and tumbling over each other in play. One of them may begin to toddle off to look out for adventures.

The old mother wolf has been lying near with her head resting along her forepaws. Suddenly she will raise her head, and stare hard at the wanderer. In a moment he will stop and look at her, and an instant later will come trotting back. Nothing is said, there is no sound, but the sharp young cub understands what is wanted of him, and does it at once. That is obedience.

It is what the human Wolf Cubs might do, too—see what is wanted of them, and do it without waiting to be told or ordered.

That is how wolves, when they grow up, become such good hunters. The pack work together, and obey the orders of the chief wolf. Each one of them, when hunting a hare or a buck, would be glad to seize it and eat it for himself, but the chief wolf would not allow this.

The pack have their different duties, just like a team of football players. Those who first find the buck have to run quickly ahead of him to head him off from the refuge he wants to make for, while those following behind run easily, so that if the leading wolves become tired, they can then go on in their places, and run the buck down.

If he is a fighting buck, with horns, and turns on them with his back to a rock, they form up round him, and calmly sit down and wait for their chance. One or two will pretend to attack him, and when he rushes at them some of the others will dart in and pin him from behind.

Or, when hunting some shy animal, some of the pack will keep driving him forward slowly, without attempting to rush him, as he might be too quick for them.

But while they are going slowly, they send one or two of their best hunters round at a great pace on to the path ahead of him. There they hide themselves, and await his coming. The hunted one, thinking only of the enemies who keep for ever quietly following along behind him, forgets to keep a good look-out ahead, and suddenly finds himself attacked and borne down by the new foes.

So, you see, wolves in a pack all have their parts to play; they obey the wishes of the chief wolf of the band just like players in a football team play up to the wishes of their captain. He does not have to shout his orders to them.

When you are playing you do not expect the captain to tell you every time you are to make a rush, or when to pass the ball to someone else on your side; you do all that for yourself. You know what the captain wants of you, and you do the right thing without waiting to be told. You " play the game " not only to amuse yourself, but so as to help your side to win.

That, after all, is the main duty of a Scout—to " play the game."

## THE LAW OF THE WOLF CUB PACK

### *1. The Cub gives in to the Old Wolf.*

In the jungle the old wolf is wise and knows what is best for successful hunting, so every cub obeys him always and at once. Even when the old wolf is out of sight the cub obeys his orders because it is the business of every wolf in the pack to " play the game " honourably.

And so it is in *our* Wolf Cub Pack. The Cub obeys the orders of his father or mother or master, whether they are there or not to see him do it. The smallest Cub can always be trusted at all times to do his best to carry out what he knows the older people want.

### *2. The Cub does not give in to himself.*

When the young wolf is hunting a hare to get meat for himself or for his pack, he may find that he is getting tired and wants to stop; but if he is of the right sort he will not give in to himself, he will "stick to it" and will keep pressing on; he will do his best and have another try. In the end he will find that the hare is just as tired as himself—and he will get his dinner.

So in our Pack. A Cub may be given a job to do, such as to skip or to learn to swim; he may find it difficult or tiring, and if he had his way he would like to chuck it. But a Cub does not give in to himself, he will stick to it and have another try; he will *do his very best*, and in the end he will succeed all right.

Now when you go home try and remember the things that you have learnt, because as a Cub you will always be practising them, namely:—

The Rock Circle and the Parade Circle,
The Grand Howl,
The Salute,
And the Two Laws of the Cubs.

THE BALOO DANCE

Now we will form the Parade Circle, and try the dance of BALOO, the bear. He was the animal in *The Jungle Book* who taught the Law of the Jungle to Mowgli. He was a good-natured, burly old thing, very like a big policeman.

When therefore the order "Baloo" is given, every Cub will

turn to the right and follow his leader, marching very slowly and stiffly, as proud as Punch, with his stomach forward, and his elbows stuck out, chin in the air, looking left and right in a haughty way; and as he goes along he gives out the two Cub Laws in a loud voice, so that everybody shall know them—" The Cub gives in to the Old Wolf; the Cub does not give in to himself."

When the Cubmaster gives the signal or order to halt, the Cubs at once stop, turn inwards, and become themselves, standing strictly at the " Alert " till they get further orders.

Other forms of this dance may be found in the pamphlet on " Jungle Dances and their Variations." Here is one of them which one of your Old Wolves (and especially your Baloo, if you have one) may like to act with you.

The Cubs squat in their lairs (six corners). Baloo (preferably an Old Wolf or a Cub Instructor) ambles, bear-like, into the centre of the clearing (hall or open space) and squats down.

BALOO (calling)—" Little brothers! Little brothers! "

CUBS (running from their lairs and squatting, as for the Grand Howl, in a circle round him)—" Baloo-oo-oo."

BALOO—" Little brothers, this is the Law of the Wolf Cub Pack—' The Cub gives in to the Old Wolf, the Cub does not give in to himself'." (While Baloo is speaking, the Cubs look at one another and nod in assent).

(The Cubs then crawl round in their circle, clockwise and say the following words twice, keeping movement and words in time).

CUBS—" We *hear* the *Law*, we *hear* the *Law*, and we'll *learn* the *Law*, we'll *learn* the *Law*." (Repeat).

(The Cubs then turn to face Baloo, sitting back on their heels and giving emphasis to the underlined words by hitting one fist into the palm of the other hand).

CUBS—" And we'll *do* our *best*, Baloo, to *keep* the *Law*." (An extra big thump is given on the word ' keep ').

BALOO—" Well said, little brothers, well said." (Then turning to any Cub he chooses in the circle)—" Little brother, what is the second Cub Law? "

CUB—" The Cub does not give in to himself."

(Baloo repeats this question to another Cub, or to two more if the circle is large. To any of the answers throughout, he may reply—" That's right! ", " Good! ", etc., if he chooses).

BALOO (to a different Cub)—" What is the meaning of this Law? "

CUB—" Think first of others."

BALOO (to another Cub)—" And? "

CUB—" Keep on trying."

(These questions and answers are repeated as above).

BALOO (to another Cub)—" What is the first Cub Law? "

CUB—" The Cub gives in to the Old Wolf."

(Question and answer repeated as above).

BALOO—" Now, little brothers, all together—What is the meaning of the first Cub Law? "

CUBS (quickly changing from sitting on their heels to the squatting position and throwing up their heads like a dog howling)—" Obey-ey-ey. Obey-ey-ey. Obey-ey-ey."

(Baloo then waves them away and they scamper back to their lairs, while Baloo ambles out of the clearing again.

Baloo should see to it that as many different Cubs as possible are asked a question).

### THE BAGHEERA DANCE

BAGHEERA was the black panther who could climb trees, or creep silently and quite unseen in the shadows by night. He was the crafty and skilful hunter, brave and enduring.

Although he could be fierce and terrible when he liked, he had a kind heart, and he taught Mowgli how to hunt and get his food.

For the *Bagheera Dance* each Cub becomes a panther.

The Pack being in the Parade Circle, each Cub moves along in a crouching position, looking out to the right and left for game to hunt. Suddenly game is in sight. Every Cub squats down, turning his head and gazing towards the centre of the circle, where he must imagine there is a deer feeding. In order not to be seen, he quietly gets on to all fours, and turns towards the centre, and then crawls backwards a few paces, in order to get a little further away from the deer, so as not to frighten him. Then every Cub begins to crawl slowly towards the centre. As they get nearer, all creep closer to the ground and more slowly. When they get near, all lie flat till the leader says "Now!" when they all spring forward on to the imaginary deer with a yell, seize him and tear him to pieces. They all fall outwards and run jumping back to their places in the Parade Circle, carrying and biting imaginary lumps of deer meat.

During the dance every Cub must watch the leader, and instantly do the same thing as he does.

## Mothering Day

One of the first Wolf Cub Packs to become efficient was the 1st Westminster, which adopted my son Peter as its chief, although he was then only a few months old. He attended a meeting of the Pack and marched along the front of the ranks—(in his nurse's arms!).

I think one of the most interested onlookers at the meeting was my aged mother, who was then in her ninetieth year. When the Cubs gave her three cheers, as she sat in her window, she was much affected, and she told me how much she wanted to thank them. She felt that, as they were her grandchild's "own," they were her own grandchildren.

Talking of my mother, I should like to remind Wolf Cubs of an old English custom which they would do well to keep up as part of their duty to their parents—the Old Wolves of the First Cub Law. It is this:—

On a certain day in the year, everyone used to pay a special honour to his mother. For the Protestant and the Roman Catholic religions it was on the Sunday in mid-Lent. But for boys who did not belong to those particular forms of religion, it would do just as well, if not better, to keep it on their mother's birthday.

The thing to do is on that day to give or send to your mother a little present, just as a mark of honour and affection.

If she is dead, you can put a few flowers on her grave—or, if you are far away from where she is buried, you can send a little money to the clergyman of the parish, and ask him to have the flowers put there. Or do something that you know she would like you to have done.

In any case, it is a good thing specially to think of and honour her who brought you into the world, and who nursed you and brought you up. Try to do things that will make her feel proud that you are her son, and never do anything that would cause her to feel grieved or ashamed. She has done much for you; do this for her.

### Game: Sentry-go

You will remember the story of the young French soldier who was on guard in the forest one dark night, when suddenly he found himself surrounded by the enemy. A bayonet was pressed against his chest, and a harsh whisper in his ear said:

" One word and you are dead! "

By keeping still and doing nothing he could save his life; but he took a big breath and shouted the alarm with all his might.

As he lay on the ground dying, and heard the bugles sound the alarm, and the noise of the regiment rushing to arms, he knew that by giving his life he had saved his comrades—so he died happy.

In the same way every man who is an explorer, a soldier, or Scout, has to Be Prepared to go through danger and hardship for the sake of his companions; and, sometimes, even, he has to be ready, like the young soldier, to die for them.

Often, too, it is very dull and uninteresting work that he has to do for them.

At the end of a long day's march, with sore feet and aching body, he has to do his spell of sentry-go round the camp while his friends sleep. However dead-beat he may be, he still keeps on the watch for enemies, wild beasts, or other dangers, for he knows his comrades sleep because they trust to his alertness.

Nor would he ever think of waking up the next man who is on duty one minute before the proper time, for no good Scout is a shirker. It is far more often that he tries to do *more* than his share of work for the others.

It is just the same whether he is risking his life for his comrades or washing up the pots after supper for them. He is always ready and willing to do things which a shirker would leave with the murmur of " It's not *my* job! "

In the same way a Wolf Cub here at home is always ready to do his bit of work for the Pack—scrubbing the floor of the Den, putting a bulb in the electric light, or whatever happens to want doing.

Here is a game in which one boy does the dull work of " sentry-go," while the others have a more active and enjoyable time. He does it because it is his duty.

Two Sixes take part. Cubs on one side wear a piece of red wool round their arm, and the other blue wool.

One red Cub is given a place from which he is easily seen all round. He continues walking up and down on a certain beat of ten yards.

On his chest, slung round his neck like a sandwich-board, he wears a card not less than twelve inches square, with a design on it.

Every time he completes ten beats he changes it for another design. He has altogether a supply of six cards with a different design on each, which might be something like this:

+ Z □ O V Φ

The blue Cubs have to crawl near without being seen, and make written notes of the design as they appear in turn.

On another beat a blue Cub is in the same way doing sentry-go with another lot of designs, and the red Cubs are spying on him and making a report.

The sentries do nothing except walk up and down and change their cards, but the rest can capture one another by snatching away the coloured wool from their arms.

The moment a boy loses the wool he is " dead," and out of action for the rest of the game.

There is no limit as to where Cubs may be placed, but Akela decides as to how many Cubs shall be told off to capture the other side, and how many shall go and spy on the enemy's sentry, and read his signals or card signs.

At the end of the game, the umpire takes in all the reports and counts up how many correct reports there are. Every one of the six designs that is correctly down on a Cub's report counts as one mark to his side, and Cubs are put on their honour not to compare their reports with one another.

Perhaps some of you may think that the sentry will have rather a poor time, but is is good practice for him in learning to do his share of the work for others without getting much fun out of it for himself.

He will just say:

" It's all in the day's work."

### Playing the Game

Even wild beasts like wolves have some sense of duty and of "playing the game" for the good of others.

For instance, one wolf will go into a piece of bush country and thoroughly hunt it out, moving backwards and forwards through it, silently pushing his way through the difficulties, driving the rabbits, buck, and birds before him, without trying to rush in and catch them for himself.

Out near the end of the wood, or close by a runway, the other wolves are lying hid, comfortably waiting there till the game is driven within reach of them, so that they can pounce out and catch it.

If one wolf can show such an example of unselfish work to help the others, surely you, a human Wolf Cub, can do the same among your companions, and "play the game" so that they may be the better for it, even though you may have a poor time yourself in helping them.

# FOURTH BITE

MOWGLI AND THE BANDARLOG—KAA—THE WOLF CUB PROMISE—DOING YOUR DUTY—THE GOOD TURN—THE CUB GRIN—THE HUNGER DANCE OF KAA.

## Mowgli and the Bandarlog

A LONG time ago, when I was going to India for the first time, my elder brother, who had been there, taught me that the correct way of addressing an Indian gentleman was to say to him: "Choop u bunder ke butcha jao," which, he said, meant "Good morning, sir!"

When I used it to the Indian gentlemen I found they did not like it, and when I enquired more carefully into what it meant, I found that it did not mean "good morning" at all, but that I was saying to them, "Shut up, you son of a monkey, and get out!"

You may call a boy "a young monkey" in England and it means very little, but to call a man "a monkey" in India is the greatest insult you can put upon him.

Some of you have been lucky enough to read Rudyard Kipling's yarns in *The Jungle Book*. One of them tells of Mowgli's adventure with the monkeys—or Bandarlog. Mowgli is a boy who has been brought up with the wolves, has become one of the pack, and is very friendly with all the animals of the jungle.

He once said to Baloo the bear and Bagheera the panther that he rather liked the Bandarlog—they were so lively and cheerful.

But Baloo explained that he was quite wrong, and that he ought to have nothing to do with the Bandars. They have no law like the wolves have; they only use talk which they have overheard from others; they think themselves very funny and clever, but really they know nothing and are silly; they boast a great deal about what they are going to do, but they never do anything; they chatter and talk instead of working; they are evil and dirty.

No one in the jungle will have anything to do with them. They are cowardly and get away into the trees and throw nuts and sticks at wounded animals. They never can remember anything; they are always going to have splendid laws of their own, but they always forget them.

I think that we can sometimes find boys who ought to be among the Bandarlog—who chatter and talk a lot and do very little; who are dirty and untidy; who are cowardly and spiteful, and who obey no laws and have no discipline such as the Wolf Cubs have.

One day the Bandarlog got hold of Mowgli. They had watched him through the trees while he was building a little house for himself out of branches and creepers, and they thought what a fine thing it would be to get him to teach them to make their own houses.

So one day, when he was sleeping, they crept down and seized him, and two of the strongest of them, grasping him by the arms, dashed up into the tree-tops with him, and then rushed him along between them for miles, leaping from tree to tree, and taking him away from his friends.

Now and then he got glimpses of the earth, far below between the branches, as they dragged him through the leaves and twigs. Now and then they would spring across an open space from one tree to another, landing with a jerk on a waving bough.

And then with a cough and a whoop they would fling themselves into the air, outward and downward, and spring up suddenly, hanging by their hands on the lower branches of the next tree.

So, bounding and crashing, whooping and screeching, the whole tribe of Bandarlog swept along the tree-top roads with Mowgli as their prisoner.

As he went he gave the Jungle Call to the other animals for help, and, high up in the sky above him, Chil, the kite, saw what was going on, and watched where the monkeys took him to and then told it to Baloo and Bagheera.

These two struggled through the forest as well as they could in the direction which the monkeys had taken, but Baloo was old and slow and could not keep up with the Bandarlog.

### Kaa

Then they came across Kaa, the great serpent. He was a good-natured, slow old thing, and badly wanted his dinner, so was easily persuaded to join in the hunt of the Bandarlog. Bagheera further told him that these monkeys had spoken insultingly of him, calling him a " footless yellow earthworm."

Old Kaa was not easily roused, but this disrespect made him

very angry, and when Baloo said, " Will you not come and help to catch the monkeys ? " he said, " I think I will, especially as they called me ' Yellow Fish.' Fish indeed! "

"It was far worse than that," said Bagheera, " worm—worm —footless yellow earthworm they called you."

Kaa was now thoroughly roused to join in with Baloo and Bagheera, and they made their way to an old ruined town where the monkeys lived and liked to play at being men.

Bagheera, in his keenness, got ahead of the other two, and when he saw the monkeys gather round Mowgli he dashed in and boldly attacked them.

But there were thousands of them, and they all rushed for him at once and soon overwhelmed him, and he was obliged to take refuge in a deep pool of water, until Baloo came up and also tackled them.

Then there was a glorious fight; but in order to make sure that Mowgli should not be taken from them, the monkeys took him on to the roof of a small summer-house and dropped him down through a hole into the place from which there was no escape. He found it full of poisonous snakes, but he at once gave the jungle hiss of the snake, and they became friendly and did him no harm.

Bagheera and Baloo were having a rough time and were getting rather the worst of it in battle, when old Kaa appeared upon the scene, and, gathering all his strength, he rushed for the crowd of monkeys and butted in with his hard head, knocking them right and left, and frightening them still more with his hiss, for the monkeys all knew that they were the favourite food of the python, and in terror they turned and fled.

Then the three faithful animals turned to get Mowgli out of his prison, and Kaa succeeded in doing it by gathering up his enormous strength and butting a hole in the wall with his own head. Mowgli was thus able to escape.

Then Kaa commenced a curious twisting and turning, out in the open, and hissed to the monkeys who were crowding in the trees round about and told them that he was going to dance the Hunger Dance; and as he twisted and turned himself about, the monkeys could not resist watching him, until they could no longer control themselves—and he called to them to come to him, and they gradually came nearer and nearer, until he was able to seize those that he wanted, and to crush them up in the folds of his body, and then to swallow them down, one after another, until he had had a full meal of them.

And that was the end of Mowgli's adventure with the Bandarlog.

## THE WOLF CUB PROMISE

I don't think any boy wants to belong to the Bandarlog—that is, the silly-ass boys, who tear about without any real work to do or games to play or laws to obey. Wolf Cubs are not like them —they have their duties to the Pack to carry out—they enjoy themselves just as much—indeed a great deal more than the Bandarlog because they have games with proper rules and work that is really useful.

Like the Scouts, a boy before becoming a Wolf Cub has to make a Promise. It is this:

**"I promise to do my best,**

**"To do my duty to God, and the Queen,**

**"To keep the Law of the Wolf Cub Pack, and to do a good turn to somebody every day."**

### Doing your Duty

When a fellow promises to do a thing, he means that it would be a terrible disgrace to him if he afterwards neglected or forgot to carry it out; in other words, when a Wolf Cub promises to do a thing, you may be perfectly certain that he will do it.

1. *To God.* To do your duty to God means never to forget God, but to remember Him in everything that you do. If you never forget Him you will never do anything wrong. If, when you are doing something wrong, you remember God, you will stop doing it.

You are taught to say grace before dinner, and to return thanks to God after it. Well, I think you ought to do the same after anything you have enjoyed, whether it is your dinner, or a good game, or a jolly day. God has given you the pleasure, so you ought to thank Him for it, just as you would thank any person who gave you something that you liked.

2. *To the Queen.*—I have told you how wolves in a pack all obey the chief wolf. So it is in our nation. The British people are a very big Pack, but they have their one Chief, Her Majesty

the Queen. So long as they look up to her, and obey her, their work will be successful like the hunting of the pack, or the football match, where all obey their captain.

If everybody started to play the game in his own way, there would be no rules, and there could be no success. But if we "play the game" and back up, as the Queen directs, our country will always be successful.

And in the same way, as a Wolf Cub, you must obey the leader of your Pack and Six.

3. *To keep the Law.*—Every game has its rules. So if you play the game properly you obey the rules. These are the Rules or Laws of the Wolf Cub game, which you learned in the last bite.

### The Good Turn

But now about *doing a good turn to somebody every day.*

Wolf Cubs have a patent dodge for making themselves happy. How do you suppose they do it?

By running about and playing at Wolf Cub games? By exploring the country? By getting to know all about the ways of animals and birds?

Yes, they do all these things, and make themselves happy; but they have a still better way than that. It is very simple. They do it by *making other people happy.*

That is to say, every day they do a kindness to someone. It does not matter who the person is (so long as it is not themselves!)—friend or stranger, man, woman or child. Though, like the Knights of old, they prefer to do it to a woman or child.

And the kindness, or " good turn," need not be a big thing.

You can generally get a chance of doing an act of politeness in your own home, such as helping to do some little job about the house; or you can, if away from home, take a little child safely across the street, or do something of that sort.

Be always ready to carry a parcel for anybody, to give up your seat in a crowded bus, or show people the way; to open doors for ladies, to help old women, blind men, or children to cross the street, to give water to thirsty dogs or horses, to protect birds from having their nests broken into, and robbed by other boys—these and hundreds of other kinds of good turns any Wolf Cub can do, and must do, if he is acting up to his promise to do Good Turns.

And you must never take a reward for doing a good turn; if, when you have carried a heavy parcel or called a taxi for an old lady, she offers you some money, you should salute and say, "Thank you, ma'am, I am a Wolf Cub, and it's my duty to do you a good turn. I cannot take any money for it. Thank you all the same."

If you take money for it, it is not a good turn, but just a piece of work that has been paid for.

Some boys, when they have done a good turn, go and brag about it to other boys, and to their parents and friends, as if they had done the finest thing in the world. That is not the way with Wolf Cubs or Scouts—they keep quiet about what they have done.

One day an old gentleman, a friend of mine, was attacked in a back street by a rough, who hit him in the stomach and snatched away his gold watch, and ran away with it. A Boy Scout, however, was near, and he alone dashed off in pursuit. He was not able to catch the thief, but he pressed him so close that the man, fearing that he might get caught with the watch in his possession, dropped it, and ran on.

The Scout picked up the watch, and as he was unable to overtake the thief, he came back to the old gentleman, gave him back his watch, went and called a cab, and got him into it, and then went off without saying who he was, or to what Troop he belonged.

The old gentleman asked me to find the boy so that he might reward him, but I was never able to do so. The Scout had done his duty, he did not swank about it, or tell others. He just did it because it was his duty, not because he expected to get praised or rewarded.

That is the way with Scouts—and so it is with Cubs.

Wolf Cubs have sharp eyes. Have you ever noticed that some Scouts and Cubs tie a knot in the ends of their scarves? This is a good dodge to remind a Cub to do his good turn for the day. He leaves the knot in the end of his scarf to remind him that, having done one good turn, he can do another.

### The Cub Grin

Then there's another thing, which, if you have the sharp eyes of a Cub, you will have noticed, and that is that in each of the pictures of a Cub, he is grinning.

Well, if you look at a real wolf, or even a dog when he has been running about, he wears a big grin on his mouth. So, too, the boy-Cub should always be smiling. Even if you don't feel like smiling—and sometimes you may feel more like crying—remember this, that

**Cubs Never Cry**

In fact, Cubs always smile, and if they are in difficulty, in pain, in trouble, or in danger, they

**Always Grin and Bear It**

That is what our soldiers and sailors and airmen do in war-time, so I am sure a Cub can do it.

A very young boy, named Francis Palmer, belonging to the Wolf Cubs of the 18th Bristol Group, was knocked down by a motor-car, his left leg broken in two places, and the side of his face badly cut about.

The boy was naturally in great pain; but, to the astonishment of the doctors and nurses, he never cried or complained. One of the doctors asked him why he was so brave, and his answer was:

"I am a Wolf Cub, and so must not cry."

THE HUNGER DANCE OF KAA

The leader will be Kaa's head, and the rest of the Pack will tail on behind him, each holding the Cub in front of him, and will follow the head wherever it goes, moving as slowly as possible, and keeping step with the Cub in front of him

The head will quietly glide along on a track like the figure of eight, and will then wind his tail up into a circle, gradually getting smaller and smaller, until he turns round and works his way out again in the figure which the Scouts call the "Spiral."

Every Cub will keep on hissing during the whole performance and will walk sliding his feet along without making the slightest noise, so that the whole body sounds like a snake rustling through the grass, making occasionally the louder hiss which is a snake's way of calling to his friends.

When Kaa has thus coiled and uncoiled himself, the leader gives the command "Bandarlog," and at once the snake breaks up and each Cub runs about in his own way, imitating the monkeys.

One will run as if on urgent business in a certain direction and will suddenly stop, sit down, and look at the sky. Another will dance on all fours round and round without any real object. Another will hunt his own tail. Others will climb imaginary branches and sit down and scratch in the middle of it. One will keep running round in a figure of eight. Another will creep on all fours up to some imaginary enemy and then suddenly sit down and look up at the stars. Another runs after his own tail, walks a few paces, and then runs after his tail again. Another will keep prancing, pick up an imaginary straw and examine it and prance again. Another turns head over heels, sits up and scratches himself. Another will walk very hurriedly for a few paces as if on important business, stop, forget what he was going for, scratch his head and walk rapidly again in a new direction, and do the same thing over again.

In fact, do any silly things you like such as monkeys do—but don't take any interest in what anybody else is doing. Be very busy all the time and do all the different things in turn. The whole time you keep on giving the monkey's call. All will be in a state of confusion doing aimlessly silly things, and all will at the same time give the monkey's cry—" Goorrukk, goorrukk, how, how, goorrukk

Suddenly the leader shouts "Kaa." The monkeys freeze with horror, for they know, only too well, what their terrible enemy will do to them.

The Cub who forms Kaa's head stands up with arms outstretched, thumbs clasped, head down, and slowly swings his body to and fro. He hisses once and all the monkeys take an unwilling step forward. He points out one of them. The frightened victim crawls forward between his legs and is "swallowed," and then tails on behind the leader, as in the first part of the Dance. Perhaps a dozen monkeys go this way, one after the other, and so re-form the body of Kaa; the others slowly move round to the back and retake their places as his tail. When all have joined up, the snake moves heavily round in a circle, and then lies down and goes to sleep after his heavy meal.

This is done by all lying down one after the other, starting with the tail.

As soon as the head of Kaa has wound round into a fairly close circle, each Cub must take short steps. The last Cub in the tail then sinks down very slowly; the pressure of his hands upon the shoulders of the Cub in front draws him down also, until all the body of Kaa is lying down except the front three. These three, led by the head of Kaa, sway for a moment, the head looking round and about, before finally sinking to rest.

# FIFTH BITE

THE GOODFELLOWS—HOW TO MAKE YOURSELF USEFUL—GAME: *Zulu Boy*—THE DANCE OF SHERE KHAN'S DEATH.

## The Goodfellows

OUT in the jungle there lived an old Owl with great round yellow eyes and two little tufts on his head like ears. Silly children were afraid of him because he only came out at night, and gave a weird hooting cry which they thought sounded ghostly; but any jungle boy knew that he was a wise old thing and kind to everybody. In the village there lived a tailor who had two little sons, Tommie and Johnnie. They lived with him and their old grandmother, their own mother being dead. Although she loved them both, Grannie was always having to find fault with the boys because of their laziness and forgetfulness and untidiness. They used to tear about the place yelling and playing their games, upsetting the furniture, breaking the crockery, spoiling their clothes, and generally making themselves a nuisance. They never thought what trouble they were giving to other people so long as they had a good time themselves.

Then Grannie told them how different it had been in the house in years gone by when the Goodfellow had come there. "What was a Goodfellow?" the boys wanted to know.

"The Goodfellow," said Grandmother, "was a little wee man who came to the house before anyone was up, and he swept the hearth and lit the fire, drew the water and got breakfast ready; he tidied up the rooms, he weeded the garden; he did every kind of useful work, but no one ever saw him. He always slipped away before the people of the house got up. But he was the greatest blessing to everyone. All were happy, and home was bright and clean."

So Tommie and Johnnie wanted to know how they could get a Goodfellow to come and help in their house and so to save them from having to do the many odd jobs that their Father and Grannie were always asking them to do.

They begged their Grannie to tell them how they could find a Goodfellow, and she told them that the best way was to go and find a wise old Owl and ask him, as he probably knew all about the Fairies and could tell them where to look for a Goodfellow.

So Tommie, the older, went out after dark, and when he heard the old Owl calling he imitated his cry and so got near him and had a talk. Tommie told him his troubles; how he was always being bothered to work when he wanted to play, and if only he could get hold of a Goodfellow to come and live in the house he would not have to do any more jobs himself, but could have a nice easy time.

"Ohoo! Hoo-hoo-hoo! Hoo-hoo-hoo-hooooo!" said the old Owl. "You see that pool over there. Go to the north side of it when the moon is bright, then turn round three times and say:

Twist me and turn me and show me the Elf—
I looked in the water and saw . . .

To get the finishing word of the rhyme look down into the water and there you will see the Goodfellow, and his name will fill in the rhyme you want."

So when the moon was up, Tommie went to the pool and turned himself round three times and cried:

"Twist me and turn me and show me the Elf—
I looked in the water and saw . . ."

But when he looked into the pool, he saw nothing at all except his own reflection.

So he went back to the Owl and told him how he had seen no one there except his own reflection in the water when he had hoped to find a Goodfellow who would come to the house and do all the work.

Then the Owl said: " Did you see no one whose name would complete the rhyme I gave you? "

He said: " No one."

And the Owl said: " Who did you see in the water? "

Tommie replied: " No one but myself."

Then the Owl said: " Would not the word ' myself ' make the rhyme? "

And Tommie thought of the rhyme:

> " Twist me and turn me and show me the Elf—
> I looked in the water and saw myself."

" But I'm not a Goodfellow."

The Owl replied: " No, but you can be. You can be a Goodfellow if you try. You are a strong little boy. You could sweep the floor; you are clever enough to lay the fire and light it; you could fill the kettle and put it on to boil; you could tidy up the room; you could lay the breakfast things; you could make your bed and fold up your clothes; you could do all these things before anyone else was up, so that when your Father and Grannie came down they would think that Fairies had been at work."

Goodfellows are the small people who live in the house and who do good there.

In some houses instead of Goodfellows there are Boggarts. These are little demons. When people want to be quiet, for writing or reading, or when they are feeling ill or tired, the Boggarts begin to yell and scream and rush about the place.

When the house is clean and tidy they come and upset everything, breaking the furniture and the crockery and leaving everything untidy for other people to clean up. They are dirty and lazy themselves, and don't do a thing to help their parents.

Boggarts are horrid little beasts, very different from the Goodfellows.

But the Goodfellows are not really Fairies, they are just ordinary boys and girls living in the house who make themselves into

Goodfellows by getting up in good time to do their good turns, instead of lying in bed and behaving like Boggarts.

Goodfellows do their work quietly without wanting to be thanked or rewarded for it. They do it because it is their duty to their father and mother and family. It may sometimes be a trouble to them if they are feeling tired or want to be playing, but they must remember that it is their Duty, and Duty comes before everything else.

So in our story, Tommie and Johnnie after being put up to it by the old Owl slipped out of their beds early in the morning.

They cleaned up the place and lit the fire; put the breakfast all ready and slipped quietly back to their bedroom; so that when Father and Grannie came down expecting to have to do all the work themselves, they were astonished to find everything already done for them, and they believed that the Fairies had come.

Day after day this went on, and the boys got more fun out of doing their duty than they had ever got out of playing rowdy games, and it was only a long time afterwards that their parents discovered who were the real Goodfellows.

So every Cub can be and should be a Goodfellow in his home by doing good turns every day for his father and mother, and without making any fuss about it.

A Cub is never a Boggart.

And he does not merely do Good Turns at home, but also when he is out and away from home; to his school-fellows or schoolmaster when at school; to his fellow Cubs or his Cub-master in the Den; to people he sees in the streets or the tram or the village.

Whenever he sees a chance of making himself useful to any-body the Cub should do it—because it is his duty. And he must not take any reward for doing it.

### How to Make Yourself Useful

Do you make your own bed in the morning? If you do not, why shouldn't you do it? You are perfectly well able to do it, and you would save other people a lot of trouble if you made it for yourself.

Do you know, I always make my own bed myself, and put away my clothes and tidy my own room, and I am sure that any Wolf Cub can do the same. Also, as I am generally up before anybody else in the house, I don't wait for somebody to come and lay and light the fire, but I do it myself—and I like doing it.

*Bed-making.*—Examine your bed and see how the sheets and blankets are laid and tucked, and do the same with it to-morrow without a word to anyone. How surprised they will be to find their work already done.

Don't forget in making your bed that all the sheets and blankets should be stripped off and aired. The mattress turned end over end so that the upper side last night night will be the under side to-night; this prevents it becoming knobby and holey. When you re-lay the sheets and blankets, put them on very carefully and smoothly, without a wrinkle, so that no one could have done it more neatly.

*Fire-lighting.*—(See Eleventh Bite).

*Cleaning Windows.*—A wet wash-leather to clean, and a dry one to polish it, make a window very bright and nice.

*Cleaning Boots and Shoes.*—This you can learn best from watching a bootblack at his work, and noticing all the different dodges he has of cleaning and polishing his customer's boots. I love cleaning boots, and it is almost as satisfactory as cleaning all the brass-work with a soft rag and " Brasso."

*Wash up* plates, cups, knives, and forks, but don't be clumsy and chip or break the cups. The water must be hot in order to wash off the grease. Dry and *polish* them afterwards.

*Sweep Carpets.*—If your mother has not got a carpet sweeper or vacuum cleaner sprinkle damp tea-leaves out of yesterday's teapot on the carpet and sweep them up; they collect and keep the dust.

*Wash Clothes, Handkerchiefs, and Socks.*—Soap the things in lukewarm water, and leave them rolled up to soak. Then wash in fresh water. Rinse out in fresh cold water, and hang out to dry.

*Take baby out in a pram*—but don't leave it to go and play with other boys. You are on Goodfellow Duty and therefore, like a sentry, not allowed to leave your post. Keep out of the roadway, and away from the danger of motor-cars, bicycles, etc.

*Run messages* as fast as you can, and without making stupid mistakes or forgetting what was told you as ordinary boys do.

These are just a few ideas on being a Goodfellow in your home.

### GAME: ZULU BOY

One Cub is the Zulu boy who is painted white and turned out into the bush to be hunted by the tribe.

Instead of being painted white, in our game he wears a white cocked hat made of paper, which he must not take off during the game.

At a certain hour he is sent out into the jungle to hide himself. The "jungle" is the country or streets for 600 yards in any direction round a central well-known spot, such as the church, or school, or tall tree, etc.

He is given ten minutes' start, in which time to get away and hide himself.

Then the tribe (or pack) are told off into pairs, and are let loose in different directions to hunt him. They can track him, or ask passers-by if they have seen a boy wearing a white cocked hat; and if they find him they can chase him until they capture the hat.

But the pair of hunters must be there together to do it; he cannot be captured by a single Cub.

The white boy must not hide in any inhabited building unless a rule is made allowing it, but he may ride in a cart or car of any kind, and he must keep his hat on all the time.

If he succeeds in keeping his hat uncaptured for an hour, he wins the game.

### THE DANCE OF SHERE KHAN'S DEATH

Now back to the Jungle for the Dance of Shere Khan's Death. The bullying tiger's last day came when rudely awakened from a sleep in a dry ravine of the Waingunga River. At dawn he had killed and eaten a pig, and had drunk, too. Mowgli, with the help of Akela and Grey Brother, divided a herd of buffalo in two, and drove them into the ravine from opposite ends. Shere Khan, unable to clamber up the sides of the ravine after his big meal, was trampled to death beneath the feet of the terrified buffaloes. It was a dog's death. Now for the Dance. First the Pack form a circle, and turning to the left walk round singing the following words to the tune of *Frère Jacques:*

Mowgli's hunting,
Mowgli's hunting,
Killed Shere Khan,
Killed Shere Khan,

Skinned the Cattle-eater,
Skinned the Cattle-eater,
(Yell) *Rah-rah-rah!*
*Rah-rah-rah!*

(For after Shere Khan was dead Mowgli skinned him, although he had a quarrel with old Buldeo the Hunter first, and had to ask Grey Brother to hold the man to the ground until he promised to go away. Mowgli took the skin to the Council Rock afterwards, as you know.) Now return to the song. One step is taken to each line, and the song is immediately repeated, with everyone turning about, and moving in the opposite direction. The actions are as follows: LINE 1, move off with right foot and right hand, the hand is held to shade the eyes in the attitude of a Scout peering over the country. LINE 2, repeat with left hand. LINE 3, a vigorous stabbing movement with the right hand, as though stabbing a tiger. LINE 4, repeat. LINE 5, both hands raised in front of face, imitate action of skinning, by tearing the hide part. LINE 6, repeat. LINE 7, dance round to the right waving the arm above the head. LINE 8, repeat.

For the second part, Cubs get down on all fours facing to the centre of the circle, with the leader outside. This part of the dance consists of a series of taunts to the dead tiger by the leader, the Pack responding to each by growling and crawling a little towards the centre of the circle. There are four taunts in all. Both taunts and growls start fairly softly and increase gradually in noise and anger. There should be no movement or sound from the Pack between the growls. The four taunts are: Lungri, Frog-eater, Burned beast of the Jungle, Hunter of little naked Man Cubs! By the time of the fourth growl, the Pack should have reached the Rock Circle.

You begin the third part of the dance by kneeling back on your haunches, hands hanging loosely by the sides. The leader should already be in place in the centre by the Council Rock.

He kneels back in the same way, stretches both hands above his head, and says slowly and dramatically, "Shere Khan is DEAD!" The Pack then stretch their arms up in the same position and, taking their time from him and keeping their hands in the same position, bow forward three times till heads and hands touch the ground, saying, "Dead-dead-dead!" Then all jump up and shout "Hurrah!" excitedly three times, and drop to the ground as though shot in mid-air. After lying *in dead silence* for about five seconds, the signal is given to get up, and the Dance of Death is over. The dance is not nearly so hard as it sounds from the description, and if each part is tried separately before putting them all together, any Pack can learn it.

### The Dance of Shere Khan's Death

There is another version of this dance which some may prefer.

The actions are the same, all except Line 7, but, instead of *singing* the words " Mowgli's hunting," utter them in as dramatic a way as possible and when you come to the yell at the end throw up your hands with a great shout of " Woof! "

You can, if you like, repeat this cry of joy at the end of the dance instead of the word " Hurrah! "

But the great thing to remember *is* that it really is a fine piece of acting if you put every ounce of yourself into it.

If you want to entertain your fathers and mothers and friends, it is good to do the Dance of Tabaqui, and immediately afterwards the Dance of Shere Khan's Death.

# SIXTH BITE

### UNIFORM—THE INVESTITURE OF A TENDERPAD—THE SIX—TOTEM POLES

### UNIFORM

THE wolf cub of the jungle is like many other animals, he has four legs, a head, and a tail. So has a goat, or a pig, or a giraffe—but these animals are not all clothed in the same kind of fur, nor are they of the same shape or colour. You can tell a wolf from these by his shape and the colour of his fur, and all wolves are exactly like each other. So with the boy Wolf Cubs—they are like any other boys in having each a head, and two arms and two legs, but you can tell a Wolf Cub at once, because he is clothed in a different way from the ordinary boy—he wears the Cub uniform, which is a jersey and shorts and stockings, and a green cap with yellow piping, and scarf of the colour of his Group.

And like the cubs of the jungle he keeps it smart and clean, he does not allow mud and dirt to remain on it, and he takes care not to get it torn and ragged in playing about among the bushes.

Remember, too, that with the boy Wolf Cubs the uniform means something more, it means that you are now one of a big brotherhood. It goes all over the world. There are your brother Wolf Cubs everywhere in the British family of nations—in Australia and New Zealand, in Africa, in Canada, in India, as well as in other countries—all doing the same work and all wearing the same uniform.

People think a great lot of a boy who is dressed in this uniform, because they know he is not an ordinary boy, but that he can be clean and smart and active, and that he can be trusted to do his best to obey orders or to do good turns for other people.

That is what is expected of you because you wear this uniform.

So be sure, each one of you, to carry out this idea, not only when you are at a Pack meeting, but when you are at home, or in the streets or lanes away from the Pack. Always think of your *Duty*. When you are in uniform you are " on duty."

You are like a soldier or a sailor wearing the Queen's uniform. Remember how these gallant men have got wounded and have suffered pain and hardship, and very many have given up their lives, merely to get their duty done, without caring what trouble it brought upon them.

You, too, can show people that, as one of the Wolf Cubs, you can stick to your duty and do it though it may be a trouble to you, and even though it may bring you into danger. That doesn't matter.

And what is DUTY?

Why, it is just carrying out the Cub Law and Promise. So to be a true Wolf Cub you must know these by heart, understand them, and carry them out at all times.

To-day, therefore, we are going to see that each New Chum remembers what he has already learned.

The Cub's Promise,
The Cub Law,
The Salute,
The Grand Howl.

I expect that your Akela will have a little talk with you about these very important things before he can be sure that you are ready to become a Wolf Cub and make that very solemn Promise.

### INVESTITURE OF A TENDERPAD

The Pack is in the Parade Circle and the new boy who is to be invested comes to the centre to stand in front of Akela. He may be escorted by his Sixer or by an Assistant Cubmaster.

The boy's cap and badges are held in readiness by an A.C.M. or are lying at Akela's feet.

Cubmaster: Do you know the Law and Promise of the Wolf Cub Pack, the Grand Howl and the Salute?

Recruit: Yes, Akela, I do.

Cubmaster: What is the Law?

Recruit: The Cub gives in to the Old Wolf. The Cub does not give in to himself.

Cubmaster: Are you ready to make the solemn Promise of the Wolf Cubs?

Recruit: Yes, Akela, I am. (Then he repeats, phrase by phrase after Akela:) I promise to do my best, to do my duty to God, and the Queen, to keep the Law of the Wolf Cub Pack, and to do a good turn to somebody every day. (While the Promise is being made the whole Pack stands at the Salute.)

Cubmaster: I trust you to do your best to keep this Promise. **You are now a Wolf Cub and one of the Great Brotherhood of Scouts.** (Gives him his badges, and his cap, which he puts on himself, and shakes hands with his left hand. The Cub changes the badges from his right hand into his left hand, and salutes the Cubmaster with his right hand. Then he turns about and salutes the Pack. He pauses for a moment at the " Alert " while the Pack salute in return as if welcoming him into the Pack.) He then joins his Six.

If the Group Scoutmaster is present at the Ceremony, it is very likely that he will give the new Cub the Group Scarf, to show that he is now a Member of the Group.

The ceremony ends with the Grand Howl, in which the Tenderpad is now able to enter for the first time.

### The Six

Now you are no longer a new chum but a Tenderpad, wearing the uniform of the Pack; and you are something more than this. You are not only a member of your Pack, but also of one of the Sixes which form that Pack.

A Six, as you probably know, is made up of six boys under a Leader, and these always stick together for work or for play, and each Six is called after a Wolf by its colour—either the Black Wolves, the Brown Wolves, the White Wolves, the Grey Wolves, the Tawny Wolves or Red Wolves.

Each Cub wears on his arm a triangular badge of cloth of the colour of his Six.

The Leader of the Six is called the " Sixer," and his orders must always be obeyed by the other fellows in the Six. The second boy in the Six is called the " Second," and his job is to help the Sixer whenever he can. It is up to each Cub in the Six to help to make his Six the best in the Pack.

### Totem Poles

Every Pack should own a Totem Pole. The word " Totem " is an Indian one, and simply means the " crest " or " coat-of-arms " of the family using it. The crest or coat-of-arms war usually painted or printed on most of the things that the ownes used.

Now the American Indian families had their own Totems carved when they could afford them. They were generally tall cedar posts or poles wonderfully carved. The crest was to be found at the top, and was generally a beast, bird or fish. They

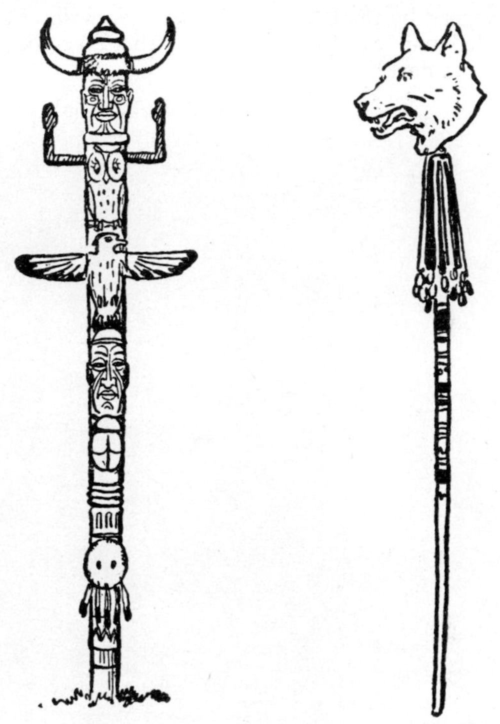

*An Indian Totem.* *A Pack Totem.*

looked upon it as a kind of mascot, and believed that it watched over them, and protected them in all danger. All Cubs belong to one large family with brother Cubs in many lands, and our crest is the Wolf Head. You wear it in cloth on your caps and jerseys, and a metal one in your buttonhole when you are not in uniform. Some Old Wolves can carve a Wolf Head from a block of wood, or even a stuffed head can be used if you are lucky enough to get one. The pole can be an ash staff, or anything that you like. Now fasten the head on top of the pole, and there you are. Always treat your Totem with care and respect, never knock it about.

Now every time a Cub wins a Proficiency Badge, a ribbon of the colour of the badge is fastened on the Pole, and the Cub's name written on a tab which is fastened to the end. Other honours earned by the Pack can be added as well, and perhaps a brass-headed nail can be driven into the Pole for every boy who joins the Pack.

# SEVENTH BITE

THE STARS—THE FIRST STAR—THE UNION JACK AND THE RIGHT WAY TO FLY IT—DRAWING FLAGS AND EMBLEMS—GAME: *Flags*—THE STORIES OF THE SAINTS—" GOD SAVE THE QUEEN."

## THE STARS

Now that you are a tenderpad, you are allowed to earn and wear two stars on your cap, to show how good you are at your work and to make you a full-blown Wolf Cub, but don't forget the Cub's Promise and the Law of the Pack, nor think because you learnt them up for your Investiture that you can drop them and forget about them. You must remember them always, and not only be able to repeat them to anybody at any time, but also to tell them to yourself every day and do your best to act up to them.

Most of you know by sight the badge of the Boy Scouts—the arrow-head with two stars on its outer wings. Do you know what those two stars mean? They are the two bright eyes of the Wolf Cub before he becomes a Scout—meaning that the Scout remembers the clever things that he learnt to do while he was yet a Cub—and that he sees everything—nothing escapes his notice, whether on the ground, in the air, round about him, far away or near.

The work necessary to win those stars may seem rather a lot for a Cub to do, but it is well worth the trouble, because when you have got your Second Star you can really feel that both your eyes are open in the Jungle. In later Bites we will talk about the Second Star, and about the badges you may be able to go in for after that.

Now I will show you how to start working for your First Star.

## THE FIRST STAR

Before being awarded the First Star a Tenderpad must satisfy his Cubmaster that he can pass the following tests:

(1) Know the composition of the Union Jack and the right way to fly it.

(2) Know in very simple form the stories of the Saints of England, Scotland and Ireland.

(3) Recite the first and third verses of "God Save the Queen," and know what to do when it is played or sung.

(4) Be able to tie the following and demonstrate their uses:—reef knot and sheet-bend.

(5) Turn a somersault.

(6) Leapfrog over another Cub of the same size.

(7) Throw a ball six times so that a Cub ten yards away can catch it. Catch a ball, both hands together, thrown to him from a distance of ten yards, four times out of six.

(8) Walk upright and with good carriage, carrying a solid article weighing about two pounds on his head without using his hands, for a distance of ten yards; turn and come back to the starting point. A Cub cap may be worn.

(9) Know why and how he should keep his hands and feet clean, his nails clean and cut, and his teeth clean; and why breathe through his nose; and be carrying these things out in practice.

(10) Be able to tell the time by the clock.

(11) Grow one of the following:—

- (*a*) a bulb in water, peat moss, sand or soil;
- (*b*) a chestnut or acorn in water, peat moss, sand or soil;
- (*c*) mustard and cress, peas or beans on flannel.

(12) Clean a pair of boots or shoes, fold his clothes neatly and satisfy his C.M. that he is doing his best to keep the Pack Den tidy and to leave no litter anywhere.

(13) Show that he understands the meaning of the Highway Code, paragraphs 1-15 inclusive.

(14) Have at least three months' satisfactory service as a Cub.

(15) Repass the Tenderpad tests. This test must be taken last.

The First Star is worn in the front of the cap, on the right side of the Wolf Cub Badge.

### THE UNION JACK AND THE RIGHT WAY TO FLY IT

The Union Jack, our National Flag, is rather a confusing one to look at, until you know what it is made up of. You know that England, Scotland, and Ireland all have their Patron Saints, namely, St. George, St. Andrew, and St. Patrick, and the flag is made up of the different crosses which represent those Saints.

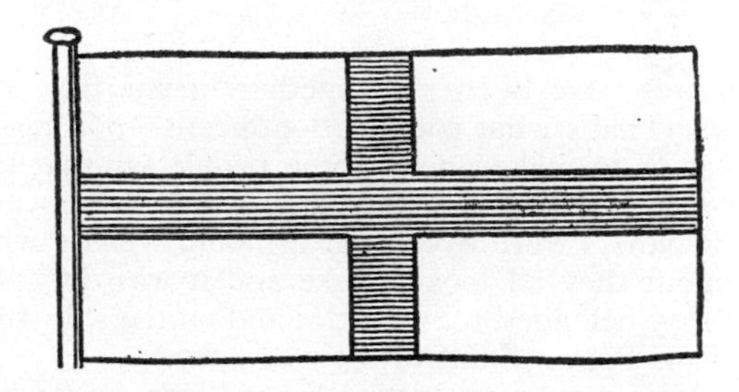

Thus St. George wore a red cross on a white flag.

St. Andrew had a white corner-wise cross on a blue flag.

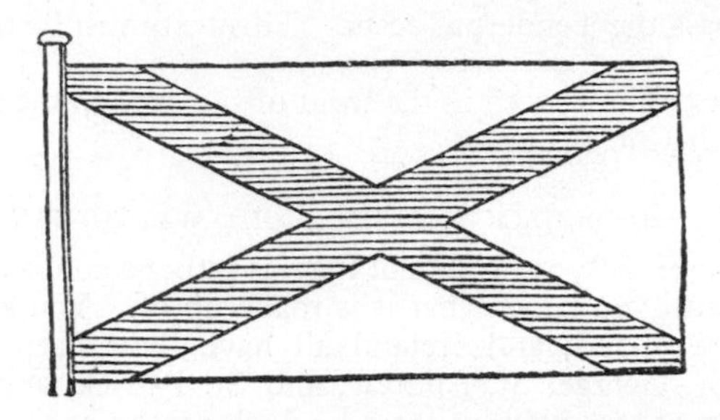

St. Patrick had a red corner-wise cross on a white flag.

And all three have been put together in one flag called the Union Jack. That's what composition means—putting together three flags so as to make one. Some people say that the word "Jack" comes from the ancient name which was given to the shirt which soldiers wore over their armour, because when they were in armour they all looked alike and it was difficult to see which side they belonged to in battle; and on the shirt they wore the cross of the Patron Saint of their country.

Thus a soldier in a white shirt with a red cross on it was known to be an Englishman, fighting under the "Jacque," or what we should call now the "jacket" of St. George.

Similarly, on our ships the same colours are flown in the form of a flag (which was also called "Jacque") down to the present day.

Your Akela will tell you lots of stories about the Saints of the three flags, and will show you how certain flowers and creatures are connected with them. You all know, for instance, that the rose is the national flower of England, and that the dragon is connected with St. George because of the legend about their great battle.

Now everybody ought to know how to fly the Union Jack. Yet there a great many people who do not know which is the right way up of the flag.

A boy would look an awful ass in the eyes of Scouts if he went and hoisted the Union Jack upside down!

Above are two pictures of the flag. The part of it nearest to the mast is called the " hoist "; the tail end of it is called the " fly." The red arms of the flag from corner to corner have a narrow white band on one side of them and a broad one on the other. The broad one should be to the top of the flag on the " hoist " side, and towards the bottom of the flag in the " fly."

The top picture shows the right way up, and the lower one the flag upside down. Can you see the difference? Study it well, and do not forget it afterwards.

### Drawing Flags and Emblems

A good way of remembering what you know about the Union Jack, and the way it is made up, is to draw little pictures about it. Here is one way in which you can set to work. It is often a good thing for the whole Six to share the work between them. Take twelve cards about five inches long and three wide. On each of the cards draw and colour with chalk or paints one of the following things:

1. The Cross of St. George.
2. A red English rose.
3. A fiery dragon.
4. The Cross of St. Andrew.
5. A prickly Scottish thistle.
6. A fish (St. Andrew was a fisherman).
7. The Cross of St. Patrick.
8. A shamrock leaf for Ireland.
9. A bishop's mitre for St. Patrick.

10. 11. 12. On these cards you can draw sham crosses or pictures such as a blue cross on a white ground, a daisy, or whatever you like. You will see the idea of this when you come to play the game I am just going to describe.

### Game: Flags

When you have finished these cards, you can play a game with them with the other Sixes. Each Six has a packet of the cards, which are shuffled up into any order. The Sixes get into file, and the cards are put in front of the Sixer, face downwards. At the other end of the Den, four squares are chalked on the floor opposite each Six. One is called England, another Scotland, another Ireland, and the fourth is called "Sham." On the word "Go," the Sixer runs out, picks up the top card, looks at it, takes it to the squares and puts it in whichever square he thinks is the right one. He then runs back and touches the next Cub, who does just the same thing. This goes on until all the cards are in the squares. Then I expect Akela will look at the cards and see whether you have all put them in the right squares, and will decide which Six played best.

## The Stories of the Saints

Having learnt about the Union Jack you will now want to know something of the three patron saints themselves. (A patron saint is, by the way, someone under whose protection a country has been placed.)

*St. George of England.* We know little about his life except that he was a Christian and on that account was put to death in the year 303 in Palestine, but it is rumoured that he once visited Britain when he was in the Roman army. In the thirteenth century, after the Crusades, he was adopted as our patron saint. You will all know the legend and the picture of St. George slaying the dragon and this is a dramatic way of describing the victory of good over evil.

The rose is said to have been the saint's favourite flower and so it has become the emblem of our land. St. George's Day is April 23rd.

*St. Andrew of Scotland.* St. Andrew was the brother of Simon Peter and he was one of our Lord's first disciples. Both of them were fishermen which shows us why the emblem of Scotland is a fish. We know that he was a simple, kindly-natured man and courageous enough to defend his faith, for he was put to death by the Romans, and it is said that he was bound to a X-shaped cross, and that he died on November 30th.

The thistle is an emblem for Scotland, for it is said that when the Danes invaded the country on a dark night one of them accidentally trod on a thistle with his bare foot. His cry of pain gave away the whereabouts of the enemy.

*St. Patrick of Ireland.* It is thought that this saint was born in Scotland about the year 389 and that he was brought up as a Christian, and we know that when he was only sixteen he was captured by pirates and taken to Ireland. However, after some years he escaped to Gaul, but he returned to Ireland to teach and to preach, for tradition has it that he had heard a divine voice telling him to take up this work. Later on he was made a bishop and so the bishop's mitre became an emblem of Ireland. On St. Patrick's Day, March 17th, the Irish wear shamrock, for it is said that the saint used a shamrock leaf in order to explain to the people the mystery of the Trinity.

### " God Save the Queen "

You will always want to join in when " God Save the Queen " is sung, and therefore you should know the words of the National Anthem.

" God save our gracious Queen,
Long live our noble Queen,
God save the Queen!
Send her victorious,
Happy and glorious,
Long to reign over us,
God save the Queen!

Thy choicest gifts in store
On her be pleased to pour,
Long may she reign!
May she defend our laws,
And ever give us cause
To sing with heart and voice
God save the Queen! "

The Queen is the Head, or Akela, of the whole British family of nations, and so you learn these verses as part of your Promise to do your best to do your Duty to the Queen. Stand at the Alert whenever you say them or sing them, and think what the words mean as you do so.

# EIGHTH BITE

OBSERVATION—TRAINING YOUR SENSES—WEATHERCOCKS AND STATUES—BIRDS'-NESTING—STALKING—FINDING YOUR WAY BLINDFOLDED—THE WOLF HAS A SHARP NOSE—A WOLF HAS SHARP EARS—A NEWSPAPER MADE OF SNOW—TRACK READING —PETS—GAMES AND PRACTICES—OBSERVATION TRAMPS.

*Now this is the law of the Jungle—as old and as true as the sky—*
*And the Wolf that shall keep it may prosper, but the Wolf that shall break it must die.*

. . . . . . . . .

*The Jackal may follow the Tiger; but Cub, when thy whiskers are grown,*
*Remember the Wolf is a hunter—go forth and get food of thine own.*

RUDYARD KIPLING.

This means that the jackal is a sneaking sort of beast, who does not hunt and get his own food, but who creeps about when the tiger goes hunting, and then gets some of what is left when the tiger has finished his meal.

The jackal is just like the worthless kind of man, who never earns his own living, but sneaks about begging and living on other people's earnings.

But the wolf is very different. He hunts his own meat, like the manly fellow who earns his own living and makes his own way in the world without leaving it to other people to help him. So you, my dear Cub, are learning to do the same.

When a wolf hunts animals for food, he does so by smelling where they have gone.

A man, who has not the same power of smell, hunts animals by following their tracks; and for the Scout this tracking is his regular way, not only of hunting, but of getting information.

Now tracking and stalking are fine things to do, but if you are to be a good tracker you want a great deal of practice and training.

It takes seven full years to train a real tracker in India. I am afraid you will have to wait until you are a Scout to do real tracking, but there are plenty of things which you can do while you are a Cub which will help you tremendously later on.

### Training your Senses

Before a Scout can be a successful tracker, he must be able to notice every small thing that may help him to reach his object. He has not only got to *see* everything, but use his ears and nose and hands. Above all, he's got to use his mind, so that he can think out the meaning of the things he notices.

As Cubs, then, you must learn to use your eyes and ears and nose and hands and mind. There's a list for you! It will give you plenty to do, and I am going to show you how you can set about it, not only when you are with the Pack but all day long, until it becomes a habit to notice everything.

When I was the age of a Wolf Cub, I used to notice the number on the collar of every policeman that I met, and then remember where I had seen him. Then I used to get a friend to come for a walk to one of the points where the policeman was on duty (a policeman on " point " duty is one who remains always about the same spot for regulating the traffic and so on—not like the policeman on " beat," who moves about over a certain district of his own).

When we were in sight of the policeman, but a good way off, I would shade my eyes and stare hard in his direction, and gradually spell out his number and the letter of his division. Then we would walk past him, and my companion would think that my marvellous eyesight had read them correctly!

### Weathercocks and Statues

It is not a bad thing to get to know by sight all the weather-cocks in the town. I used to keep a little notebook, in which I drew pictures of the weathercocks that I saw. Very few people look up and notice these.

On the top of the Royal Exchange in London there is a huge golden grasshopper as weathercock. I suppose thousands of people pass it every day, and yet very few ever notice it. They don't keep their eyes about them like a good Scout or Wolf Cub does.

If a Manchester Boy Scout were asked where is there a statue of St. George and the Dragon, he would probably at once tell you that on the top of Queen Victoria's statue in Piccadilly there is a little statue of him.

Houdini, the great conjurer, used to do many of his tricks by noticing, in one glance, a number of small articles and remembering them. He learnt this first while a boy, by looking in at a shop window for a few seconds, and then, turning his back on it, would tell his companions all the different things that were on view in the window. That is awfully good practice for Wolf Cubs. Try it.

You can also read the numbers of motor-cars as they pass you and notice the time at which you saw them. Then remember them, and later on write them down; it is good practice, and may some day be useful, because sometimes a motor-car is "wanted" by the police for knocking somebody down and then running away. If the number of the car is published by the police, you may be able to report that you saw the car at such and such a place at such and such a time.

Many of you, I know, are keen on taking down the numbers of railway engines. At the same time don't forget to notice the different classes of engines and anything else that catches your eye. It's all good training in observation.

### BIRDS'-NESTING

You have to notice small signs, and to have very sharp eyes, if you want to observe the habits of birds and their nesting.

Of course, Scouts and Wolf Cubs want to find birds' nests—not with the idea of robbing them of their little eggs, but of watching how the birds make their nests, what sort of eggs the different kinds of birds have, and how they feed and bring up their young ones. You can do this by stalking and watching.

It is only rotters who go and pull nests about and take the eggs. Scouts and Wolf Cubs do their best to protect the nests.

Of course, you can find nests after a deal of prying about into bushes, but the more sporting way is to watch the birds and see where they go and return. In fact, with many of the wilder birds it is the only way to find out where their nest is. In some cases it is a pretty difficult job.

Take the plover, for instance, or even the more common bird, the skylark. You see him rise up from the ground and go singing up into the sky, but if you go to where he rose you don't find his nest there. He always runs along the ground after leaving his nest for some distance before he rises; and when he comes down again he does not land at his nest, but some way from it. A skylark, like the willow-warbler, builds his nest on the ground.

The great titmouse builds in holes in trees, but also very often in most quaint places, such as in the neck of a pump or in a jar.

The nuthatch always makes his home in a hole in a tree.

### Stalking

The spring is the most interesting time of the year for studying Nature, both birds and flowers.

The swallows and other birds are just beginning to arrive from far away across the seas to spend the summer in Great Britain. The ordinary fellow, who is not using his eyes and ears, will not find half the fun that a Wolf Cub does in a ramble along the woodside or hedgerow.

Quick ears will discover the willow-warbler, or the chiff-chaff, the little, restless, brown fellow with his sharp piping note; and it will need good eyes to spot him and to follow him in his cheery, busy skipping from twig to twig.

It is good to discover the thrush's nest, and the bright-eyed mother thrush sitting on her eggs. She can be made quite tame if you are nice to her and show that you mean her no harm.

It is a very interesting thing to keep a notebook of all the birds you see and the date on which you saw or heard them first. You can then compare the dates again next year, or with some other fellow's notes.

Note down on what day you first heard the cuckoo, or saw the first swallow of the year, or the first skylark or nuthatch.

If you can draw pictures of the birds and of their eggs, it makes the book all the more interesting.

Also, a list of all nests that you discover is a good thing to keep.

Young wolves learn to look after themselves in the wild. They learn to watch birds and animals day by day so as to learn their habits, just as a boy Wolf Cub also does.

But the *boy's* object is to know more about them, and to take a friendly interest in their doings, whereas the young wolf does it because he then knows best how to hunt them and how to catch them for his dinner.

When the young wolves surrounded a flock of plover feeding along the ground and hitched nearer and nearer to them, sinking their grey bodies in the yielding grey moss till they looked like weatherworn logs, the hunting was full of tense excitement, though the juicy mouthfuls were few and far between.

But then there came the ducks to all the ponds and pools, and the young wolves learnt to decoy the silly birds by rousing their curiosity.

They would hide in the grass near the water while one of them went and played and rolled about on the open shore till the ducks saw him and began to stretch their necks and to gabble their amazement at the strange thing which they had never seen before.

Shy and wild as he naturally is, the duck must take a peck at every new thing.

Now silent, now gabbling all together, the flock of ducks swimming on the water would veer and scatter and draw together again and finally swim in towards the shore, every neck drawn straight as a string, the better to see what was going on.

Nearer they came, nearer and nearer still, until suddenly a swift rush out of the grass sent them all headlong splashing and quacking with crazy clamour.

But one or two always stayed behind with the wolves to pay the price of their curiosity.

### Finding Your Way Blindfolded

A real Scout does not only trust to his eyesight, because he has to work just as much by night as he does by day, and he cannot, of course, see so well in the dark, so he has to use other senses, such as hearing and smelling and feeling.

I once had to guide a large force of soldiers by night through a dark wood to attack the enemy. I had been there the day before, so I found my own footmarks, and followed them by feeling them as I went along.

Every Scout has to work in the dark, so I advise every Cub to learn how to do it.

It is very good practice to get up in the dark every morning, have your bath or rub down, clean your teeth, do your exercises, put on your clothes, and even tie your tie and brush your hair without ever turning the light on. You soon get to do it quite easily.

Also you can practise finding your way blindfolded.

Then you find how useful it is to have other senses.

You can listen and hear sounds which will help you to know the direction. You may hear the church clock strike, or a whistle at the railway station, or the call of a curlew in the marsh—all such things may help to know your direction when you cannot see it.

Or you may, by the smell, know that you are passing a stable, or the grocer's shop, or the farmyard, and guide yourself by that means.

## The Wolf has a Sharp Nose

There was an old Arab guide in Egypt, who was totally blind, yet he knew the way, even in the desert, by the smell of the sand. He would take up a handful now and then and smell it to see if he were on the right track. He knew the smell of each camping ground when he came to it.

On one occasion his companions thought they would play him a trick, so they brought along a bag of sand with them from their last camping ground, and when they arrived at the new one

*Wolves out on the prowl.*

they handed him some of this sand to smell, saying they had just picked it up.

The blind man smelt it, looked puzzled, and smelt it again, and then said he was extremely sorry; he had made some blunder and had brought them back to their old camp again.

He was quite miserable about it till they told him laughingly of the trick they had played him.

When we were at war with the Zulus many years ago, I was awakened one night in bivouac by a curious scent in the night air. It was the smell of a native.

I at once woke up my companions, but they could not smell it. But, then, most of them were smokers, and a man who smokes generally cannot smell so well as a man who does not.

So you will find that most real scouts do not smoke.

Well, I still felt that the enemy were somewhere near us, and so we all kept awake. Very soon we could hear them creeping up in the grass, hoping to surprise us, and to catch us asleep. Instead of that, they were themselves surprised by a volley from us, which sent them flying.

So you see how valuable the sense of smell can be to you. Here is another case which happened in France.

A man carrying a package presented himself at the home of a rich banker. As the banker was away, his mother took the parcel. The stranger declared that what it contained was of great value, and he demanded a written receipt.

While the lady was leaning over the table to write it, the man took a knife and stabbed her in the back. Her sister ran to her aid, and the man stabbed her also, then escaped.

The ladies, both of whom were only wounded, asserted that this same man had previously visited the bank under the name of Jamet.

Jamet was searched for everywhere by the police, but they were not successful.

However, the head of the detective department took away the package which had been left by the man, and found in it nothing more than an old railroad guide. He also found one important thing—the book had a peculiar smell, that of a tannery.

Inquiries were made by the police at the tanneries of Gentilly, just outside Paris, and they discovered that a man who occupied a high position in one of them had recently been to the home of a Parisian banker.

So he was brought before the women, and they recognised him immediately, and he confessed.

So you see how valuable it is to be able to notice small signs, and then to put them together and read their meaning.

## The Wolf has Sharp Ears

In the South African War I was in camp close under a mountain, and far away up on the crags above us I heard a baboon give a cry of alarm.

There were hundreds of men in camp, but I do not suppose many of them heard the cry, or, if they did, they did not pay much attention to it.

But to a Scout it would mean a good deal.

Why should a monkey high up there in the cliffs suddenly become alarmed and call a warning to his friends? I got out my glasses, and carefully scanned the mountain.

Presently I saw two or three men's heads amongst the rocks. As they carefully kept their bodies hidden I guessed that they were Boer spies watching us. So I secretly sent out two parties of men to climb the back of the mountain, and to come at these fellows from behind and capture them.

This they did, and we found it was just as I expected; they were the enemy's scouts spying our doings, and had alarmed the monkeys by their movements.

## A Newspaper Made of Snow

How can a newspaper be made of snow? Well, when winter comes along he sends an army of little white fairies to make a newspaper to tell you the news.

The snowflakes are the fairies as they come flying down in

*Birds who live in water only waddle on their great flat feet, with their toes turned in, like old Mother Flat Duck or Yellow Duckling.*

hundreds and thousands and millions and billions, till they cover the ground and spread a white sheet all over the country.

This is their newspaper, and anyone who is sharp can read its news. At first it looks all white and blank, that snow. But if

*Hens walk with one foot after the other.*

you look closer you see little specks and marks, which, if you can only read them, give you interesting news.

Let's go for a walk in the snow and see what it has to tell us.

Hullo! What's this?

Master Sparrow has been out in the snow. How do I know?

*Brother Rabbit out for an airing—note his tracks in the snow.*

Well, because small birds who live in bushes generally hop, both feet together.

If it had been Miss Chaffinch, her feet would have been smaller, and her tail would have just touched the snow every now and then, and would have made a slight brushing mark upon it. If it had been Mrs. Thrush, her feet would have been bigger and her hops larger.

Bigger birds, and those who live upon the ground, such as pheasants, hens, and peacocks, generally walk, one foot and then the other.

Then those who live in water only waddle on their great flat

*Madam Cat out hunting.*

feet, with their toes turned in like old Mother Flat Duck or Yellow Duckling, or like old gout-toed Alderman Goose.

What is this?

Master Sparrow had stopped here and fought with a lump of bread which he has stolen. Then he had gone hopping on with it in his beak, because it was a biggish piece of bread—judging by

*Old Towrow, the dog, chasing Madam Cat.*

the mark of it in the snow—and yet none of it is left lying there and he could not have eaten it all, so he must have carried it on.

Yes, look! There is the bread lying on the ground farther on over there, and the footprints hopping right up to it.

But what is this that crosses Master Sparrow's path? Why, it is Brother Rabbit out for an airing.

And just beyond, where the bread lies, Master Sparrow's footprints suddenly end. He has flown away.

Perhaps he was frightened by Brother Rabbit coming along? No; his footmark is on top of that one left by Brother Rabbit, so he must have come some time after Brother Rabbit had passed that way. And, besides, I expect that if the bread had been left there before Brother Rabbit came, he would have had a nibble at it. Don't you think so?

But what could have made Master Sparrow suddenly end his hopping and drop his bread and fly away?

*Mr. Giles is very angry with Towrow.*

Oh! I see?

There are some other footprints. Who is this who walks so carefully that her hind feet tread almost exactly where her fore feet were, so that instead of leaving the prints of four different feet in the snow there seem to be only two?

It is Madam Cat! Out hunting, too, for her footsteps get closer and closer, as she stalks nearer and nearer to Master Sparrow, and her tail switching nervously just brushes the snow here and there.

But what is the meaning of this sudden change? She springs from her long hind legs, falls half round to her right, and then springs away, galloping off with long bounds to the left! Oh, it is because old Towrow the dog is after her. There you see his footprints, galloping, digging deeply into the snow, and kicking it up in his violent bounds as he tears after the cat.

And how angry old Mr. Giles, his master, is. You can see here where he stopped in his walk to yell at Towrow.

Oh, yes; and see there? He threw his stick at Towrow. And poor Towrow crept humbly back to his master, bringing the stick in his mouth (for, you see, Mr. Giles' footmarks do not go where the stick was, but the dog's tracks go there and back to Mr. Giles, and the stick is no longer laying on the snow).

And so all ends well; no harm has been done to anyone.

Mr. Giles has gone home with his stick digging in the snow, and Towrow running behind him; Madam Cat has scampered off with her tail in the air; Master Sparrow is chirping on the chimney top; and Brother Rabbit is safe and snug in his warm, dry burrow.

So that ends the news of the day.

"What becomes of the Fairies?" you ask.

Well, when they fall to the ground they die like other people; they lie cold and white until the sun comes and calls them to wake. Then they melt away and disappear, but their spirits fly up to Heaven again, and they crowd together in great white clouds, and sail across the sky.

*Poor Towrow creeps humbly back to his master, bringing the stick in his mouth.*

Then, when you want more news on earth they come flying down as snowflakes to the ground, and spread again their newspaper for you to read—if you know how to read it.

## Track Reading

Zadig was a wonderful scout in Persia. One day one of the best horses belonging to the King ran away, and could not be found. Zadig was wandering about in the woods when some of the Royal servants came up and asked whether he had seen the runaway.

He replied:

"Do you mean a well-bred grey horse, about fifteen hands high, with a tail about 3½ feet long, wearing a bit with gold bosses on it, and shod with silver shoes, going lame in the off foreleg?"

" Yes; where is he ? "

" I don't know; I have not seen him."

So they arrested him, thinking he had stolen the horse. But shortly afterwards the horse was found and brought home, so they questioned Zadig further, and he explained it thus:

" I saw on a path in the wood prints of a horse's feet, showing the horse was trotting when he passed there, but the off fore-foot made shorter strides than the near fore, so I guessed he was lame. The hoof marks were small, so they were those of a well-bred, valuable horse. There was dust on the bushes on both sides of the path, but this was brushed off here and there by the tail of the horse as it swung from side to side. The path was 7 feet wide, so the tail must have been 3½ feet long.

" At one point a tree bent down over the path, and one branch was just five feet above the ground. In passing under this the horse had touched it with his back, and had left two or three hairs sticking to it, so I saw that he must be a grey horse fifteen hands high. (A ' hand ' is a measure of four inches.)

" He had, when trotting along, struck a stone with his foot, and had so knocked off a little chip of silver from his shoe; and, similarly, he had stopped at one place to pluck a mouthful of grass close to a stone, and had rubbed off a few specks of gold on the stone alongside his mouth, which showed me that he must be wearing a gold-bossed bit."

That is the way that a Scout reads his information, but it means that he keeps his eyes open and allows not the smallest sign to escape his notice. It will be a long time before you are clever enough to do that.

### Pets

It will help you to study and understand the ways of animals and birds if you can keep a pet, even if it is only a small one to start with such as mice or a guinea-pig. You must ask your mother about it first, of course. One of the Scout Laws is that " a Scout is a friend to animals," so get ready for the time when you will be a Scout by being kind to animals you meet. If you have a pet, there is a lot you can do for it, such as punctual feeding (you like your own food regularly, don't you ?), keeping it and its living-place clean, and so on.

### Games and Practices

Here are a number of games and practices for sharpening up your senses.

*In the Pond.*—Cubs form a circle round an Old Wolf just outside a chalk line. When the Old Wolf gives the order " In the Pond," all jump in. On the order " On the Bank," all jump out. If the order " In the Pond " is given when all are inside the circle, none must move, and none must move if when you are on the bank the order " On the Bank " is given. Such orders as " On the Pond " or " In the Bank " must be ignored, as they are traps set to catch you. The Cub with the least mistakes wins.

*O'Grady.*—Cubs form a circle and the Old Wolf gives various orders, but no order must be obeyed unless it starts with the words " O'Grady says." A Cub loses a life for each mistake he makes.

*Touch Iron.*—During any game the Old Wolf says " Touch iron," " Touch wood," " Touch something yellow," etc., and at once all the Cubs run to do so. The last to touch loses a point.

*What is it* (*Taste*)?—All Cubs taking part are blindfolded. Then each tastes a number of well-known flavours. The Cub who recognises the most wins. Here are a number of things with strong tastes: peppermint, liquorice, cheese, caraway, onion, etc.

*What is it* (*Smell*)?—A number of paper bags are put in a row two feet apart. Each has a different article in it which smells, as coffee, tobacco, onion, leather, rose leaves, orange peel, and so on. The Cub has five seconds at each to sniff the smell. When he has tried them all he writes them down or tells them to the Old Wolf in their correct order.

*What is it* (*Touch*)?—All Cubs taking part are blindfolded. A number of paper bags with objects inside, such as rice, lump sugar, tea, etc., are passed round the circle. The Cub who names the most things correctly wins.

*What is it* (*Hearing*)?—All Cubs taking part are blindfolded. An Old Wolf then makes a number of noises, such as pumping up the tyre of a bicycle, shutting a door, scraping a chair on the floor, etc., and the Cub who guesses the most correctly wins.

*Stalking.*—A Cub sits blindfolded in the middle of a circle. At a signal from an Old Wolf, a Cub from the circle tries to creep in noiselessly and touch the Cub in the centre. If he succeeds, he goes into the centre instead of the Cub already there. If the Cub in the centre hears him, and succeeds in pointing at him before he is touched, he goes back to his place in the circle.

*Draw a face.*—Players in circle. The Old Wolf draws a face in the air:—

First the outline, clockwise; then right eye, then left eye; nose downward; mouth right to left, all with the *left* index finger. Each Cub tries to draw the face in exactly the same order and in the same way.

## Observation Tramps

Take the Pack for a walk through town or country and assign marks for certain objects noticed by the way.

As an instance:—

Horse going lame, 8 marks.
Magpie, 3 marks.
Flock of seven birds, 3 marks.
Pebble shaped like a bird's egg, 3 marks.
Oak tree, 1 mark.
Red garment, 1 mark.
Weathercock, 1 mark.
and so on.

Each boy on seeing an object that counts will report to the Old Wolf in a whisper, and the marks due will be recorded against his name.

At the end of the walk these will be totted up and the winner will be declared.

# NINTH BITE

A NIAGARA FALL ACCIDENT—WHAT A SCOUT WOULD HAVE DONE—THE USE OF KNOTS—SWIMMING—BRITISH SEAMEN—"PLAYING THE GAME"—JACK CORNWELL, V.C.—THE WOLF CUB'S LAIR—HOW TO MAKE A LAIR.

## A Niagara Fall Accident

When I was in Canada some years ago, an awful scene was witnessed at the Niagara Falls. It was mid-winter. Three people, a man and his wife and a boy of seventeen, were walking across a bridge which the ice had formed over the running river, when it suddenly began to crack and partly to break up. The man and his wife found themselves on one floe of ice quietly floating away from the main pack, and the boy was on another.

All around them the water was covered with other floating blocks of ice, grinding and bumping against each other, so that swimming was impossible, and no boat could get to them had one been available. So there they were at the mercy of the current, which here wandered slowly about, but gradually, slowly and surely, carried them down stream towards those awful rapids a mile away.

People on the banks saw their dangerous position, and thousands collected, but not one seemed able to do anything to help them. The course of the river would bring them under two bridges, which spanned the river just before the rapids.

For an hour the poor wretches were floating along before they came to this point. On the bridges men had got ropes (the bridges were 160 feet above the water), which they lowered, so as to hang in the way of the drifting people.

As they came along the boy managed to grasp a rope, and willing hands proceeded to haul him up; but when they had got him a certain distance, poor fellow, he could hold on no longer, and he fell down into the icy stream, and was never seen again.

The man on the other floe also grasped a rope, which he tried to fasten round his fainting wife, so that she, at any rate, might be saved; but the tide was now rushing them along, his hands were numb, he failed to fasten the rope, it slipped from his hands, and a few seconds later both he and his wife ended their tortures by being sucked under the waters in the heavy, swirling rapids.

### What a Scout would have done

It is easy to be wise after an event, but this disaster is worth thinking out. What would you have done had you been there, seeing that it is the duty of a Cub to think of a plan and to carry it out on such an occasion?

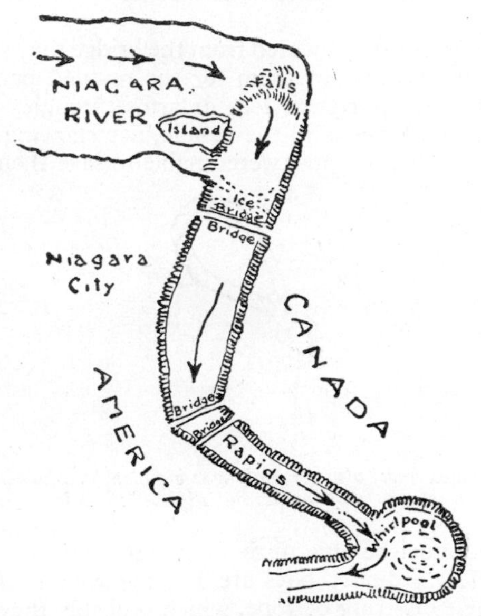


*This sketch map shows you where the ice accident took place.*

One of our Canadian Scoutmaster told me that he was travelling in a train shortly after this accident, when some of his fellow travellers were talking it over. They did not know that he was connected with the Scouts in any way, and one of them said:

"Well, I believe that if any Boy Scouts had been there they would have found some plan for saving these poor people."

So you see what people expect of Scouts now. The only thing is to Be Prepared to do what is expected of you.

It is easy to be wise after the event, but it would be useful and interesting to think out what might have been done, so that if anything like it happened again, and you were there to see it, you would know what to do. I have drawn a sketch map to show the position.

### The Use of Knots

One thing to be noticed in this accident, and that is the value of being able to tie knots, as all Scouts can do. People often think: "What is the good of learning so simple a thing?" Well, here was a case in which that knowledge might have saved three lives.

When the ropes were lowered from the bridge they should have had a loop or two tied in them for the rescued people to put round them, or to put their legs or arms through. As it was, the ropes had no loops, and the people, not knowing how to tie bowlines or overhand loops, were unable to save themselves.

*An* Overhand *knot, also for making a big loop, is a lubber's knot, which is very easy to tie, but difficult to undo again.*

Every Cub must be able to tie knots properly.

What duffers ordinary boys are at tying knots! They make a sort of tangle of string or rope, which probably they can never undo again, but the moment it is put to a strain it somehow slips and undoes itself, just when you want it to hold! That would never do for a sailor or for a bridge builder.

Knots are quite easy to learn, and as soon as you know them you can teach other people how to make them.

For your First Star, you have to learn two of the most useful ones. Use rope or cord—not string—when learning them, and as soon as you think yourself a swell at knot-tying, try doing it in the dark or when blindfolded! You will then probably find that you are not so good at it as you thought.

But remember you cannot always have it daylight when you want to tie a knot. Your tent may blow down in the night, or your horse break loose, or your sail may want reefing; there will be many occasions when you will have to tie ropes in the dark, and you will then be glad that you learnt how to do it beforehand.

It is difficult to follow a description in a book when you have never tied a knot before, so get Akela or your Sixer to show you how they should be done.

Reef-knot *is for tying up parcels and bandages.*

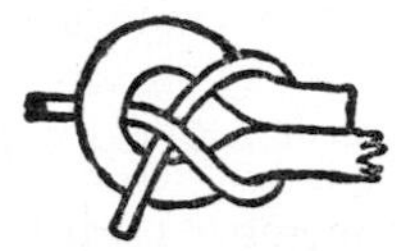

Sheet Bend, *or common bend, for joining ropes of equal or unequal thickness together. Make loop with one rope and pass other end through and around whole loop and bend it under its own standing part.*

## British Seamen

A fine type of British Sea Scout is the deep-sea fisherman. He spends his life sailing out to the fishing grounds far away in the wild North Sea. It is a hard, cold life, with constant danger in a small though very seaworthy boat.

But it is just this hard, rough life that makes our seamen such tough, reliable men.

It is these deep-sea fishermen who, though doing their work unnoticed in peace time, came to be so jolly useful to our fleet during the war, by sweeping the seas for mines all round our coasts. These mines were floating iron bombs spread about by the enemy to blow up our ships: but the mine-sweepers, doing their dangerous work skilfully and well, picked up hundreds of them and so saved our ships.

Then there are the sailors who man the thousands of trading steamers and ocean liners running from Britain to every corner of the world. We do not see much of them about our streets, but we hear of them in the papers now and then.

There are shipwrecks and fires at sea, collisions and founderings, but in almost every case of disaster we read the good news of acts of gallantry and obedience to orders in the face of danger on the parts of our sailors.

Bluejackets of our Royal Navy we do see about the streets occasionally; and fine fellows they are, strong, cheery chaps, who can turn their hand to any job that may be required of them.

Their pluck and discipline are well known, but don't you think it must mean double-extra pluck in a man to go down as they do and work in the bottom of those great steel battleships in a sea fight?

There they are, doing their duty down under the iron decks in the ammunition stores, or tending the turbine engines, or stoking the furnaces, shut in like rats in a trap, while far above them their brother bluejackets are getting all the excitement of firing their guns, and seeing something of what is going on around them.

### "Playing the Game"

I remember Lord Beresford taking me over his ship one time, and as we crawled about in the low chambers near the bottom of the ship, where the watertight doors kept the men imprisoned and unable to escape in the event of the ship going down, he said:

"These are the plucky men, the ones who work down here doing their duty unseen, getting none of the fun and none of the glory; but without them the ship would never get along, and the battle could not be won."

But these men are just what we would like every man in the country to be. Working away at his duty, helping in his own place, unseen, unnoticed, but doing it because it is his duty, and not because he expects to get fun out of it or glory.

I used to play football for my school, and for a long time I was goalkeeper.

Well, I felt I was very much like these naval enginemen and stokers; I should have liked to be playing up, continually getting the ball, and dashing along with it among the cheers of the onlookers, but instead I had to stand there alone, cold and unnoticed, in goal.

Still, when the enemy did come and make an attack, having got past our backs, then it was that the success or failure of the match depended on the fellow who had been doing his duty unseen; that was—the goalkeeper.

Do not forget that, Cubs. Do your duty, though it may not be pleasant, or it may be unnoticed by other people. Still, you must stick to it, because that means "playing the game," not for your own glory or excitement, but that your side may win.

## Jack Cornwell, V.C.

Many hundreds of your brother Scouts served on the ships of the Grand Fleet and the Battle-Cruiser Squadron during the war of 1914-1918. Admirals and officers of their ships wrote to me telling me of the good discipline and fine spirit shown by them.

Some of the officers told me they liked boys who had been Scouts better than those who came to the Royal Navy from training ships, because they could be trusted to do their work without having somebody always there to look after them and to see that they didn't idle their time. Scouts can be relied on to do their duty no matter what it cost them.

It cost one of them his life. That was Jack Cornwell.

He was on duty with one of the guns on board H.M.S. *Chester* in the big sea battle off Jutland in June, 1916. The crew of his gun were all shot down except two. Many a man would then have run away or taken cover as he could not possibly work the gun by himself: but he stood there, though badly wounded, in case he should be wanted. He stuck it out in pain and suffering, with his comrades dead and dying around him. He afterwards died of his wounds, but he had done his duty nobly and had shown that a Scout could be trusted to " stick it out " even though he died for it.

Even a Wolf Cub is not too young to be a hero. Here at any rate are two examples which happened to come next each other in the newspapers.

" The Wolf Cub Pack is going strong and has in its ranks the youngest boy in Great Britain to hold the Royal Life-saving Society's certificate for proficiency in life-saving. The award is also held by many of the Scouts."

" The Wolf Cubs attached to the 9th Glasgow Group have got a good example in the deed of one of their members, Walter Pitkeathly, who lost his life saving his younger brother.

" On April 29th, Pitkeathly, who was ten years old, and his brother were playing near a water-filled quarry, when the younger boy fell into the water. Walter without hesitation jumped in to the rescue, and although he succeeded in bringing his brother to the bank, he himself fell back into the water exhausted and was drowned."

## The Wolf Cub's Lair

I once crawled onto a wolf's den to see what sort of place he lived in. It was a low cave under an overhanging rock in the side of a dry earth bank. The hole was partly natural and partly dug out by the wolves.

Once inside, the wolf was safely sheltered from bad weather, and from view, and from attack by any big animal, since the entrance was so low that he could only just crawl into it himself.

It was not unlike the wolf's cave described in *The Jungle Book*, where Shere Khan came and tried to get hold of Mowgli, whom the wolves had rescued from him.

The wolves and Mowgli were safely inside the cave, but the entrance was too low for Mr. Tiger to get in, so he could only glare at them angrily from outside.

In the wolf's cave which I examined there was a stone which stuck out in the back wall of the lair, and I found behind this stone a second small cave which had been dug out, evidently by the young wolves, and they had thus made for themselves a little home of their own.

Well, that is an example to you Cubs. You should be able to make for yourselves dry, comfortable homes when out in the woods or plains. It is much better fun to make your own shelter than to buy ready-made ones.

You can begin by making one in your own garden.

### How to Make a Lair

The kind of shelter you make depends on the kind of material you have with which to make it.

A very simple one can be made out of old sacks, which you stitch together with string till you have quite a big sheet of sacking. Then if you tie one end firmly to a fence or hedge and prop up the other end on two poles or sticks, you will have a splendid den to go to when the sun is very hot, and you can play all sorts of games in it. You can decorate it, too, with painted pictures of wolves and other jungle animals drawn on the sacking. It will not be of any use for you to spend the night in because it will not keep the rain out, but when you grow up into a Scout you will be able to do lots of sleeping out, and that is great fun.

I have spoken of a real wolf's lair being a very comfortable sort of cave; so it is—for a wolf, but not for a man.

Caves are generally damp and dark and "earthy," and therefore not healthy. Tenderfoots often dig out caves for themselves to camp in, but no real Scout ever does; for he knows that living in such a place soon makes you ill.

Also one Boy Scout, at least, has been killed by such a cave falling in on him while he was digging it.

I expect many of you have got a corner of the Pack Den, or a bit of wall, which belongs specially to your own Six. If you have, it's up to you to make it look as cubby and bright as possible. If you have a corner, perhaps you will be allowed to screen it off with lengths of sacking, painted with trees and jungle animals. Put your thinking caps on and see how you can best use the space that has been given to you. You can get sets of pictures of the jungle animals, and special cards to paint your Six colours on, and you can cut interesting bits out of the illustrated papers. In fact, there are lots of things you can do to make your Pack Den look a real Den, even though you may have to take the things down after your meeting and stow them away. Get your Sixer to talk to Akela about what can be done.

# TENTH BITE

HOW TO GROW BIG AND STRONG—LEAP FROG AND SOMERSAULTS—WALKING—HOPPING AND THROWING A BALL—BREATHING THROUGH THE NOSE—NAILS—TEETH—GAME: *Toothbrush and Germ*—FEET—TELLING THE TIME—GROWING THINGS—CLEANING SHOES—FOLDING CLOTHES—TIDINESS—THE HIGHWAY CODE—GAME: *Road Safety Relay Race*—SERVICE—GAME: *Arrows.*

## How to Grow Big and Strong

In our Army years ago we used to have a battalion of very small men—who were not big enough for the ordinary regiments. They were called the "Bantams." At first people were inclined to laugh at them for being so small, but they very soon showed

*A Ghoorka*

that at fighting they were as good as anybody else. A small man can have a big heart and plenty of pluck inside him.

Our Ghoorkas—the little warriors in the Indian Army—have shown this. They are splendid fellows and dress very much like Boy Scouts, so that when you meet one you might at first think he was a Scout who had got " overdone " with sunburn.

So even though a Wolf Cub is small, he too can be just as brave and as strong as a bigger boy if he likes to make himself so.

I will tell you some of the things which you can do to make yourself big and strong and healthy.

The main thing is to keep the blood inside you strong and plentiful. The blood to your body is what steam is to the engine; it makes it go well or badly according to the strength of the steam. But also your blood is food to the body, like water to a plant, it makes it grow: if it doesn't get enough it remains small and weak and often withers and dies.

How can I get *good* blood and *plenty* of it when it is all made for me inside me?

Well, it is made from the food you take in through your mouth, and to get plenty of it you must take in food that is good for making blood, good healthy meat and vegetables, and bread and milk.

That is the way to get plenty of blood, but you must have it also *good and healthy*, and this again you can arrange for yourself, nobody can do it for you.

When you have taken in your food and have chewed it well and have swallowed it, it goes down into your stomach, and there the good parts of it go off into the blood, and the useless part of it passes out of you at the other end. If you let this useless part of it stay inside you too long—that is, for more than a day—it begins to poison your blood and so to undo the good of taking in good food.

So you should be very careful to get rid of the poisonous part of your food at least once a day regularly. That is the secret of keeping healthy and well.

Then you can strengthen your blood by putting fresh air into it. The blood wants air, and it keeps passing through your lungs, in the middle of your body, trying to get some of the air which you breathe in through your nose. So help the blood as much as you can by taking in deep breaths of good fresh air. Don't give it stuffy old air that has been shut up in a smelly room, but plenty of real cold fresh air out of doors.

For this you should breathe out all the breath that is in you and then suck in, through yout nose, as much air as you can hold in your chest till it and your ribs swell out to their full extent. Do this every now and then in the day—when you are in the fresh air—and it alone will help you to grow and to be strong.

But also, besides the good food and fresh air, there is another very important thing you can do for your blood, and that is to give it exercise.

As I have told you, the blood is like water to a plant and feeds the body or the part of the body to which it runs. It will always try to reach every part of you—but if you help it to do so that part will grow all the faster. That is why runners and football players get such strong legs; because by continually exercising them they get the blood to run more fully in their legs, and thus these grow in size and strength.

In India you will sometimes see a native holding his arm up over his head. He does this as punishment to himself for something that he has done wrong before God; and he vows that he will hold up his arm for the rest of his life and will never use it. And so from want of exercise the blood does not run properly—the plant is not watered—and gradually the arm becomes thinner and thinner, more and more withered until it is nothing more than skin covering the bones, quite useless.

Therefore, if you want to grow in size and strength, exercise every part of your body. You can do this by

### Leap-frog and Somersaults

I have seen many boys playing leap-frog. Some of them do it splendidly, but some of them are more like sacks of coke tumbling

" *This is the end of a 'head-over-heels,'* not *this.*"

over a coal-heaver's back than anyone leaping! When you first learn, try going over someone about your own size, or a little smaller. Get him to stand with his back to you, to bend down and tuck his head well in (if he stands with his feet a bit apart and grasps his leg with both hands he will be least likely to topple over). Now take a run up to him, put both your hands on his back and leap over—legs well apart. Try and go over absolutely squarely and put as little weight on him as you can.

Turning a somersault is rolling head-over-heels on the ground. The important things to remember are that you should keep your shoulders rounded and your chin tucked in. Don't be content with just managing to roll over. See if, after turning, you can get up without having to use your hands to help.

## Walking

Some fellows walk, others slouch! Which do you do? You can tell walkers from slouchers as soon as you see them together. The walker is straight, there's a spring to his step and an intelligent look in his eyes. The sloucher has round shoulders and looks

*Water-Carrier.*

dull, for, as he goes along, he never sees very much more than the ground.

Try walking with a weight upon your head. Get a weight of about two pounds—not anything too stiff or too solid—and see how far you can walk with it flat on your head. If you slouch it will soon be on the floor, but if you walk with your shoulders straight and your chin slightly up—well, there's no knowing how soon you'll be able to rival a muffin man! If you find it very difficult, because you've got a funny shaped head, try it with your Cub cap on!

Perhaps you have seen pictures of water-carriers in the East. Imitate *them*—no, not with the aid of Mother's best bedroom jug, that would be a Boggart's trick, but with something that will not hurt if it falls to the ground.

### Hopping and Throwing a Ball

Hopping is a matter of practice. Try to hop like a bird and not like an elephant. Here again you must hop on your toes and not on your flat foot. This exercise teaches you how to balance, and you should try hopping a figure-of-eight course on the right leg when bending to the right, and on the left leg when bending to the left.

Throwing and catching a ball is matter of practice and good eyes. When you try to catch a ball, make a cup of your hands, and when the ball strikes them draw them back a bit and grip hold of the ball at the same time. If you hold them out flat,

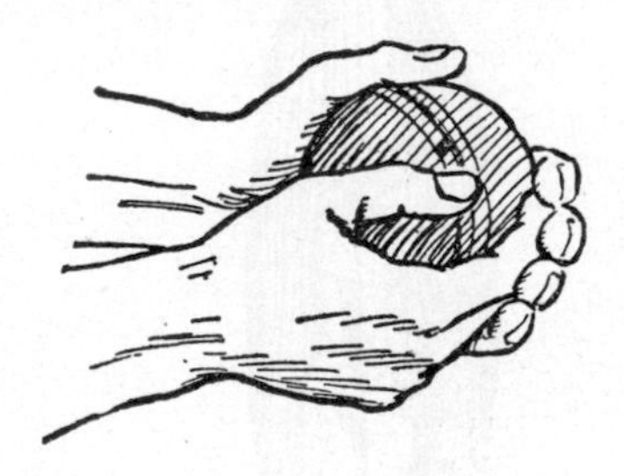

the ball will bounce out again; if you hold them wide apart the ball will slip through. Watch the ball from the time it leaves the other fellow's hand and move to where you think it is going to land. Do not stand still all the time and expect him to do all the hard work for you. The test for the First Star is to throw a ball six times (using either hand) so that a Cub ten yards away can catch it. Catch a ball, both hands together, thrown to him from a distance of ten yards four times out of six.

All these will help you to grow into fine, strong men, but you must not forget the other three things that help too—namely, to eat enough good wholesome food (but without over-eating, as that will help to poison the blood); also to have your daily "clear" regularly, to clean out the poisonous stuff from inside you: to breathe plenty of *fresh* air by deep breathing and by having your window open so that the fresh air can come into the room where you live or sleep.

These things you must practise for yourself; they cannot be done for you by other people, so it rests with you either to make yourself big and strong and healthy or to let yourself be a poor feeble little creature.

Now can you remember the four things which you have to do? What are they?

Wholesome food.
Daily clear.
Fresh air.
Body exercise.

### Breathing through the Nose

You will notice that I have said, in talking about breathing, that you should draw the breath in through the nose.

Why not through the mouth?

It is for this reason. Your throat at the back of the mouth is very delicate, and apt to catch cold and to get sore, and if you breathe through the mouth the cold air strikes it at once and may give it a chill; but if you draw in your breath through your nose it gets warmed in passing up it, and goes into the throat as it were through a back door but nicely warmed.

But there is also another reason why you should breathe through your nose.

There are little beasts floating about in the air called germs. They are so tiny that you cannot possibly see them with the naked eye, but with a very strong magnifying glass it is possible to look at them.

They are squirmy-looking little beggars, and very dangerous, because if they get inside you they may give you an illness of one kind or another.

If you breathe with your mouth open you are very likely to get some of these down your throat and into your stomach, where they are likely to do a lot of harm. But if you breathe through your nose they will get caught up in the sticky juice inside your nostril and you get rid of them again when you blow your nose.

Also when you are doing hard work you will, if you keep your mouth open, soon get dry and thirsty, but this is not the case when you breath through your nose.

Your mouth was given to you to eat with, your nose to breathe with, so why not use them for what they were intended?

The Red Indians in Western America teach their babies to breathe through the nose, by tying up their mouths by day and night. But their reason is in order to prevent them from snoring, which happens with a fellow who sleeps with his mouth open. And snoring in a country where you are surrounded by enemies would be very dangerous for you, as they could easily find out when and where you were lying asleep and stick a knife into your ribs.

## Nails

Before eating a meal you should always wash your hands, and you must at no time allow your nails to be dirty.

The reason for it is that these poisonous little germs, which float about in the air, live on dirt and are very liable to get on to your hands and to hide under your finger-nails, therefore you should always be careful to keep these clean, especially before handling your food. Nails, both on fingers and toes, should he kept properly trimmed with scissors.

People very often suffer lameness and great pain from the nail of their big toe growing down into the toe at one side. This is often caused by leaving the nail to grow too long until, by the pressure of the boot, it is driven to grow sideways into the toe. So you should be careful to cut your toe-nails frequently, every week or ten days, and they should be cut square across the top, not rounded, and with *sharp* scissors.

Finger-nails should also be cut about once a week to keep them in good order. They can be rounded to the shape of the finger to prevent the corners catching and getting torn.

Biting the nails is very bad for them.

## Teeth

A man came up to an officer to be recruited for the Army, and the officer examined him as to his strength and height and eyesight, and then looked at his teeth—after which he said: " You are a fine big man, but I cannot take you into the Army, because your teeth are bad."

And the man went away rather astonished, and told his friends that they wanted soldiers nowadays not only to kill the enemy but also to eat him. The truth was that a man is no use as a soldier unless he can, if necessary, bite hard biscuit and tough meat.

Unless a fellow can chew his food well the good does not come out of it in his stomach to go to make blood, which, as I have told you, is so necessary for health.

So, whatever you do, try to keep your teeth sound and strong.

There is no part of you that poisonous germs attack more readily than your teeth. They get in between them and burrow inside them, and bring about that awful pain known as toothache, and the teeth decay and have to be pulled out; and consequently your food after that does not get properly chewed.

But you can prevent this for yourself if you take the trouble to clean your teeth properly and to brush and wash away these germs out of your mouth.

The first thing is to have a toothbrush. This you can buy for a few pence at any chemist.

The thing is not to forget to use it every morning and every evening, when you get up and before going to bed, and also if possible after your midday meal.

Attack those germs with a brush and get them out from their hiding places between and behind the teeth, and swill them out with mouthfuls of water, so that they don't get a chance of burrowing and destroying your grinders.

There are no chemist shops in the wilds of Africa, and yet the natives there have splendid teeth, and they keep them clean by continually brushing them after every meal with little brushes made out of bits of stick. They take a short stick and hammer the end of it until it is all frayed out like a paintbrush.

## Game: Toothbrush and Germ

Cubs in circle, hands joined, arms fully extended. One Cub in centre is a toothbrush, a Cub outside the circle is a germ. The object of the game is for the toothbrush to catch the germ. All the Cubs may try to prevent the germ from entering or leaving the circle by lowering their arms or closing up, but the toothbrush may enter and leave freely.

### Feet

Your feet have a worse time than the rest of your body, because they are shut up in shoes and stockings all day. The result is that they need to be washed very frequently.

You can't walk far if your feet give out. Feet often get blistered because you let them get damp from perspiration, and leave the damp stockings on them, so that the skin gets all soft, and therefore rubs very easily into blisters or raw places.

You can prevent this by often taking off your shoes and giving your feet and stockings a good drying, so that the skin does not remain soppy.

Soaping or greasing the feet before putting on your stockings is not a bad thing for preventing rubs.

*Blisters.*—If you get a blister on your foot, you should take a little care about it, and you can get rid of it easily; but if you are not careful, the skin rubs off, and may make a nasty sore.

This is the way to treat it. Take a needle, hold it for a few seconds in the flame of a fire or match, in order to kill any germs that might be on it. Then run it into the blister sideways, close down to the flesh. You will not feel any prick from it. Then press the water out of the blister through the tiny hole made by the needle.

### Telling the Time

Long ago, when nearly all a man's time was taken up in catching, killing, and eating his dinner, and in resting after all that had happened, no one needed to know the exact hour of the day or night. Now people have so many things to do that they need to know the time to the " very second."

If you have learnt your weights and measures at school you will know that 60 seconds make a minute, 60 minutes make an hour, 24 hours one day and night.

Here is a clock face. You will notice that there are two hands (a big one and a little one), twelve figures, and sixty little lines on it.

The little hand moves slowly round the clock face and when

it is pointing at or near a figure, that figure is the hour of the day or night. (If you take another look at the picture you will see that the little hand is pointing near 12.)

The big hand moves far quicker, for it tells the minutes and has to pass all those sixty little lines—from twelve back to twelve—while the little hand is going between two figures.

The twelve figures really only mark the hours, but, because it would be such a nuisance to have to count those little lines every time we wanted to know how many minutes it was to, or after, a certain hour, clockmakers have arranged them so that every one of them marks five minutes—the figure 2 is twice five minutes after the hour, that is ten minutes past; the figure 8 is four times five minutes before the *next* hour, that is twenty minutes to. The 3 is a quarter of sixty minutes (three-times five) past; the 6 half past, and the 9 a quarter to the hour.

Can you tell me what the time would be if the little hand was between 3 and 4 and the big hand at 5 ? Why, twenty-five past three, of course.

Now make yourself a model clock with hands that move. You'll soon be an expert, and when a poor old lady who can't see very well asks you what the time is you'll be able to tell her and not have to say, " I don't know."

## Growing Things

Most of you, no doubt, like watching things grow and it is more fun if you have a hand in it yourself. So here is your chance for, before gaining your First Star, you must grow one of the following:—

(*a*) A bulb in water, peat moss, sand or soil;

(*b*) A chestnut or acorn in water, peat moss, sand or soil;
(*c*) Mustard and cress, peas or beans on flannel.

Choose which you would like to do and then start straight away, for none of these things grow in a night. (*See* page 182).

## Cleaning Shoes

Like making my own bed, or folding my own clothes, I like cleaning my own shoes.

There is a great satisfaction about getting a good polish on to your shoes through your own work. It is almost as pleasant as polishing up brass-work with a tin of " Brasso " and a soft rag.

For shoe cleaning you should have:—

1. An old knife to scrape off the mud.
2. A hard brush to brush away the dirt.
3. A blacking-brush to rub the blacking in.
4. A tin of blacking.
5. A soft brush to put the shine on.
6. A soft rag to put the polish on.

If you are using boots for rough country wear, or for camp, the best way to clean them is not to polish them, but to rub grease all over them, and especially into the seams, with an old tooth-brush. Any grease will do—oil, vaseline, tallow, or mutton fat.

If you want to keep dry-footed, don't forget to grease the soles as well as the uppers.

## Folding Clothes

The motto of the Scout is " Be Prepared," which means " Be Prepared" to do your duty at any time of day or night.

Soldiers and sailors, firemen and policemen, and other such men as have to be ready to turn out any time of the night always make a practice of putting their clothes neatly in place so that they can find them at once, even in the dark, and get into them quickly.

So Scouts and Wolf Cubs should do the same, and be careful to fold them and stack them in the order in which they want to put them on.

You should practise a few times jumping out of bed and slipping into your clothes in the dark, and you will soon see how much more quickly you can do it if you have them all laid ready instead of having to hunt about for them in confusion.

It may some day be the means of saving life.

Then sailors and soldiers have to keep their clothes in a very small space. A soldier, as you know, carries a change of clothing and all sorts of other things, like brushes, razor, soap, etc., in his kit-bag on his back. In order to get their things into such a small space they have to fold every article very neatly and very tightly, otherwise it will not fit in.

So if you are going into camp, you will have to be able to fold and pack your things in the same way into a small space.

You cannot do this well unless you are in the habit of always folding your things neatly, so you should do this with your clothes in your own home.

And it is good for the clothes. They keep in much better condition, and they look much better on you when they have been carefully kept in this way.

Also, if you should be away from home, and you want one or other of your things sent to you, you can tell other people exactly where to find them when you have everything in good order in your own room.

### Tidiness

One of the First Star tests is that you must satisfy Akela that you are doing your best to keep the Pack Den tidy and to leave no litter anywhere. I think that's important, don't you? Most people seem not to mind where they throw their litter—cigarette ends, bus tickets, orange peel, and bits of paper are left strewn around.

When Scouts and Cubs grow up we shall hope that there will no longer be people who throw these things away. They will take the trouble to put them into the proper bins for the purpose or take them home.

It makes the streets not only look untidy, but also makes them dangerous, owing to people slipping on banana and orange skins, and thereby very often breaking their limbs.

And dangerous also because the rotting fruit helps germs to grow, which then can get into the air and poison people. I heard the other day of a Cub who could not think of a good turn to do, but he saw a banana skin lying in a bin where it was safely out of the way, and he put it back on the pavement so that if another Cub came along he would have his chance of doing a good turn by removing it!

Cubs who live in the country don't get such a chance of mopping up paper in the streets; but they can do an equally useful work in the lanes near their homes by uprooting the thistles and other weeds that grow along the sides of the roads. It not only makes the lanes look neater, but it will also be a blessing to the farmers, because many of these weeds, especially thistles and groundsel, seed in such a way that their seeds are blown by the wind into the neighbouring fields and gardens, and there start a lot of fresh weeds growing.

Therefore a Cub who destroys one plant prevents thousands of others springing up in the neighbourhood.

It is therefore a very satisfactory business to walk out with a spud, or even with a stick, and to cut down a few hundreds of these enemies every day.

On the gates of a park in Scotland these words have been put up:—

*Please Remember*

Banana skins and luncheon scraps,
Orange peel and choc'late wraps,
Broken bottles, torn rags,
Kodak cases, paper bags,
Cigarettes and matches spent,
Cardboard plates and papers rent,
Tins and suchlike odds and ends,
Spoil this place for other friends.
Dirt and papers in pretty places
Slam park gates in people's faces.

So Cubs must be very careful not to be "litter-louts." Don't scatter your toffee papers about the streets or on your camp site. Keep them in your pocket until you can put them in a rubbish bin or in the fire. Be proud of your Pack Den, and see that each one of you does his bit to keep it neat and tidy, so that when a visitor comes to see you he may see how good a Pack you are by the tidiness of your Den.

### The Highway Code

Far too many people, grown-ups as well as children, are still killed every day on the roads in the town and the country, largely through carelessness. You, Cubs, by using your eyes (and wits!) can be useful here, not only to yourselves but to many other people. Akela will tell you which parts of the Highway Code apply especially to you, and you can play games which will help you to remember this. Here is one of them:—

### Game: Road Safety Relay Race

Make a pack of eighteen cards for each Six, *viz.*, six red, six yellow and six green. Each pack is placed face downwards on the floor, in front of each Six, in file.

Each Cub in turn runs up to the pack and draws a card. If it is red he goes back to the Six to await another turn. If yellow the Cub stands aside to await the "All Clear." If green, the Cub races up to the Old Wolf at the end of the den and hands it over. The yellow Cub may also run when anyone in his Six gets a green.

The first Six to reach Akela wins.

### Service

I expect you have some Rover Scouts in your Group (perhaps some of them help to keep you Cubs in order!). Well, their Motto is "Service," and they have to search out all sorts of ways of doing good turns and real hard work for others. But Rovers aren't the only people who have to serve. Cubs have to do their best in this way too.

That is why you have to have at least 3 months' satisfactory service in the Pack before you can get your First Star. (Most of you will take a good deal longer than 3 months, for Akela will want you to learn everything very thoroughly before he will let you pass.) You will be expected to turn up punctually at each Pack meeting, and to try your hardest when you get there. But just turning up to Pack meetings regularly is not enough. You must have obeyed orders, you must have done your best to help the other Cubs of the Pack, you must have joined in games and work with all your might. But, above all, you must have shown that you are really trying to do your best to live up to your Cub Law and to keep the Promise, not only when you are with the Pack, but at all times—at home, at school, in the street.

When you have done all that, you will have deserved to win your First Star, and will be rightly proud to wear it when Akela hands it to you.

### Game: Arrows

(So called because the questions represent the arrows with which the Cub gets wounded.)

The Cubs sit round in a ring, while the Cubmaster sits in the middle. The Cubmaster then asks questions round on the knots, flag test, etc. If a boy fails to answer the first question put to him, he folds one arm, as if it was in a sling. If he fails to answer the second, he folds the other. When he fails the third time he kneels, and at the fourth he lies down and is " dead."

# ELEVENTH BITE

THE SECOND STAR—LIGHTING FIRES—OUTDOOR FIRES—BUSH FIRES —HOW TO SAVE A PERSON FROM BURNING—MAKING TEA—(BOWLINE) AND ROUND TURN AND TWO HALF HITCHES—RUNNING WITH A MESSAGE—POINTS OF THE COMPASS—TELEPHONE—SKIPPING—SWIMMING—GAMES.

Now you have got one eye open, and are ready to start getting some sight into the other one. You are bigger and stronger and perhaps a bit wiser by this time, and the things which you will have to do will be rather more difficult. That makes it all the more satisfactory, when we learn them and pass the tests, doesn't it?

## The Second Star

Before being awarded his Second Star a Cub must satisfy his Cubmaster that he can pass the following tests:—

(1) Swim 15 yards *or* skip with both feet together 15 times forward and 15 times backward, the Cub turning the rope himself.

(2) Use a compass to show a knowledge of the eight principal points.

(3) Be able to tie the following and demonstrate their uses:— Bowline and round turn and two half hitches.

(4) Understand the meaning of thrift in all things and be carrying it out in practice. Show evidence of the care of his Cub uniform.

(5) Produce a satisfactory model or article made entirely by himself in wood, metal, cardboard, clay, plasticine or similar substance; or an article knitted or netted, woven or carved; or a set of at least eight sketches drawn by himself in colours (chalk or paint) of National flags, or animals, or flowers, with the names clearly written.

Models made in Meccano or other partly constructed materials are not admissible.

(6) Lay and light a fire, indoors or out-of-doors.

(7) Make a pot of tea.

(8) Run or cycle over a stated route with a verbal message of 15 to 20 words, including figures, and repeat it correctly. Be able to use the public telephone; know where and how to ask for assistance in an emergency (ambulance, fire, and police).

(9) Show how to clean and dress a cut finger, cover a scald or burn. Understand the danger of dirt in a scratch. Know the simple treatment for shock (not electric). Understand the necessity for summoning adult help.

(10) Observe and point out from life three birds (not domestic), three trees, and three other natural things such as insects, flowers, fishes, the choice to be made by the Cub in each case.

(11) Demonstrate the safe way to use a pocket knife, strike a match, guard a fire and handle an iron. Understand the dangers of broken glass, rusty nails and frayed electric flex. Know the safe way to plug in and disconnect domestic electric appliances; or how to light a gas fire or ring; or how to light oil stoves or lamps.

(12) Have at least nine months' satisfactory service as a Cub.

(13) Repass the First Star Tests. This test will be taken last.

### Service

You remember the story of the Goodfellows, the good little chaps who did useful work about the house before the other people were up, and you remember the Boggarts, the little rotters who did nothing but run about and make a lot of noise and leave things untidy and dirty.

Cubs don't want to be Boggarts. Their job is to be like the Goodfellows and to be useful in their homes and helpful to other people, especially their fathers and mothers.

In order to be a good Cub a fellow must know how to lay and light a fire.

### Lighting Fires

It is much more fun lighting a fire out-of-doors than indoors, but it takes a little more skill and a lot more care, because fire is a very dangerous thing if you don't know how to control it properly. You may not have a chance right away for learning how to light an out-door fire, so let us start with an indoor one in a grate.

Laying and lighting a fire indoors wants some practice, if the fire is to burn up quickly and brightly, so you can practise this while you are Cubs.

First of all, you must clean out the grate, get rid of the ashes of the old fire, and sweep the fireplace quite clean.

Many people waste a good deal of fuel by throwing away the cinders. You should pick out all the cinders and only throw away the powdered ashes.

Cinders mixed with coal give a lot of extra heat to a fire and save money.

Here is a tip which I use for dividing the ashes from the cinders.

If you haven't got a sieve use an old wire fire-guard. Shovel the whole of the ashes of the fire into it and let the ash run through to go into the dustbin, and keep the cinders that are left to go into the fire.

In laying your fire be very careful to do it the right way; if you don't the fire won't light, and you will have all the trouble of laying it over again.

Beginners generally put too much paper, too little wood, and too much coal on at first. You only want a small amount to start with, especially of coal, because the weight of it squashes down on the fire and chokes it.

Tear up a newspaper and roll into loose balls and long, loose screws, and lay these in the bottom of the grate—but don't use too much paper. Get some dry sticks—white wood is best—and lay these very lightly on the paper; build them up firmly (as if you were building with bricks), so that they will not fall in and crush down when the coal is added, but will allow plenty of air to get in. Now add small pieces of coal, putting them on carefully with your fingers. Don't shovel coal on, or put on dust and cinders to start with. When all is ready set fire to the paper all along the bottom of the grate—using one match. Watch your fire until it is burning up well, and the wood has caught—don't go away and hope for the best! Once the wood and coal are well alight you can add coal with the shovel, and also the cinders you picked out of the old ashes. But it is possible you may be expected, at times, to light a fire with damp wood or hard old pea-sticks, bad coal or coke and cinders, in a bad fireplace. This is difficult, but a Cub must not let himself be beaten. Here are a few tips. Try and get hold of just one little piece of *dry* wood. Cut this up into *shavings*, as a Scout does to light a fire in the open. Start quite a small fire, with paper and your shavings and a few sticks; this is sure to catch, and you can add sticks and coal gradually. A candle end is, of course, a help—but one doesn't expect a Cub to have to use that—it is wasteful for one thing, and makes a beastly smell! A very good tip is to get hold of the grease-proof paper the butter or margarine has been wrapped in—that starts a lovely blaze; it is really worth saving it up for the job! Or old paper the paraffin oil can has been standing on is very good—but take care, as it blazes up very easily, and *never* pour paraffin on the fire.

### Outdoor Fires

First you must make sure that it is a safe place to light a fire, somewhere that it cannot spread or do any damage; also that you have permission to do so.

Akela will choose the place for you, until you are a Scout and have learnt all the rules of a backwoodsman.

Remember to begin your fire with a small amount of very small chips or twigs of really dry dead wood lightly heaped together, and a little straw or paper to ignite it; about this should be put little sticks leaning together in the shape of a pyramid, and above this bigger sticks similarly standing on end. When the fire is well alight bigger sticks can be added, and finally logs of wood. A great thing for a cooking fire is to get a good pile of red-hot wood ashes, and if you use three logs, they should be placed lying on the ground, star-shaped, like the spokes of a wheel, with their ends centred in the fire.

A fire made in this way need never go out, for as the logs burn away you keep pushing them towards the centre of the fire, always making fresh red-hot ashes there. This makes a good cooking fire, and also one which gives very little flame or smoke for the enemy to detect from a distance.

### Bush Fires

Every Scout knows how important it is to see that his cooking fire is quite out before he leaves it. He pours water over the hot ashes, so that there is not a spark left which might set fire to the grass round his camp. This in summer-time is a great danger, because once you start a grass fire you never know where it is going to stop.

Old scouts are very careful about cutting away, or burning bit by bit, the grass round the spot where they are going to make their camp-fire, so that, when that is alight, it will not spread to the surrounding veldt.

*The lee side of a rock is all right—*

Then, when they have finished cooking, old campaigners are very careful indeed to pull their fire to pieces, and to tread it all down, and pour water over the smouldering ashes, so that there is not a spark left that might later start a new fire.

Grass and forest fires are never started by true Scouts, but only by silly, careless tenderfoots.

*—the lee side of a fire is another thing.*

A bush fire, when once it is lit, blazes and spreads at a tremendous rate, and in a few minutes is much too big for a man to stop. Then it rushes across country, burning crops and woods, cattle and farms, and even villages and towns, as it goes along.

That is why a real backwoodsman is very careful about his camp-fire. This carefulness is a regular habit with him, so that, even when safely burning weeds in a back garden, he first cuts away anything that is likely to catch fire, and when the weed-burning is over, he carefully tramples out the last remaining spark before he goes away.

Remember that sand or earth is often as good as water for putting out a fire.

Tenderfoots, in trying to stamp out a fire, or to beat it out with sacks or branches of trees—which is the right thing to do—often go the wrong way about it, and get to leeward of the fire. Do you know what that means?

To windward means towards the wind—that is, on the side on to which the wind is blowing, the windy side. The lee side, or leeward, is the opposite side.

The lee side of a house or a rock is a good place to get to when a cold wind is blowing. But, in the case of a fire, it is a bad place to get to, because the smoke and flames and sparks are all carried to leeward.

But that is very often the side to which a tenderfoot goes in order to stop a fire spreading. I have heard of one boy who badly burnt himself in doing so.

### How to Save a Person from Burning

If you see anyone catch fire in this way, remember the first thing to do is to cover him up as quickly and as tightly as possible with your coat, or a blanket, or carpet. Fire cannot go on without air; the more air or wind you give it the better it burns.

If a person whose clothes have caught fire starts to run, the fire will flare up at once. You should make him lie down and roll him up at once, tightly, in a blanket, and smother the fire. Then go for help.

### Making Tea

When you have made a good fire you will want to cook something on it. It is fun to roast sweet chestnuts or potatoes in the embers, but the most useful thing is to boil water for tea. One of the Old Wolves will show you the right way to do it, especially how to lift the billy or dixie off the fire when the water is boiling and the handle is hot enough to burn you badly if you are not careful.

If you can't get a chance to make an out-door fire you can make your pot of tea for the Second Star Test indoors in the ordinary way, and this is a very useful thing to be able to do anyhow, for Good Turns.

There is a right way and a wrong way to do it, and I'm sure your Mother will soon tell you if something went wrong, and help you to do it properly next time.

## Round Turn and Two Half Hitches and Bowline

In your First Star you learned two very useful knots. Here are pictures of two more that you must learn before you can win your Second Star.

They are neither of them very difficult, but it will be much easier for you to learn them if Akela or your Sixer show you how.

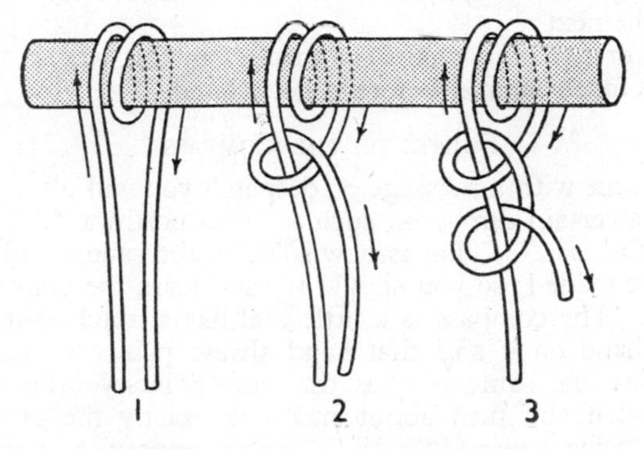


*Round turn and two half hitches. For fastening a rope to a pole or spar.*

*A* Bowline *is a loop tied with a knot which cannot slip and which at the same time will not jam, and so can be untied easily. This is it before you pull it tight.*

## Running with a Message

This is another test for the Second Star, and too many fellows when they are put to the test think only of the running—that is, of how quickly they can get there with their message, and they think too little of the message itself.

You should put this subject the other way round in your mind. It should be " Learn the message and run with it."

Pay careful attention to the wording of the message, say it over to yourself, and again to the sender. Be sure that you have got it right and that you understand it before you start; and then keep repeating it to yourself as you go along so that you are certain to deliver it right at the other end.

If you don't do this you are sure to bungle up the message, so that if you get there faster than anybody else it is no use after all, and you have to come back and take it a second time.

And the same way in passing on a message. Be sure that you have got it correctly from the last speaker before you pass it on to the next.

If one or two of a chain are careless in this way, a message gets very much altered before it gets round.

### Points of the Compass

When sent with a message or despatch you will often be told to go in a certain direction, such as " Go northward," or " Go towards the east." That is how soldiers and sailors and Scouts always are guided; so you should try and learn the points of the compass. The compass is a little dial like a watch, but it only has one hand on it and that hand always points to the north. If you face the same way as the hand points you are looking north, and if you turn about and look exactly the other way you are facing south. South is exactly opposite to north, and east is exactly opposite to west. When you are facing north the east is on your right and the west on your left hand.

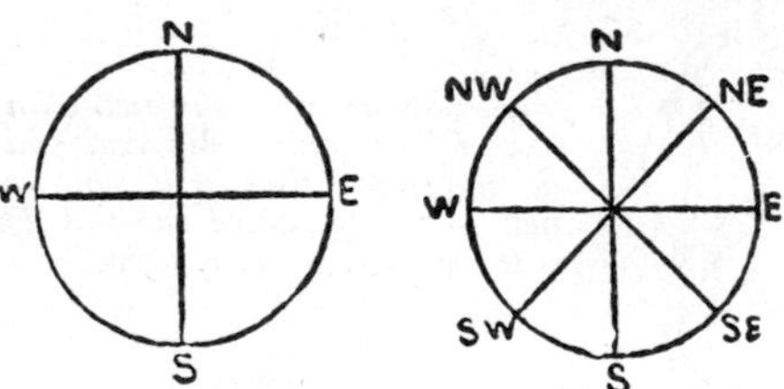


That gives the four points of the compass: North, South, East, West.

Supposing you have not got a compass, you can tell the different directions by the sun.

> Of the stars in the heavens the Sun is the best:
> He comes from the East and sets in the West.

If you are up early and see where he rises, you know where the east is. At midday the sun is due south.

Then half-way between each of the four main points there are four others which are easily remembered: N.E., S.E., S.W., and N.W.

### Telephone

There are many other ways of sending messages. One way is signalling with flags, lights or buzzers. In different parts of the world, messages are sent by means of drums and horns. The telephone and wireless are more modern ways of sending messages. At first you might think that they have nothing to do with the jungle or with Cubbing, but that is not so. In the jungle, both men and animals have ways of sending messages to each other which seem to be mysterious to us, just as when we speak to each other on the telephone it must seem mysterious to them. So it is right that in Cubbing we should make use of these modern inventions and learn how to do so. You have to be able to use the public telephone if one is available near where you live. Your father and mother, Akela, or a friend will be able to show you how to do this. This is a test that must be done in practice; you can't learn it out of a book.

Some Cubs, however, live in places where there are still no telephones and they have to know how to ask for assistance if something such as an accident or a fire happens. The way in which they do this will depend on where they live, but they have to find out how to do it in order that they can prove themselves as useful as possible and to know what to do when the occasion demands it.

### Skipping

Fetch your rope—it doesn't need to be a beautiful expensive one with wooden ends, but it should not be too thin and light—and have a try. If you have never learnt to skip at all, get two friends to turn the rope for you at first and use all your brain in learning to jump properly and at the right time. Stand straight upright, shoulders down, your toes just touching the rope. Are you ready? Right! There it goes over your head. Now jump, heels together, toes out, and as you land let your knees bend slightly outward. Do a little jump in between each big one—when the rope is over your head—this will help to keep you steady and in time.

Now try turning the rope yourself. Start with it in front of you and keep your back straight all the time. Don't land like an elephant on your heels—practise being as nimble as a mountain goat (if you can) and make no thump at all by jumping on your toes. You will have to skip fifteen times forward and fifteen times backward and alone, for your Second Star, so I should take care to practise at home.

Some boys think that skipping is girlish, but Cubs are more sensible than that. They know that footballers and boxers use this sort of exercise to help to make them fit.

### Swimming

If you have not yet learnt to swim it is high time you did. It may take a bit of "stickability," but so does skipping, and neither of them would be much fun if they were as easy as falling off a log.

The younger you are the easier it is to learn to swim, so this is a grand time to start and you'll find it useful all your life. There are many wonderful stories about Scouts and Cubs who have saved other people's lives, because they had learned to swim and because they were brave. Perhaps you'll have to be rather brave while you are learning, but it's all good practice, and remember that everybody can learn to swim if they really make up their minds that they are going to succeed, and keep on keeping on until they do.

Of course you'll need to be taught how to do it properly, so don't go off to try by yourself in streams or ponds, where you may easily drown before you have a chance to learn.

### Games

*Whispering a message.*—Each Six stands in file behind the Sixer, with about two yards between each Cub. The Sixers are told a message by Akela which they must take back to their Sixes and whisper to the next Cub. That Cub repeats the message to the Cub behind him, and so on. The team which passes the message down to the end most correctly wins.

*Compass running points.*—Mark out a circle on the ground, and the eight points on it, the north being marked with the arrow head. Place a Cub at each point, and one "out." Akela calls out two points and the Cubs at those two points have to change places before the Cub who is "out" can reach one of the points.

# TWELFTH BITE

KNITTING AND WEAVING—THRIFT—MODELS—COLLECTIONS—SCRAP-BOOKS—A WOLF-CUBS' BAND

## Knitting and Weaving

One of the things that a Cub ought to be able to do is to knit. This is not at all difficult to learn, and it comes in very useful when making things for yourself or for other people.

It is particularly useful if you go out into the wilds later on as a pioneer or explorer.

Shackleton's men in the Arctic expeditions were all able to knit their own socks and mitts, and I have known many hunters and travellers and soldiers, especially those from Scotland, who could always knit their own stockings.

Weaving and plaiting is also a most useful knowledge.

When I travelled in Kashmir I found the mountain sides so steep and slippery that it was impossible to climb them in ordinary English boots, and I had to do as the natives did, that is, to wear " Chaplis," or shoes woven out of grass.

These were most comfortable, and gave one a grip which enabled one to go up or down a mountain side so securely, that I felt I would have no hesitation in walking up the wall of a room and along the ceiling like a fly!

But, as you may imagine, shoes made of grass don't last very long, so one wanted a new pair every second or third day.

The consequence was that I had to make them for myself, and I used to do this by wearing a long rope of grass and coiling it round my neck and then plaiting it into shoes as I walked along on the day's march.

Similarly, I found it most valuable to be able to make baskets. In the wilds you cannot buy portmanteaux and handbags wherever you like, but you want something for carrying your meat when you have shot your game, or for carrying your fish, fruit, berries, or wild vegetables.

There are plenty of twigs about and rushes. The thing is to know how to weave them into baskets. It is quite easy to learn and very pleasant to do.

Of course, in a civilised country you can always sell these things when you have made them, and they bring in lots of money for you or your parents or your Pack.

### Thrift

The next test is perhaps a little difficult to grasp as it asks you to understand the meaning of thrift in all things and be carrying it out in practice.

Actually the word thrift has come to us from Iceland, and the people on the island know what thrift is and are strong, sturdy, and independent. There is a little flower, a sea pink, that is called " thrift " for precisely the same reason that it can live and give happiness by its appearance to others in places where there is very little soil and where it is blown upon by hard, cold winds.

You have to learn, therefore, to be careful about all that you have, your food, your clothes, your little bits and pieces, and your money. It is much nicer, for instance, if you can make your own swords and other things that you play with, instead of buying them in a shop, or expecting someone else to give them to you. In just the same way, the Pack as a whole can make things for itself—skipping-ropes, clock faces, and so on—instead of buying them. You want to take a pride in your uniform and clothes, and not damage them unnecessarily and be always giving trouble to other people to clean and mend them. Food should not be wasted.

Take care of your pennies and they will soon turn into pounds.

A man named Astor, when he was a boy, learnt how to make whistles and flutes, which he then sold for a few pence. He put his pennies in the bank, and in a few years he found that they had mounted up into pounds; and in the end he became one of the richest men in the world.

Young wolves in the autumn got more food than they could well eat. There were plovers to be caught and ducks and geese to be stalked.

The geese would settle at night on a sand-bar, well away from rocks and bushes or anything that might hide an enemy, and there they would go to sleep in little groups on the open shore.

As the night darkened, four shadowy forms would lengthen out from the nearest bank of shadow, creeping onward to the sand-bar with the slow patience of the hours.

Creeping slower and lower, these shadows gradually got nearer and nearer to the flock, until there was a sudden rush, a terrific clamour of wings smashing into the water, and the hoarse startled cry of the frightened geese.

A minute later the four shadows would be trotting back to the woods, each carrying a burden thrown over its shoulders, with his jaws tightly holding the neck of a fine goose.

Sometimes the wolves, when they wanted an exciting tussle, would tackle some of the big seals which had come ashore to sun themselves on the rocks. The wolves would creep in between the seals and the sea, so that when the alarm was given the seals found their retreat cut off as they floundered back towards safety.

A wolf rarely grips and holds his enemy, he generally snaps and gashes it over and over again until he kills it. But in this case he had to hold tight on to his prey to prevent it escaping into the sea, and the seals snarled and bit back savagely, so that the wolves had a lively time of it.

But with all this plentiful amount of food of geese and ducks and fish and seals, the wolves had really more food than they could possibly eat.

But wolves are not fools. They knew that the winter was coming when the whole land would be covered thick with snow, and the rivers would be frozen over, and that it would be very difficult for them then to find anything to eat.

So they made hay while the sun shone. They killed all the food they could get, and the cubs were taught by the old wolves, after hunting day and night and killing what they could, to drag their game into safe hiding-places between the rocks.

Here they piled snow over the meat after pushing it into a cranny between rocks, and in this way prevented the scent leading other animals to dig it out, and at the same time kept it cold and frozen till the time came when they would want it.

And that is just what the boy Wolf Cub should do. If he finds he can earn money at any time, he should do his best to earn as much as possible and then to put it safely away in the Savings Bank and not to spend it. He should remember, like the wolves did, that some day bad times may come when he may want to use his supply, and if he has carefully stored it in this way he will be ready to meet hard times.

It is not enough for you to go to your mother and ask her to give you sixpence to put in the Bank. You should have saved " by your own efforts," that is, by putting aside something regularly out of your weekly pocket-money instead of buying sweets. Or perhaps you can do some jobs of work for someone, and earn a little money in that way. Then you will be able to go on savin up your money bit by bit, until you have quite a nice sum in the Savings Bank "for a rainy day."

## Models

But don't expect to become rich all at once. To get to big things you have to begin with little things.

Before you get pounds you must have your pennies; just as before you grow to be a big man you must be a small boy.

Before you build a big ship you must make a model of it.

Now most of you Cubs will want to make something big some day, whether it is an aeroplane, or a house, or a boat, or an engine.

But the first step is to be able to make a model of it.

When the great Tay Bridge was built a model of it had to be made first on a small scale, and before the great ship *Queen Elizabeth* was made she was first modelled like a toy ship.

So a Cub who is going to do big things should try and make his models first. If you are going to make a big box, make a small one first.

If you want to make a house, build a cardboard one to begin with; or you can make your little Man-of-War in clay, or your engine in tin, and so on.

Also it is useful to be able to draw the outline of such things before you start to make them. Every fellow can draw a little bit, and if he practises it he will soon get to do it well.

Every Scout has to be able to draw a map. He would be called a fool if he couldn't do it.

## Collections

And I am sure that every Cub has got a collection of some sort or other, or if he has not already got one, he is going to make one whether it is foreign stamps or sea-shells or postcards.

Well, these collections are very nice to have, but is is ever so much more fun if you make a collection of your own drawings.

For instance, fellows who are fond of flowers can draw pictures of all the different flowers they find, using coloured pencils or paints. The flowers thus drawn will never fade like the real ones if picked; and in time you will have a splendid record of all the different flowers you have found.

Some people may say that flowers are too difficult to draw, so in that case make a collection of all the flags of the different nations.

A Cub can draw these with coloured pencils and a bit of paper; and he could add to them the flags of the different British Overseas Dominions and the flags of the Naval signalling code.

You can find out more about collections when you come to start to win your Collector's Badge (see page 164).

## Scrap-books

Cubs should keep scrap-books. These may be made very interesting, containing pictures and photos and cuttings from newspapers. They should be all neatly arranged and pasted in, and the books will, no doubt, be awfully interesting to their owners a few years hence.

I know it, because I have kept scrap-books all my life, and I find them not only most interesting, but in many cases valuable for reminding me of things that happened long ago.

My first book begins with a portrait of my father and mother, and then a picture which I drew when I was only three years old! It is not much of a thing as pictures go, but still it is amusing to see what I tried to do when I was so young a Cub as that!

But some of the greatest fun is in making the scrap-book up and sticking things in. It really is quite an art to have it neat and clean and tidy. This is the way I start to work.

If possible, I get an album with thin cardboard leaves, because plain thin paper is apt to cockle up when you stick anything on it; but, of course, any book will do better than nothing.

It is best to have the album about twelve by eight inches in size, because a smaller one gets filled up in no time, and so often you may want to put a big photograph in.

On the front page, write your name and the date of commencing the book. It is always nice to start at the beginning of a year, or on your birthday, so that you have a book for each year as I have, or else for two complete sections of your life.

For instance, if you are at school, you might have a book in which to put pictures of your school and your friends there, and programmes of school sports or concerts—you will enjoy immensely looking at it when you are a grown-up man; and then, perhaps, have a second book for your home life and your holidays.

But, of course, making a scrap-book is only an extra hobby, and it cannot interfere with your other Cub work and games, so you must not be perpetually playing with the sticky paste and cutting up paper and making your room in a mess.

The best plan (at least, I have found it so) is to have a fairly big envelope in which to put all the things you think likely to be interesting to keep.

Pictures of Scouts in camp, and interesting stories out of papers, and photographs of all kinds, will then be collected tidily, ready for you to sort out in a spare hour on a rainy day.

Of course, if you can take photographs yourself, they are particularly nice to keep; but that is rather expensive. The very nicest and best plan of all is to draw things in your book yourself.

If you are good at drawing in this way, you will perhaps be able to go in for the test and win your Artists' Badge (see page 153).

When the time comes for sticking your " scraps " into the book you will want some paste. Flour or starch paste is quite easy to make, and this is how it is done.

Put one and a half teaspoonfuls of flour (or lumps of starch) in a little basin. Pour in a little cold water and stir it into a thin paste. Then pour in boiling water, stirring all the time, until it is a thick, blue-looking paste; and do not forget to put in a few cloves to prevent it going sour.

Besides that, you want a paste-brush, a pair of scissors, and something by way of a waste-paper basket (for snipping and cutting makes the room very untidy), a pencil for writing down names and dates under the pictures, and an old newspaper.

The newspaper is an excellent thing which I myself find extremely useful, and therefore recommend to you; you place the photo face downwards on the newspaper and smear the back of it all over and its edges and corners with paste, and then put it in its right position in the album. The place where you smeared it on the newspaper is then all sticky, but by doubling over the sheet you get another clean " smearing-place."

Very often, photographs have a dark edge all round, and it is nicer to cut that off; it also looks very neat if you just clip off the corners.

### A Wolf Cubs' Band

Packs of wolves when they run about in the jungle make what they call music; nobody else calls it music, but it amuses them and makes them feel cheerful.

Why should not a Pack of our Cubs therefore make its music too by having a band? By a band, I do not mean one of those expensive affairs with brass trumpets and highly decorated drums, but one which has instruments that do equally well and cost nothing.

The first thing, of course, for a band to have is a *Big Drum*. This means getting an old biscuit box or a petrol tin and a couple of drum-sticks. These may be shank bones from the butcher, or stout sticks with a rag knotted round the end.

Cymbals? Well, you get them ready-made from the kitchen (if Mother is kind) in the shape of two saucepan lids.

Triangle? *Of course* you must have a triangle, and have a good big one while you are about it—by carrying a pair of tongs slung from a loop of string and beating them with a big door-key.

Trumpets and flutes and fifes and all other wind instruments are played through the mouth of the performer.

You can either whistle or hum or howl the tune, but it sounds all the better if you buzz it through a comb covered with a piece of thin paper.

The Conductor is really an important person in the show, and if he is a good actor he will shine as a conductor.

But really the band is not so ridiculous as it seems if you like to play it carefully, in good time and in good order.

You can if you like make music instead of a noise, and by singing very softly in a quiet hum at times, and then loudening up into a tremendous chorus at others, it will really sound well and do you credit.

One of the best drum and fife bands I ever heard was made by a number of boys drumming on kerosene tins and loudly whistling the tune, and the effect was splendid as they marched down the street.

A household band might consist of first and second combs, tongs, pair of tin mugs, saucepan lids, biscuit tin, and tea-tray.

For muffled drum effects, a tea-tray beaten with a banana is most realistic.

## THIRTEENTH BITE

PACK HOLIDAYS—COMFORT IN CAMP—HOW TO MAKE YOUR BED—HOW TO PACK YOUR KIT—IN CAMP—THINGS TO REMEMBER—THE CAMP STOMACH-ACHE.

### Pack Holidays

Some of you Cubs may be lucky enough to go off with Akela and other Old Wolves for a few days for a Pack Holiday, which is really very much the same thing as camping, the chief difference being that, instead of sleeping in a tent, you sleep in a Group Headquarters, or a school or other suitable building. This doesn't mean that you will be staying indoors except at night for you will want, of course, to get out as much as ever you can.

You will have to make just the same preparations for a Pack Holiday as you would for a Cub Camp and so, as practically everything applies equally to both of these, I am going to begin straightaway to talk about Cub Camping.

### Comfort in Camp

Every Scout aims at being a good camper, because you can't be a backwoodsman or a pioneer unless you can look after yourself in all weathers in the open. You Cubs will have to leave *real* camping until you become Scouts, and what fun you will have to look forward to then! But possibly Akela may arrange to take some of you to camp in the summer, if you are very good Cubs. If you do go to camp, there are several things you ought to know, if you are to make yourselves comfortable.

People talk of roughing it in camp. Well, a tenderfoot may find it rough and uncomfortable, because when he goes into camp for the first time he puts up his tent on a nice green patch of grass down in a hollow, and the rain comes on in the night and floods him out.

He probably pulls all the cords of his tent as tight as they will go; in the night the dew or rain comes and shrinks the cords so that they drag the pegs nearly out of the ground; a breeze springs up, out comes the pegs, and down goes the tent!

There are lots of ways in which a tenderfoot suffers in camp. But there is no roughing it for an Old Scout; he knows how to make himself quite comfortable.

A good Cub knows that his camp should be on a dry and fairly high place, protected from the north and east winds (those are the chilly ones); that all good Pack camps have a jolly barn or hut where the Cubs can have sing-songs or play games if the weather is horrid.

A Cub knows too that if he is to have the best possible camp he must start getting ready for it some time beforehand and not leave everything to a scrambled last minute.

How are we to start this getting ready? By saving money? Yes.

If you are going to camp, have a Camp Bank, and every Cub should pay something into it. It doesn't matter how small that something may be, provided that you really try to help your parents by doing a little towards paying for your pleasures—and camp is a pleasure, isn't it?

This saving is part of the getting ready, but you should also learn some of the things that have to be done in camp.

### How to Make your Bed

It is a great thing to be able to make your bed so that in the morning you find yourself still covered over. First put your

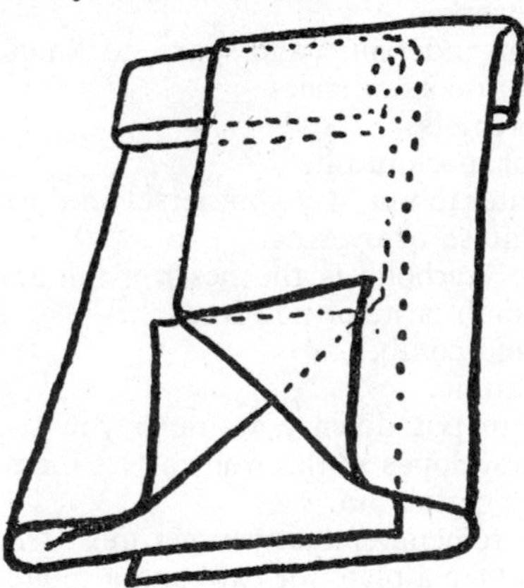

ground sheet down with the shiny side on the ground, then put the palliasse with the straw in it on top. Take one blanket and fold it in halves, then fold the other one the same way and put it under the top half of the other with its edges against the other's fold—you get in the middle and you have two thicknesses of blanket under you and two over you. If you look at the drawing carefully you will see that you can't fall out, and your toes won't get cold if you fold the bottom over and pin it.

With the two thicknesses of blanket and a properly filled palliasse under you, you'll be as warm as toast and far happier than any Tenderfoot Tim who thinks that things *over* you are all you need, and lets all the damp and draught in to chill him!

### How to Pack your Kit

It is a jolly good idea to have one real practice of this at home before the actual packing day arrives—you may find that you need a bigger kit-bag, and it's as well to know that in time to buy or borrow one.

Write out a list of the things you think you will want, even if you have a list from your Cubmaster to guide you, then turn your bed into a shop and put all the things out on the counter. You will have something like this list of things on it.

Two blankets—woolly ones are better than smooth ones.
Pyjamas or a warm shirt to sleep in.
A pair of gym. shoes for games.
An old pair of shorts and a shirt to wear and tear in camp games and work.
A spare vest or undershirt, and spare stockings.
A spare pair of boots or shoes.
Some handkerchiefs.
An overcoat or mackintosh.
A coat or sweater to put over your jersey in the evening besides your mackintosh or overcoat.
A towel, soap (carbolic is the best), a flannel, a toothbrush and some tooth paste or powder.
A hairbrush and comb.
A bathing costume.
A little book to put down how much you spend, and some paper and envelopes so that you can let them know at home how you are getting on.
It's as well to remember that you get most frightfully hungry at camp, so take a plate (or two) and a mug, a knife, a fork, and a spoon; deep enamel plates and mugs are the best because they don't break if a silly ass sits on them.

If the Pack does not possess ground-sheets and you are camping in tents you will have to get hold of one—and be sure that it is a good one.

Persuade your Sixer to be decent and bring a mirror so that you can part your hair without it looking like forked lightning.

By this time the bed looks fairly full and you wonder how ever you are going to get all the things into a kit-bag.

Some boys put their overcoat in their kit-bag first and then get mad because it rains and they have to empty everything out to get it. Start with your gym. shoes and swimming costume, then the change of clothes, pyjamas, and blankets—with anything that might get broken in the middle. It is best to have a little waterproof bag for your soap—don't pack the carbolic in your mug, it makes the tea taste funny! Right on the top have your ground-sheet and (if you have room) your mackintosh, and just underneath your towel and washing things.

Don't forget to mark your things, so that you can see which are yours and which aren't.

## IN CAMP

Now that we've packed our kit let's be off, shall we? Write your name and the place to which you are going on a label and tie the label to your kit-bag. Get someone to help you carry your kit to the station or wherever you are meeting Akela.

When you are in the train don't lean against the doors or stick your head out so far that a passing train knocks it off!

And when you are in camp remember that as you are there to have a splendid time you must keep in mind the Cubs' patent dodge for making themselves happy—that of helping other people and particularly Akela.

Do just as you are told and don't rush about like a Bandar.

Keep your things in your kit-bag till you know where you are going to sleep, and when your spot has been settled unpack your things and make your bed.

When you are told that it is time to go to sleep, shut your eyes and do your best—don't keep everyone else awake by dancing a Highland fling on your bed or having a pillow fight with your next-door neighbour.

When you wake up in the morning imagine you have been born without a tongue and keep it absolutely still, until it's time to get up.

This is the sort of way your day will be spent.

7.30. The Camp gets up. Turn your bed over double so that the others don't walk on it. When you wash don't do the job half-heartedly, but strip—it is worth it. Throw your dirty water into the proper pit and hang up your towel to dry on the clothes-line.

Wear your old clothes at this time of the morning and your gym. shoes without stockings as the grass will be very wet.

8.15. Breakfast.

8.45. Camp jobs. After breakfast, each Six and Cub will have certain jobs to do, such as to tidy their own tents and the hut, and see that there is not a scrap of paper or rubbish anywhere about. Each Cub will have to bring out his blankets and hang them on a fence or a clothes-line to air, put his ground-sheet outside his tent with his kit neatly piled on it, and get himself into correct uniform above the knees. This is the time for each boy to have his daily "clear."

10.0. Inspection—of you and your kit and of the camp site.

10.15. Prayers, Flag-break, Grand Howl.

10.30. Camp games and other morning stunts.

12.0. Bathing (perhaps).

1.0. Dinner. Wash up. Each Cub will do his own washing up with the aid of a mop, a bowl of warm, soapy water, and a drying towel.

1.45. Rest time. You will not be allowed to move about, but there will be Canteen and Bank, and one of the Old Wolves will read an exciting book or something of that kind.

2.45. Games or expedition.

5.0. Tea and another wash up.

5.30. Get beds made. Camp games and free time.

7.0. Flag-down.

7.15. Supper.

8.0. Camp fire.

8.45. Prayers. Wash and get ready for bed.

9.15. Lights out.

### Things to Remember

The most important thing is the Cub grin. Don't grouse if the porridge is burnt or some other Cub sits on your bread and jam.

Before you go, and the whole time you are away, say to

yourself, " I am going to make this the jolliest camp there ever was FOR THE OTHER CUBS."

When you leave, leave nothing but your thanks and a good name.

Remember that trees are alive and that you would not like to have an arm or a leg torn off! Be especially careful about fruit trees; even if you see apples lying about on the ground, remember that it does not make them yours, it is just a splendid chance for a good turn; pick all the decent ones up in a basket and take them to the owner. Never go hunting for wood without a grown-up with you in case you make a mistake and take things that you shouldn't touch.

Long grass is probably going to be cut for hay, and it is very difficult to cut it with a machine if it is all lying down on the ground.

Let gates just look the same after your Pack have been through them as they did before you came anywhere near, and just note that they have a nasty way of breaking if you swing on them!

Leave cows, pigs, horses, and all manner of animals alone. No, I'm not so worried about their hurting *you*, but of your hurting *them*.

A bad camp can always be traced by the rubbish and paper that are left about in and near it. When you see any rubbish lying about in your camp don't wait for " Joe " to pick it up! Do it yourself.

*Akela's Story at Camp Fire.*

### The Camp Stomach-ache

"What sort of cake do you like?" said the old gentleman to the boy.

"Oh, I like plum-cake, and seed-cake, and currant-cake, and ginger-cake, and lemon-cake, and——"

"Here, that will do!" cried the old gentleman. "If you go on like that, you'll have another kind of cake—one that you *won't* like—and that is—stomach-ache."

But even without eating too many cakes, you can get this painful experience, especially when you are in camp, unless you are a bit careful.

So, if you want to have a good time in camp, and not be sent home ill after a few days of it, remember these few hints and carry them out.

*Fruit.*—Don't eat too much fruit. A little of it is a very good thing, especially if it has been cooked or stewed. But fruit that is over-ripe, or that is not quite ripe, is very apt to give you "gripes."

*Water.*—Then water is often dangerous, unless it comes from a filter or good spring. Often a clear and cool-looking stream carries the drainage from a farm higher up, and, although it may look clean, it may contain rank poison.

*Washing.*—Wash your hands before each meal, because your fingers, and especially the finger-nails, are apt to get dirt on them—and, although you don't notice it, may contain little germs of poison.

*Flies.*—Also do all you can to keep flies out of your camp, because they are fond of settling on any filth, and then they come and settle on your food, bringing the poison on their feet.

Remember that a fly can carry on its feet enough germs to poison a man.

Flies don't flourish when everything is kept clean. Don't therefore allow any old scraps to lie about the camp, but carefully sweep them up and burn them, and then the flies don't get a chance.

Don't put out jam-jars for the little chaps in striped yellow and black football jerseys. You only make them come all the more. Keep all sticky sweet things covered up and safe.

*Latrines.*—Be careful to have your daily "clear" regularly, and if you don't, go to Akela and get some medicine. Cubs go to camp because they are old enough and big enough to look after themselves in this way.

*Dry Rub.*—When I was in camp in Zululand, we were far from any water where we could bathe. But washing is so good for keeping you fit and well. So we used to go out in the early morning, while the long grass was all wet with dew, and roll in it. Thus we got wet all over, and then, after rubbing ourselves with rough towels, we were just as clean and refreshed as if we had had a bath.

You can always get enough water to damp a towel, wherever you are, and this rub-down should never be missed, at least once a day. It does you a world of good.

*Dry Clothes.*—Lots of tenderfoots catch cold in camp, but a Scout only catches cold when he has to sleep in a stuffy house.

The reason for catching cold in camp is not really from being in the open air, but chiefly because fellows let their clothes get damp, and this gives them a chill.

Watch any old campaigner in camp, and you will see he is very careful to change his clothes the moment they are damp.

*A Cub Camp.*

In West Africa, I never got fever when everybody else was ill with it. I had two shirts; one I wore, the other I carried hanging on my back with the sleeves knotted round my neck. This shirt was drying all the time while the one I was wearing was getting damp. (It was mighty hard work marching, you must remember.)

Directly we halted, if it were only for a few minutes, off came my damp shirt, and on went the dry one. In this way, I did not sit still in a wet shirt, catching the breeze and getting a chill, as so many did. The consequence was that I kept fit and well when others got sick and in many cases died.

As I have already mentioned, wear gym. shoes and no stockings in the early morning while the grass is still wet.

# FOURTEENTH BITE

SAFETY IN THE HOME—DIRT IN A WOUND—BURNS—SCALDS—SHOCK—GAME: *Stepping Stones*—PRACTICES—OBSERVATION IN NATURE—INVESTITURE OF THE TWO-STAR CUB.

### Safety in the Home

Every day lots and lots of people are hurt and some of them are killed because of accidents in their homes which ought never to have happened if they had been a little more careful.

When you learnt the Highway Code you found out how to look after yourselves and other people on the roads, but it's just as important indoors.

Most of the accidents that happen are due to burning. A fire should have a guard in front of it or somebody's clothes may swing into the flames, or a piece of burning fuel may fall out on the hearthrug and set the house on fire. Or a hot iron may be left standing on something which may catch fire, instead of on its proper rest. Even the head of a match may fly off and cause damage if it is not properly struck. And if they are left about for a baby to play with, of course there will be trouble.

Babies, too, have a habit of snatching at anything they can reach. If it happens to be the tea-pot or the handle of a saucepan of scalding water, they may be terribly hurt. Pots and pans on the stove should be placed so that the handle doesn't stick out invitingly, as even a grown-up may knock into them and send the contents flying.

Very old people are nearly as bad as babies, if they are a bit wobbly on their feet or short-sighted. If other people leave things lying about in dark corners or on the stairs, Granny may have a bad fall and old bones break more easily than yours.

There's a right way and a wrong way to use a knife or any tools, and there are many other ways in which people can be badly cut.

Electricity and gas and oil stoves and lamps can all be killers if they are not properly handled.

Cubs should know about all these things and should always be careful to do them properly, so that there are no accidents in *their* homes.

### Dirt in a Wound

Our soldiers have to keep themselves particularly clean, and great trouble is taken to get hot baths for them every day. And why do you suppose they go to this trouble?

It is because if a man gets wounded when his skin is dirty, the wound very often festers and gets worse, but if his skin is quite clean, the wound heals up very quickly.

That is why you should keep yourself clean and should often wash your hands, because you are always likely to get a cut finger or to graze a bit of skin off your knuckles, or do something cheerful of that kind; and if your skin is clean it will heal up quickly, but if you let dirt get into the cut it may get hot and swell and fester, and take quite a long and painful time to get well—all because you were not careful to keep the wound clean. So if you get a scratch or a cut, put a dab of iodine on it and all will be well.

A gentleman was dancing at a ball with a lady when a comb in her hair came loose; in putting up her hand quickly to catch it she accidentally scratched her partner's nose. He thought nothing of it and did not take care of it, probably letting the dust of the ballroom get into the little wound, and the result was that it festered and poisoned his blood, so that he died within a week or two.

So be careful to keep all wounds, however small, well washed, and covered up so that dust cannot get to them, and they will quickly heal. But the covering must be particularly clean and free from germs.

Keeping them covered from the cold air also makes them smart less.

### Burns

If you knock some of your skin off, the flesh underneath is awfully tender, and cold air makes it burn like billy-o. When anyone gets accidentally burnt the skin is destroyed and the flesh is open to the air; so the thing to do is, cover it lightly with softest rag or *clean* paper. The surface is fearfully tender and cannot bear anything at all hard, and moreover it gets very sticky, and any stuff put directly on it is likely to get stuck to it and will cause worse agony later when you try to pull it off again.

If you are indoors you might soak your clean rag in warm water to which bicarbonate of soda has been added (see First Aider, page 175), and lay this on the burn. Put a pad of wool or a clean folded handkerchief over the dressing and bandage gently.

### Scalds

Fire burns—but water, oil, and anything hot and *wet* scald. A scald, like a burn, has to be covered up as quickly as possible; put a clean rag on it if you have nothing else. A scald is pretty sure to form blisters—be particularly careful not to break or prick these.

### Shock

When a person receives a burn or a scald, or any other injury, he gets a shock. Not an electric shock, of course, unless he has been meddling with electric wires.

When someone is hurt, you must remember to fetch or send somebody for a grown-up person as soon as possible; and you must do this even if you think you can deal with the injury yourself.

Until the grown-up arrives, keep the patient warm and quiet, and prevent other people crowding round him.

### Game: Stepping Stones

Put down small bits of board, or cardboard (nailed to the ground), or mark on the ground a twisty line of stepping-stones as if for crossing a brook—some close together, others far apart. Each Cub to try the course in turn, two tries. In the second try he carries in his hand a board about eight inches square, on which is a tennis-ball, which must not be dropped.

### Practices

Have an alarm that one boy is on fire: roll him up in the nearest material available, blanket, coat, or other boys' jackets, rug, etc.

Practise each boy at doing the thing as being the real way to impress it on their minds and memories.

Treat the patient as for a burn.

Clean and bandage cut finger.

### Observation in Nature

Do you always go about with your eyes wide open, I wonder? If so you will not find this test very difficult for it says that you must " Observe and point out from life three birds (not domestic), three trees and three other natural things, such as insects, flowers, fishes." The last bit gives you a wide choice and each one of you should try to choose something different from all the others.

### Investiture of the Two-Star Cub

Now you have come to the end of your tests for the Second Star, and if you can show Akela that, besides knowing these, you can also remember all that you learnt for your First Star, you can put a Second Star in your cap, and both your eyes will be open like those of the wolves. You will be able to be much more helpful to Akela, to other Cubs, to your parents at home and to those you meet. But you can only remain helpful so long as you keep practising all the things you have learned, not only in the Second Star but also in the First Star and the Tenderpad.

In Part II you will find details of the Badges you will now be able to try for, but before you come to that I will set out for you the kind of ceremony which Akela may arrange for you when you become a Two-Star Cub.

The Pack is formed up in Parade Circle as for the investiture of a Tenderpad, but the Cubs who have earned their Second Stars are together, bareheaded, as part of the circle. Their caps with two stars attached are with Akela, who then tells the Cubs that they have successfully passed their tests for becoming full Wolf Cubs.

He reminds them of the meaning of the two stars, that young wolves are born with their eyes shut. For some few days they grope about blindly, but gradually they begin to see and understand things. At first they see how to see and to obey the Old Wolf's directions, so you, as Tenderpads, learned the Laws of the Wolf Cub Pack and the Promise, how to make yourselves healthy and active and strong.

Then they began to see how to do things for themselves, to jump and run, to make signs to each other, to hunt and get their own food, and to be loyal to the Pack. So you learned how to make or draw things, how to tie knots, and to make yourselves useful to other people and to do your duty to Queen and Country.

Now you have shown that you have both eyes open and can do the duties of trained Wolf Cubs. So you will henceforth wear the cap with the two marks on it, which mean your two eyes are now as bright as stars, that you will see quickly and well, you will let nothing escape your notice. You will look ahead and be prepared to do what will be wanted, you will look around and see how you can help others, you will look back and so remember what has been told you. In this way you will be a smart and useful Cub.

For the presentation, Akela calls the Cub or Cubs who have

earned their Second Star, to stand in front of him in the centre of the Circle. Akela asks them if they are ready to repeat their Promise, to mark the importance of the occasion. The Pack is called to the " Alert," and then each of the new Two Star Cubs steps forward in turn, salutes and repeats his Promise, phrase by phrase after Akela. When each has renewed his Promise, Akela gives him his cap, with the two stars in it, which he puts on for himself and then steps back to make room for the next.

Then Akela congratulates them and they return to their place in the circle.

The Grand Howl follows, when the new Two Star Cubs may be given the honour of leading the Howl and calling the DYB DYB DYB DYB together.

# FIFTEENTH BITE

GOING UP—THE LEAPING WOLF—GOING UP CEREMONY—
THE NEXT STEP

" *As the creeper that girdles the tree trunk, the Law runneth forward and back*"—
*For the strength of the Pack is the Troop, and the strength of the Troop is the Pack.*

Now this is the yarn of " The Boys who were too young but wanted to Join."

. . . and the Scribe took up his pen and wrote: The great Scout Brotherhood was born in the year nineteen hundred and eight, and it grew as no other game for boys had ever grown before. Troops appeared to the North and to the South, to the East and to the West, and all the Scouts in them said to their uncles and aunts, brothers and cousins, " Yes, this is the best thing we ever did! "

Now a few years went by, and the Scoutmasters began to notice that a lot of smaller boys gathered outside the clubroom doors and looked longingly inside. These boys said to the Scoutmaster, " Let us too be Scouts," and the Scoutmasters answered, " No, you are too young, you must go away! " But the boys would not go away, so at last the Scoutmasters went to the Chief of all the Scouts and told him. " Behold!—And what shall we do? " and the Chief Scout said, " Let them prepare themselves to be Scouts. Make them Wolf Cubs, and put them in Packs together."

So the Scoutmasters went back to their clubrooms and told the younger boys who wanted to join, and the younger boys said, " Yes, let it be so. We will run with the Pack until we are old enough to be able to be Scouts."

Years passed, and everything was most nice and comfortable. And then the Chief Scout, the Scoutmasters, and the Cubmasters said to the boys who were no longer too young, " *Now* you can be full Scouts! " But many of those boys, forgetting the whole reason why they had been made Wolf Cubs, began to make excuses and said—

Yes, Cubs! You know just the sort of things they said—

That they were very happy in the Cubs and did not want to leave.

That they did not want to give up all their badges and stripes and be the least important members of the Troop.

That the Scouts were not interesting enough.

That they did not know the Scoutmaster and that all their friends were in the Pack.

They only looked at the back of the picture—at *possible* unhappiness and disappointment. They did not even give a single glance to the more important side—the side that would have shown them that Scouting is a great big adventure; that a Cub never really leaves his Pack because it is just part of the Troop, and that he can do more for that Pack as a Scout than he ever could while still a Cub, for the Scouts will judge it by the doings of those who have been in it.

The Knights of old went out into danger and battle for the sake of the good name of their Patron, their Country, or their Lady.

The Cubs of to-day can go into the Troop for the sake of the good name of their Pack.

The more dangers and troubles they expect—the more they should brace their shoulders and go forward. If anyone told you the story of a man who turned back from doing a difficult job because he was quite happy at home, you would not think much of him, would you?

The Knights went out to danger and they were pretty certain to find it—but, if you look round and see the fellows who have gone before you into the Troop, do they look miserable or half dead? I think not! Well, have a try yourself and see what happens. Worries always look tremendous if you shiver at them—make up your mind to stick to your Troop, for you are a member of the Scouts even when a Cub, you know. As soon as you were enrolled as a Tenderpad you were admitted into the Great Scout Brotherhood—do not fail when it asks you to go forward. Help to make the words at the beginning of this Bite come true.

Of course, I am not saying the Troop will be quite like the Pack. It won't be.

In the Pack you are in a sort of Jungle Nursery, in the Troop you will have to think for yourself and stand on your own feet. You will have to stop *yourself* from following a crowd if you are not sure that crowd is on a Scouty job; you will have to stop *yourself* from giving up a thing because it seems dull and hard. You will need real pluck and steadiness.

" Honour all Men, Fear God, Honour the King and Love the Brotherhood," that was the Knight's code—get on your Scout armour (your Patrol Leader and Scoutmaster will help you to buckle each bit in place) and see what *you* can do.

### The Leaping Wolf Badge

A Cub who has gained his Second Star and also three proficiency badges, one of which must be either the First Aider, the Guide or the House Orderly, may then wear a Leaping Wolf Badge on the right-hand side of his jersey (just above the place where the pocket would be if you had one!).

When you go up into the Troop the Scouts will then be able to see that you have really done a job of work while you were in the Pack, for if they only see your Service Stars they can hardly tell what kind of a Cub you have been, can they? And you and I know that some boys *are* occasionally a bit like the Bandarlog.

When you become a First Class Scout you take down the Leaping Wolf Badge for then you will have shown that you are a really useful Scout.

### Going up Ceremony

At the end of your last Pack Meeting, something like this may happen:

The Pack forms Parade Circle at one end of the Den, the Troop a horseshoe at the other.

The Pack does the Grand Howl. The Cub who is going up falls out in front of the Cubmaster who wishes him Good Hunting in the name of the Pack. The Cub then repeats his Cub Promise for the last time. He then shakes hands with every Cub in his Six, and returns to the centre. The Pack gives him three Cub cheers or a " WOOF." The Parade Circle opens to allow the boy and the Cubmaster to go to the line, where the Scoutmaster is waiting for them. The Cubmaster hands the boy over to the Scoutmaster, who takes him into the horseshoe and introduces him to his Patrol Leader. The Patrol Leader takes the Cub to his future Patrol, who makes him welcome. The ceremony may close with the Troop yell.

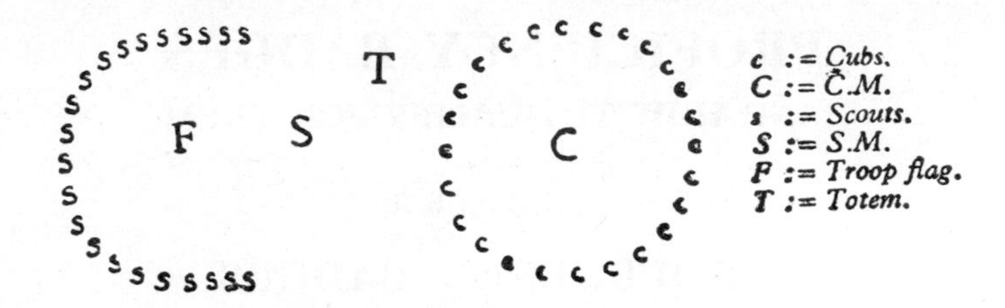


## The Next Step

You have wandered through the Jungle and your eyes have been opened to see many wonderful things. Now you go forward on your journey into the greater Land of Scouting, and Akela and the Pack speed you on your way with a cheery call of "Good Hunting." You will never forget your days with the Pack. One day, it may be, you will return to it and help other Cubs to open their eyes in the Jungle.

Good Hunting!

PART II

# PROFICIENCY BADGES

## AND HOW TO QUALIFY FOR THEM

CHAPTER I

## PROFICIENCY BADGES

THE object of the Proficiency Badges is to help remedy defects and to develop character and physical health. They should not, however, be regarded in the same way as the Star Tests. Badges are activities which individual Cubs can take up in order that they may progress further along Cub paths; they should be encouraged to take them up with a view to self-development but not at the expense of their ordinary work with the Pack.

They will start on some of these activities for themselves in many cases before they have won their Second Stars.

A Cub is allowed, if he wishes, to win and wear not more than two Proficiency Badges after he has gained his First Star, but he should at the same time be continuing to work at his Second Star tests.

There are fifteen Cub Proficiency Badges which cover a wide range of subjects, amongst which every Cub should be able to find some of special interest to him.

Proficiency Badges are granted on the recommendation of a qualified and independent examiner approved by the Local Association. They are worn on the right arm in parallel rows between the shoulder and elbow.

### THE TOTEM POLE

A Wolf Cub Pack is entitled to carry a Totem Pole (see p. 60). A ribbon can be added to the Totem every time a Cub gets a Proficiency Badge, the winner's name being written on a tab attached to the ribbon.

One object of the Totem is to make a permanent record of the Pack's achievements; at the same time it must be remembered that efficiency in badges is not a true test of a real Wolf Cub Pack. A happy family spirit counts for more than anything else.

## DIAGRAM OF BOY FAILINGS AND CUB REMEDIES

| Failings common to young boys | Cause | Education needed in | Remedy groups | Cub activities and badges for |
|---|---|---|---|---|
| Showing off<br>Bragging<br>Shyness<br>Lying | Inexperience | CHARACTER | Intelligence and perserverance | Collecting<br>Observation of Nature<br>Gardening<br>Book reading<br>Entertaining<br>Signalling |
| Mischief<br>Destructiveness<br>Carelessness<br>Impatience | Want of interest or curiosity | | Handicraft | Drawing<br>Handcraft<br>Toymaking |
| Disobedience<br>Selfishness<br>Cruelty | Disregard of others | | Doing things for others | First-aid<br>Home-duties<br>Guide-duty |
| Awkwardness<br>Poor physical development<br>Remediable physical defects | Want of knowledge and exercises | PHYSICAL HEALTH | Athletics and cleanliness | Cycling<br>Swimming<br>Athletics<br>Self-care<br>Sportsmanship |

*Artist.*

*Athlete.*

*Book Reader.*

*Collector.*

*Cyclist.*

*Entertainer.*

*First Aider.*

*Gardener.*

*Guide.*

*Handcraft.*

*House Orderly*

*Observer.*

*Signaller.*

*Sportsman.*

*Swimmer.*

## TESTS FOR PROFICIENCY BADGES

**Artist.**—1. Must draw in the presence of the examiner, with pencil, brush, pen, or crayon an original illustration of any incident or character in a simple story (size not less than seven by five inches).

2. In addition do one of the following:—

(*a*) Draw from life or memory, in pen and ink or pencil, any animal or human being he has seen.
(*b*) Draw from nature a landscape or still-life group.
(*c*) Keep a sketch-book for a period of three months.
(*d*) Illustrate a story by means of match-stick figures in a series of not less than four pictures.
(*e*) Make a simple greeting card, of his own design, using pencil, brush, pen, or crayon.
(*f*) Make a model in clay, pyruma, or other plastic material.

(Note.—*The natural bent of the boy is to be encouraged in every way; the spirit and intention of his work to count as much as adherence to academic rules.*)

**Athlete.**—These tests are divided into two classes, A and B. Class A is for Cubs from 8-10 years of age; B for those of 10-12. The tests are of the same nature in both classes, but the standards are different.

N.B.—The average height of Cubs in Class A is 4 ft. 1 in. If a Cub in this class is unusually developed (not only in height) he shall be judged in Class B. If the Cub is under-developed he should take the tests in Class A.

Must be able:—

*Class A.*

To sprint 50 yards in 10 seconds.
To jump 2 ft. 6 ins. (high jump).
To jump 6 ft. (long jump).
To climb a tree at least 15 ft., or climb a rope at least 10 ft.
To throw a cricket ball 20 yards, and catch one thrown from 10 yards.

*Class B.*

To sprint 70 yards in 12½ seconds.
To jump 2 ft. 8 ins. (high jump).
To jump 7 ft. 6 ins. (long jump).
To climb a tree at least 15 ft., or climb a rope at least 10 ft.
To throw a cricket ball 30 yards, and catch one thrown from 15 yards.

**Book Reader.**

1. Produce a list of books he has read in the previous year, name their authors and be able to tell the Examiner something about the story of three of these books. The three books to be chosen by the Cub. The three books must be of a reasonable standard, taking the Cub's age and development into account.
2. Read aloud a simple piece of prose or poetry chosen by the Examiner.
3. Show that he understands how to care for books and make a dust cover and entitle it neatly.
4. Show that he can use a dictionary.

**Collector.**—Must make a good collection of one group of objects, neatly and systematically arranged, for a period of at least three months, and know something about them, and show an intelligent interest in it. The nature of the collection should be chosen by the Cub. Suggestions are as follows:—Stamps; postmarks; picture postcards; cigarette cards; fruit papers; match-box tops; crests; coins; feathers; leaves or flowers. (For the purpose of the last two, photographic or carbon reproductions may be accepted.) A collection of birds' eggs is not admissible.

*Or*, must keep a scrapbook diary of events, etc., for a period of at least three months.

**Cyclist.**—1. Own or have the regular use of a bicycle of proper size.

2. Be able to mount and dismount properly.
3. Be able to clean and oil his bicycle and pump up the tyres. Understand the need for keeping the bicycle in a road-worthy condition.
4. Under observation go for a short ride on a specified course, showing a knowledge of the proper use of signals and of the Highway Code (paras. 62-75 and special Notes for Cyclists, pages 30-31).

**Entertainer.**—Be able to give a satisfactory performance in any two of the following:—

Playing a musical instrument (two tunes); singing (two songs); reciting; acting or miming; puppetry; conjuring.

(The first two alternatives to be well-known tunes; the performance for each of the latter alternatives to last at least three minutes.)

**First Aider.**—1. Show that he knows the meaning of "First Aid" and the need for summoning adult help.

2. Show how to dress minor cuts and grazes and know the importance of cleanliness in treatment.

3. Demonstrate simple roller bandaging of a hand and a knee, and the large arm sling.

4. Know the common causes of burns and scalds in the home and their prevention; how to put out burning clothing; the simple treatment of burns and scalds.

5. Know the symptoms of and how to treat shock resulting from burns and accidents.

**Gardener.**—1. Must care for and cultivate a patch of garden of at least 16 square feet, preferably a square of approximately 4 feet by 4 feet, for at least four months.

2. Be able to demonstrate the use of, and how to care for, the following tools:—

Spade, fork, hoe, trowel, rake.

*In the case of Town Packs where patches of garden are impossible, the following alternatives can be taken in place of* 1 *and* 2*:—*

Grow from seed three different plants in pots or in a window box for at least four months.

3. Be able to point out and name 6 garden flowers and 6 vegetables from growing specimens.

4. Distinguish and name:—

(*a*) Four common weeds, and
(*b*) Three common enemies of the garden, and
(*c*) Three common friends of the garden.

**Guide.**—1. Be able to give clear and concise directions, well expressed and distinctly spoken, to a stranger asking his way; and do so politely and promptly.

2. Know the whereabouts of the nearest police station or box, doctor, chemist, public telephone, fire alarm, railway station, petrol station, motor garage, and hotel.

3. Know how to call for Fire, Police, Ambulance.

4. *In towns.* Know the number, if any, and at least two places each way on the route of the local buses or trams up to a maximum of four routes.

**Handcraft.**—1. Make an article from odds and ends such as fire cones, clothes pegs, etc., *or* recondition two durable toys approved by the Cubmaster.

2. Make a worthwhile toy or model of reasonable size, such as a boat, engine, motor car, aeroplane or animal, *or* in reasonably correct proportions and colouring, a worthwhile composite toy or model such as a farmyard, jungle, ark with animals, cottage with furniture, or station, *or*

Make two useful or decorative articles from cane, raffia, wool, leather, wood, string or any other suitable material approved by the Cubmaster.

(Note: An article presented for the Second Star test must not be admitted for any part of this Badge.)

**House Orderly.**—Perform six out of the following eight tests, the choice to be made by the Cub, but No. 1 being obligatory:

1. Make a pot of tea and fry bacon or sausage or fry or poach an egg.
2. Prepare potatoes and boil or bake or fry them.
3. Make a bed, wash up crockery, utensils, etc.
4. Clean windows and silver or brasswork.
5. Clean and tidy a room.
6. Lay a table for at least three people for a meal of two courses.
7. Thread a needle and sew on a button *or* darn a hole in a jersey or stocking *or* mend a tear.
8. Wash and iron his scarf.

**Observer.**—1. Either:

(*a*) Observe from life and be able to describe the appearance and habits of any six living creatures (such as animals, birds, insects, fish or reptiles).

(*b*) Recognise from life and name accurately six trees and six flowers in season, preferably wild.

*or*

(*c*) Keep in reasonable detail a Nature log for a period of at least three months.

2. Find his way to an unknown spot, between 300-400 yards away by following directions given to him by the Examiner (either compass directions, or signs made on the ground, or landmarks, or a combination of these).

3. Must be able to play Kim's Game, nine objects out of twelve.

**Signaller.**—1. Must know the alphabet in Semaphore or Morse, paying special attention to correct positions of Semaphore, or the timing of Morse.

2. Be able to send and read a short simple message of ten words, slowly but getting eight out of ten correct.

3. Demonstrate the special signs in *Scouting for Boys* (viz. general answer, numbers, letters and erase).

4. Exchange a message by using a " secret " code to be chosen or invented by the Cub.

**Sportsman.**—1. Know the rules or laws of two team games such as Rugby football, Association football, cricket, hockey, rounders.

2. Show reasonable proficiency and be taking an active part in at least one of these.

3. Show a good sportsmanlike spirit in all Cub games and activities.

*Note:* Certificates must be produced for Test 2 from C.M. or schoolmaster and for Test 3 from C.M.

**Swimmer.**—1. Must be able to swim 25 yards (any stroke except back stroke).

2. Swim on back for 15 yards.

3. Be able to float on back for 60 seconds in salt water or 20 seconds in fresh water, *or* tread water for two minutes in salt water or one minute in fresh water.

4. Be able to " duck's dive " (*i.e.*, dive while standing in the water or swimming). *Or* (as alternative), perform a " honey-pot " (*i.e.*, jump with arms clasped round knees) from a board, bank, or boat, *or* dive from side of the bath.

### Presentation of Badges

It is desirable to mark the importance of winning a badge by having a little ceremony of presentation, and the opportunity of this occasion can be taken to impress upon the Cub by means of a pow-wow the desirability of keeping in practice on the subject which he has taken and of advancing in his knowledge of it as time goes on. Especially is this the case in regard to the badges which qualify for the Leaping Wolf, for by the practice of those subjects the Cub can make himself increasingly useful to others.

# CHAPTER II

# ARTIST

## Note to Cubmasters

*Cubmasters should remember that the Artist's Badge is not intended only for Cubs who have already an artistic taste and talent, but for every Cub with eyes and fingers and sense. Its object is to encourage self-expression, observation, memory, neat-handedness and concentration. Boys with any intelligence should be encouraged to go in for the badge, and their special bent be noticed and encouraged; while, if the Cubmaster possesses any artist friends he should try and get them to come and give a few hints and criticisms. Five minutes of expert advice from someone with an artistic soul is worth five hours of amateur advice from someone with merely a well-meaning instructor's soul!*

*Although adherence to academic rules is not insisted on, taste and a certain amount of artistic execution are expected. For instance, a set of grotesque attempts, handed in by a boy who is merely a "badge-hunter," and possesses no artistic talent whatever, should not gain him an Artist's Badge. But a genuine desire to express ideas, even somewhat crude, should receive encouragement.*

## Hints to Cubs

Everybody can draw if he only tries; it does not need learning.

If you practise a little, and copy other pictures to see how artists manage it, you will soon find you can get along all right.

There was a time in his life when the finest artist in the world could not draw any better than any other small boy. Don't expect to be an artist all at once—you are bound to do it fairly badly at first; but stick to it and you will do better as you go along.

It is not a matter of school learning.

In the wildest part of South Africa live some tribes of natives who are so uncivilised that they are only a little better than monkeys. They have no proper language of their own—they live in bushes and trees—they have no clothes—they don't cook their food, but eat it raw; regular savages you would call them, yet they draw awfully good pictures on the walls of the caves and rocks.

They never learnt to draw in schools. They don't know what a school is. But with a burnt stick as a pencil, and mud o

different colours as paint, they make splendid pictures of the wild animals around them.

If these Bushmen, as they are called, can make good drawings with such rough tools, on rocks and with no instruction, surely a Cub can do at least as well with nice pencils, colours, and brushes, and good paper and lots of advice.

Have a try.

Make your pencil very sharp, as that is half the battle in drawing a good sketch. You will never get a good picture at first with a blunt stump of a pencil.

The same with pen-and-ink drawing; use a hard-pointed fine pen and Indian ink.

When you draw, never put in a line or a touch without some good reason for it, otherwise your picture gets mixed.

The usual way is to think of what you want to draw and then sketch it in lightly in outline—and afterwards go over it again with darker and finer strokes.

Clean paper also helps to make the picture a good one, but you won't get clean paper if your fingers are dirty.

*Form.*—Think what you want to draw and draw it as best you can. Perhaps it is a horse with a long body, with neck and head at one corner, two fore-legs at the other, two hind-legs at the third, and a tail at the fourth.

When you have drawn him he doesn't somehow look very like the animal you see in the road.

So get hold of some artist's drawing of him and copy that.

Then you see what you might have put into your picture to make it really like a horse.

Draw a house, or a tree, a man, or anything you like. Then copy a picture of one, and so show yourself how to do it better.

There are several mistakes beginners often make in drawing the human figure. One is making the arms too short. When you have drawn your man's arms, think to yourself, " Would his arms reach nearly to his knees, if he stretched them down ? "

You will very likely find they would not reach much further than his hips! Then you are apt to make his legs too big, and give him a stumpy little body, and probably no neck. One of the greatest artists in the world, called Michael Angelo, was very keen about getting pictures and statues of the human body in right

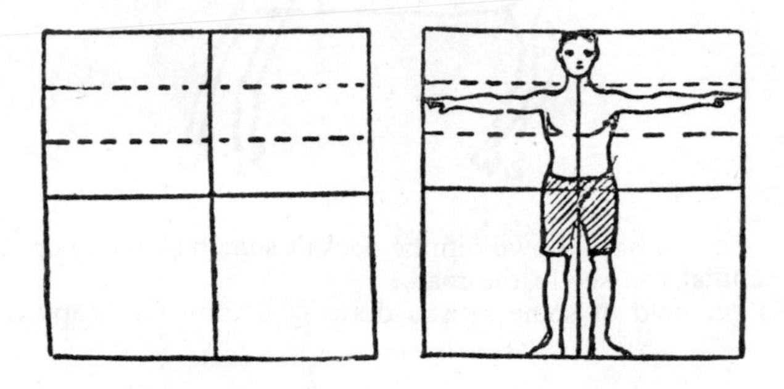

proportion, and he invented a very simple little scale. Even a Cub can make it, and test his drawings, to see if they are right. It is just a square, divided into four quarters, with the top half divided again into three parts.

If you look carefully at the picture you will see that the exact *middle* of the square is the middle of the man, and that his legs reach right to the bottom of the square. His arms are stretched out, with fingers extended, and just touch the two sides. His head fills up the top division of all—or one-sixth of the whole square. This is what Michael Angelo considered the correct proportion of the human body, so I think we can safely apply the scale to our drawings.

*Expression.*—When you have got the shape of the thing—that is, its form—you want to put some life into it.

I saw an awfully good picture the other day by a small boy of five who drew a portrait of his mother.

He might have drawn her like this.

But he didn't. It was a windy day, and he drew her like this, which I thought was very good.

Well—when mother's clothes blew out in the wind they wobbled about, so he could not well draw in fixed lines a thing that was moving all the time; but he put down what he *remembered* of the folds of her dress.

That is the way to do good pictures. To look with the sharp eyes of a wolf at the thing, and to *remember* what it looked like and put that down on paper.

A good way for getting the movement or " expression " in your picture is first to make little sketches of pin-head people till you get them doing what you want to show. Afterwards draw them on a larger size.

Here is a pin-head Scout (*a*).
Make him moving (*b*).
Make him running (*c*).
Then *draw* him running (*d*).

*Colour.*—You will, of course, want to make coloured pictures. Well, you can do a lot at first with a red and blue pencil and a black one. You can draw a Bobbie with his red face, blue coat, and black boots. It is best to draw the outline first lightly in black pencil and add the colour after.

Or you can draw a black steamer, with red funnels on a blue sea with blue sky overhead. Leave white tops to the waves, white clouds in the sky, and put in black curly smoke, which is very black close to the funnel, but gets thinner and lighter as it blows away in the distance.

When you get a lot of pencils or chalks of different colours, you can blossom out. You can copy the flowers you have collected, or draw the story you have been told.

If you have a colour box and brushes so much the better. You need not have very many colours; red, blue, yellow and brown carry you a long way—because these when mixed with each other make more colours.

Red and blue make purple.
Blue and yellow make green.
Brown and blue make black.
Red and yellow make orange.

One of the things you may do for your Artist Badge is to make a Greeting Card. You will find this great fun and far more interesting than buying one. It can be for Christmas, or a birthday, or anything you like, and you can draw and paint it, or cut your designs from coloured paper and form them into a picture by pasting them on card or brown paper. Or you may try your hand at printing from lino cuts or pin point printing, but you will have to get Akela to show you how to do these. There is no end to the fun that you can have with the help of your fingers and a little perseverance.

## CHAPTER III

# ATHLETE

### Hints to Cubs

I HAVE already said something to you in the Tenth and Thirteenth Bites on the subject of keeping yourself healthy and strong. If you aim to be an athlete it will be necessary for you to follow up these hints I have already given you, and do what you can by means of the various ways I have suggested, to make yourself thoroughly fit.

No one can be an athlete unless his heart, his lungs, his stomach, and his nerves are in really good condition.

The tests given for the Athlete Badge are different according to the Cub's age, because it would be absurd to imagine that a boy of nine can jump as high as a boy of 11, and yet we want the boy of 9 to go in for this badge, which will help his body to grow still bigger and stronger. If a Cub has won the badge when he was under 10 years of age, he is naturally expected to pass it again on the higher standard after his tenth birthday. That is only fair to other Cubs who hold the badge.

*Running.*—There is little need to give much in the way of advice in regard to training. The Cub will have to practise for himself, but he should not try and run too fast or jump too high when he first starts or he is likely to strain himself. Learn to run on the toes, with the feet pointing straight forward, not turned out; to hold the body balanced above the feet; to keep the arms fairly close to the sides and not moving too much, and to keep the head up. Don't force the pace too much, but try to develop an easy stride which carries you along with the least possible exertion. Pay also special attention to your breathing, and develop your lungs by practising deep breathing every morning and evening.

*High jump.*—In practising for the high jump, adopt the style that comes easiest to you, whether it is a straight run, or one from the right or left. It will be time enough later on to discard your natural style of jumping for one which will produce better results. Never rush at a high jump, take your run slowly and quietly, and spring off from your toes. You will soon learn how far from the bar to take off. Be very careful to land on your toes on the far side, and to bend your knees *outward* as you land. If you just bend your knees any old how the chances are that you will crack your chin against them, and that hurts like the dickens, especially if you happen to have your tongue between your teeth at the same time! Real athletes always keep their mouths closed as much as possible, and remember to think of their tongue and keep it well housed behind their teeth.

*Long jump.*—It is best to get up a good speed before taking off for a long jump, but practise taking off as near to the mark as you can without over-stepping it. This is very difficult at first, but you ought to keep at it, without jumping hard, until you can take off from the right place at least five times out of six. Then learn to jump high, and not just straight along the ground. If you stick a branch in the ground four or five feet away from the take off, and make up your mind that you are going to jump over it, you will soon learn the trick.

*Climbing a rope.*—When learning to climb a rope, start by grasping the rope with the right hand as high up as you can reach, place the left hand under the right, and then, hanging from both hands, bend your legs up as high as you can and grip the rope between the knees and more especially between the instep of one foot and the sole of the other. When you have a secure grip with the feet, bend the arms, pulling the body straight up alongside the rope. Then move the right hand as high up again as you can reach, and grip the rope hard with it. Move the left hand up under the right and grip hard with both hands. You can then relax your grip with the feet, and lift them up to catch the rope again higher up as you did at first.

In coming down the rope, never let it slide through your hands or it will burn the skin. Lower your body to the full extent of your arms, grip the rope with the knees and feet, lower the left hand till it is opposite your chest, follow it with the right. Take a good grip with both hands, relax the grip with the feet, and let them and your body slide slowly down the rope until you again have your arms fully stretched. Repeat these motions every time until your feet touch the ground again.

*Climbing trees.*—In climbing a tree, the first point is to choose one which you are allowed to climb and which is suitable for the purpose; for instance, some, like the sycamore, will leave stains on your clothes, while others, like the oak, will give you easy foothold and resting places. Beware of dead branches and test each first before putting all your weight on it. Remember that you should always be touching the tree at three points, either with both feet and one hand, or with both hands and one foot, on a branch or projection.

CHAPTER IV

# BOOK READER

## NOTE TO CUBMASTERS

*This is not one of the badges a boy can " go in for " unless he has a habit of reading something other than comics, and has a genuine liking for it. At the same time it may serve to encourage a boy to start this fascinating pursuit and to persevere.*

## HINTS TO CUBS

BOOKS are like a gigantic treasure chest stuffed full of gold and precious stones and pieces of eight—and a bit of nonsense too. It is tremendous fun exploring the chest and deciding for yourself what is valuable and what isn't, what you want to keep and what you don't like.

It's no good plunging into a grown-up book because if you don't really understand it you won't enjoy it, and reading is a thing to be enjoyed. Start with books which are meant for chaps of your age, and there are hundreds of them: adventure stories and true stories about heroes and animals and spies and sea stories . . . There are far too many to list, but somebody will be able to suggest one for you, and if there is a free library in your town there is always a kind person there who could advise you.

Keep a list of the books you read, so that you can remember what they were about and who wrote them and if you liked them.

If you are going to try and make friends with books you must be nice to them, especially if the book was borrowed. Leaving a book lying about open where it can be trodden on, is not being kind to it, nor laying it down face-down so that its back may be broken. Dirty marks on the pages will annoy the next reader nearly as much as bits of litter left lying in a nice picnic place. If you make lop-eared corners to mark your place, sooner or later they will fall off and spoil the book.

It's quite easy to make a book-mark for yourself, and it's a nice present for other book-lovers. Then you must be able to make a paper dust cover for a book to prevent its " boards " or covers getting dirty. Use strong paper and clean hands, and if you can't find out how to make a really neat job of it, ask a grown-up to show you. Then of course it must be beautifully marked with its name and author, on the back of it too, where you can read it when it is standing on a shelf, which is where it likes to be kept.

However well you can read to yourself, reading aloud is quite a different thing and takes a lot of practise. The best stories can be spoiled if they are read in an unnatural voice, making it sound unreal, and pausing in the wrong places so that it hardly makes sense. The commas and other punctuation marks are put there on purpose to show you where to pause, and the parts with no punctuation should be read smoothly but with expression. If you're reading a story about a savage tiger, don't let it sound as if you are describing a rice pudding!

Good reading aloud, or reciting poetry, can be first class entertainment if it is done well, and it a useful sort of good turn to people who are ill or blind.

When you are reciting it is not enough just to know the words by heart, though of course you must be word-perfect, but you've got to know what they mean and make your voice give expression to the meaning. Try and sound as if you were enjoying it, too!

The best Book in the World is the Bible, so try reading that sometimes, a little at a time.

The most useful book is a dictionary, and you will find it fun to look up words which you don't know and find out what they mean and how to pronouce them.

The more you read, the more you will enjoy books and will find that this is one of the best hobbies in the world.

## CHAPTER V

# COLLECTOR

### Note to Cubmasters

*Details concerning the arrangement, etc., of stamps cannot be included here, or lists of crests, etc., or instruction with regard to leaves or flowers. These must be sought in books dealing with the subjects. A few hints may be given, however, on methods which will help the Cubs to arrange their collections and scrapbooks neatly.*

*The main point is that the boy should be encouraged to work on a system, all the better if it is his own system, and should exercise clearness and neatness in describing labelling.*

### Hints to Cubs on Collecting

Of course you know how to collect postcards. Stamps you will soon learn to arrange if you get an album—they are about the best things that a Cub can gather, for they teach him about countries over the seas. Don't stick them in fast with gum, but get your Cubmaster to show you how to remove the envelope and how to use stamp mounts. So far so good—but there are other things you can collect besides these.

If you live by the sea, you can collect sea-shells. A good way of arranging them is to stick them neatly on cardboard, with seccotine—their names written underneath.

Geological specimens—that is, fossils and different kinds of stone—should be arranged in cases, or drawers in a little cabinet, or on a shelf. Not only should their names be written on the label, but also when and where you found them.

Flowers and leaves should be well pressed and dried before being stuck into the book. You should find out the correct name from some book, and write this neatly underneath each specimen, and then put in brackets its local name—that is, the name the country people call it in your part of the world.

If the leaves themselves are kept, they get very dry and brittle and frequently break into little bits. It is a good plan, therefore, to make what are known as reproductions by using photographic or carbon paper. If the former is used, place the leaf on the sensitive paper and a stout piece of glass on top, then expose to the sun or light till the sensitive photographic paper is a dark brown. The leaf will then have photographed itself on the paper which will have to be fixed! Anyone who is keen on taking photographs will be able to tell you how to do this. If you are making carbon impressions, you use the paper that is used in typewriters so as to make three or four copies of a letter at the same time. "Zanetic" is the best kind of paper to get. Place the leaf, face down, on a solid flat surface; place the carbon paper, face down, above it; put another piece of ordinary strong paper above this and with the tips of your fingers gently but firmly rub all over above the surface of the leaf, paying particular attention to the edges. This will cover the back of the leaf with carbon. Lift the papers and carefully pick up the leaf by the stalk and place it, *back down*, on the clean piece of paper or card or book on which you want to have your reproduction. Place another piece of paper above the leaf and rub as before, taking great care not to move the leaf or the reproduction will be smudged. In this way the carbon on the back of the leaf is transferred on to the clean paper and you will find there a permanent picture of the leaf which can then be neatly labelled. If carbon paper is not available or too expensive, similar results can be produced in the same way by making a soot impression. Hold a sheet of brown paper over a lighted candle until it is well covered with soot, being careful to move the paper so that it does not catch fire. Use this prepared paper thereafter in the same way as you would carbon paper.

Coins are an interesting collection, but they are rather difficult to get.

Match-box tops—I know some Scouts who collected over 150 different kinds. They had match-box tops of nearly every English make, and also some from France, Switzerland, Italy, Germany, Norway, and even Japan!

I promised to collect for them when I was travelling abroad, and I really think I got as keen as they did; and so did my friends. We would pick up old match-boxes on the snow in Switzerland, and buy them from old match-sellers in the streets in Florence. And for weeks after, my friends used to enclose match-box tops in their letters when they wrote to me! You would be surprised at the quantities of different little pictures you get in this way.

You will not get your badge unless you stick to your collecting.

It is no good collecting things just for a week or two. Try it for at least three months, and then, if you are still interested in your collection, carry on still further.

### Hints on Making Scrap-book Collections

We talked about a scrap-book diary on page 123.

*The Book.*—If you are going to stick pictures, photographs, crests, postmarks, flowers, or any other specimens into a book, don't use a penny exercise book as your album. Boys are fond of doing this; and it means that when all the specimens are stuck in they have a lumpy, bulgy book. You can get books specially meant for sticking things into, with wide backs, so that, when the pages are full, the book will be even and not bulgy. So save up enough and buy a *scrap-book* at a toy-shop or stationer's. Or you can buy loose sheets of cardboard with canvas ends to form the hinge, which you can fasten together to form a book when they are filled up.

For stamps you should, of course, have a proper stamp album, and also little invisible mounts for sticking in the stamps, so that you can take them out again without spoiling them.

*The Gum.*—Don't use quantities of strong, yellow glue, and make a sticky mess all over your hands and the table and your page. There are lots of kinds of paste and gum. Home-made paste you will find all about how to make on page 124. Or you can buy a bottle of paste, with a brush. Thin seccotine is also good stuff. Or you can get a bottle of gum. Be careful always to have very clean hands when using gum or paste, otherwise you will get black, sticky finger-marks over everything. Don't press down scraps, etc., with your fingers, use a soft rag. Be specially careful about this when sticking in photographs.

*Labelling.*—Never write the name of the specimen below it without ruling a faint line in pencil to keep you quite straight. (You can rub out the line afterwards.) Practise making neat printing letters. It is a good plan to print the name neatly in pencil first—very faint—and then ink it over. Neatness in labelling will make just all the difference to the look of your book. If you can get Indian ink use that; it looks much nicer than ordinary ink. Be sure always to spell right. But of course more important even than the spelling and neatness, is the correctness of your labelling. Always find out exactly the right name for the specimen. And get the things in the right order—not all mixed up; this is called being *systematic*. It sounds a long word, but it is a very important thing to be. Nothing in the world succeeds without *system*. Remember the proverb—"Plan your work—then work your plan."

## CHAPTER VI

# CYCLIST

### NOTE TO CUBMASTER

*There are still far too many road accidents which are often due to boys on bicycles, and these tests are designed to help to make Cubs more masters of their machines and more aware of their responsibilities, both to themselves and to others on the road. It is important that the tests are strictly observed and a high standard maintained, also that the Cub who wins this badge should be made to realise the importance of going on with the good work and even improving in the art of "roadmanship" after he has won the badge.*

### HINTS TO CUBS

A bicycle can be a very useful thing as well as giving you a lot of fun, but it can also be a very dangerous weapon not only to yourself but to other people, if it is not used properly.

It's not much good owning a bike, if you are lucky enough to have one of your own, learning to balance on it and setting off, thinking you are a cyclist. You have got to know how to look after it, to keep it in proper order and to ride it *well* so as to get the most fun and the most use out of it.

The Highway Code tells you the rules of good roadmanship, but even that is not enough for it does not tell you about the technicalities of a machine or the art of riding it.

You are told, for one thing, not to wobble about the road, and as beginners are sure to wobble you must find a quiet place to practice well away from all traffic. A common cause of wobbling is riding a machine which is too big for you. The saddle can be adjusted a little bit, and it should be low enough for you to be able to rest one foot on the ground while you are still sitting on the saddle. This may save a lot of mounting and dismounting too, though of course you mustn't put your foot down while still in motion. Another possible cause for a bad wobble is pedalling with the middle of your foot on the pedal instead of the toe. At low speeds or turning a corner your toe may catch the front mudguard and cause a bad swerve.

Keeping full control of the cycle implies three things: first, that the machine is in mechanically good condition; second, that it is the right size; and third, that the rider has road sense, which means common-sense plus some special knowledge.

It isn't really clever to ride a bike that is too big for you, as you can't control it properly in an emergency. Part of the test for this badge is that you should be able to mount and dismount properly and you can't even learn how on a bike that's too big.

Then you must know how to keep it in proper repair. It won't serve you whenever you want it to, if you never serve it. It will need cleaning, oiling and tyre-pumping very often, and occasionally more careful attention, and you should learn how to do all these things properly, and should be proud of your bike and not ill-treat it.

A whole lot of small things can go wrong with any machine, by sheer wear and tear, and they are all things that you must look out for, check and put right: tyres, brakes, chain, bell and lights. They all need attention and if they aren't kept right the bike will let you down at the wrong moment and may lead to an accident. It's no good saying afterwards: "It wasn't *my* fault; the chain slipped or the mudguard fell off. . . ." You ought to have known about it beforehand and prevented it. If it is your bike and you are riding it, anything that goes wrong *is* your fault.

Then you must know the Highway Code and the good manners that are expected of everyone who owns a vehicle of any sort on the Queen's highways. There is a special section of the Highway Code called *Notes for Cyclists* which you must learn and understand, and that just shows how important cyclists are. You must understand the road signs, which warn you what lies ahead, and the hand-signals which you and other people will use, and there are quite a lot of them which you must be able to remember in a hurry, without stopping in the middle of the traffic to think.

And you must avoid doing the silly things which so often lead to an accident. These are done all too often by boys on bikes who want to show off how clever they are by scorching or swerving or deliberately skidding. Actually they are only showing how stupid they are, because good cyclists don't do those things, and nobody admires the people who do. Other accidents are caused by boys who just don't care for anybody or anything, or perhaps it is that they just don't think, but a

Scout or a Cub should always be courteous and polite, and therefore he would not take unnecessary risks or cause anybody else to leap out of the way or jam on their brakes or even to worry unduly.

Any Cub who wears this badge will be a good cyclist, and then he and everybody else will enjoy it properly.

The 10th in the Series of Wolf Cub Books, at 1/-, is about the Cyclist Badge and will tell you all you have to know to gain this interesting and important Badge.

## CHAPTER VII

# ENTERTAINER

### NOTE TO CUBMASTERS

*This badge is not intended as an opportunity for a boy to show off, but should be used to encourage and control talent. The finished performance should really be pleasing to an audience as well as to the performer.*

*A Pack Band, as suggested earlier in this book, might be a stepping stone towards this badge, as well as being good fun. Great care should be taken over the timing and expression, as this would later be a help to a Cub when giving a solo on any instrument. A band which was all fortissimo would most certainly defeat its object.*

### HINTS TO CUBS

THE most important thing about this badge is its name. It means entertaining other people, not just amusing yourself.

So whatever form of entertaining you can do, be sure that you learn it thoroughly and go on practising until you can do it really well. Playing a musical instrument badly, singing out of tune, conjuring tricks that don't work may make people laugh—or cry!—but that is not really entertaining them.

If you have a tuneful voice or an ear for music it is a gift which has been given to you by God, and you should make the most of it. Try to find someone who will be good enough to teach you how to develop it and make the very best of it. It will give you a fine opportunity for Good Turns at Parties, or at the Scout Show, if you are good enough.

*Playing and singing.*—Don't be put off this badge by thinking that you must begin by playing elaborate pieces on the piano or violin, or whatever instrument you choose; or by singing long and difficult songs. Start with something quite simple which you really enjoy, and go over it again and again, until you feel that it is just as good as it can be, and then other people will enjoy it too.

If you go in for singing you will have a wide choice of songs: quiet ones or lively ones, old English songs or carols, and lots and lots more. But whatever you choose *keep in tune* and *don't shout!*

*Reciting.*—Poetry is not easy to read aloud or to recite from memory. It has a rhythm of its own, but the words do this without your voice making too much of the "di-*dah* di-*dah* di-*dah*." Try to read it smoothly as though it was prose, pausing at the commas and colons, and only giving the least pause at the end of each line where the words rhyme.

Of course you must know the words perfectly. It spoils the whole thing if you pause or stutter, or stop to scratch your head and shuffle your feet and look lost. But however well you know it, you mustn't gabble it off; you must understand what it means and try to make your voice express the meaning of the words.

*Acting and miming.*—In acting, as in reciting, it is not enough just to know your words and what you have to do while you are saying them. You must really try to become the character you are meant to be. Every part of you, especially your face, voice and hands, belongs to him and not to you; and you must keep on acting the part all the time you are on the stage, whether you are speaking or listening to other actors.

Miming is harder than acting. As you have no words to help you to express yourself, your face and hands, and indeed your whole body, must tell the audience what you are doing and thinking and feeling. Try to notice what other people look like when they are happy, or worried, or in a bad temper, and then see if you can register all sorts of different expressions in a looking glass. This doesn't mean pulling faces! You've got to make yourself really feel excited or suspicious or whatever it is to be, before you look the part.

*Puppetry.*—There are two sorts of puppets: the Marionettes which are worked with strings from above, or Glove puppets which you work on your hands from below.

It is fun to make your own puppets and theatre, and your local lending library will supply you with good books on how to do it.

Puppetry is really a team activity and it will probably be best if you can get some of your pals to join you, but it is possible to do a single-handed show if you practise hard enough. If so, you will find a variety show the best, including songs and recitations and, of course, a comic turn. If you have one puppet to announce the turns, he can be fixed on to a stick and easily picked up or put down while you are sliding your other hand into a glove or picking up the strings for the next turn. If you are clever you will learn to work the puppets with both hands at the same time.

Keep the puppets hanging up along the back of the stage for quick and easy handling.

You can use a record player for the music, or get a pal to play some instrument for you.

*Conjuring.*—If you want to become a Conjuror, you have a lot to learn, but a great deal of fun when you have succeeded. The first thing you must do, of course, is to learn how to work each trick thoroughly and well, and this means practise, practise and more practise.

A Member of the Inner Magic Circle has written these tips specially for you:

1. Never forget that if your audience can see how a trick is done, the effect is completely spoiled, so practise in front of a mirror until you can see for yourself that none of your movements give the game away.

2. No matter how much anyone may press you, never tell how a trick is done. All the value of a good trick is lost when the audience know the secret; people will respect you more if you politely refuse to give your tricks away, and they will want to see you perform again.

3. When you can do three or four tricks really well, you must dress them up with a few words or a little story (the professional Conjuror calls this " patter ") in order to make them attractive to your audience.

4. Another golden rule is—never tell your audience in advance what you are going to do: if you do, they will be watching for you to do it and thus have a better chance of finding out how you do it. Do not make statements such as: " I have here an ordinary pack of cards," or " This is an empty box." They will immediately suspect that they are not ordinary cards or that the box is not empty. Just say: " I would like to show you a card trick," or " In my next trick I am going to use this little box."

5. Lastly, take every opportunity to see other Conjurors; watch how they do their tricks and see how they " put them over " to the audience. If you know of somebody who is a good Con-

juror, do not be afraid to ask his advice and help; most Conjurors are only too willing to help a beginner. Don't slavishly copy a Conjuror you have seen, but learn by watching him and then go home and work out the way of doing a trick that best suits you. Never do a trick in public until you have got it off perfectly and are word-perfect in your patter. When you think you are sure, try it on Mum or Dad first. When you *know* it's right, you can then, and not until then, perform it in front of an audience.

One of the greatest Conjurors who ever lived wrote: " A Conjuror is an Actor playing the part of a Magician," This gives you a clear idea of what you have to aim at. If you want to learn more about it, there is a good book called " How to be a Wizard," by Robert Harbin.

So you see this Badge offers you plenty of alternatives, plenty of hard work, whichever form of entertainment you take up, and a lot of fun. But remember that other people must enjoy it too, before you are a real Entertainer.

## CHAPTER VIII

# FIRST-AIDER

### NOTE TO CUBMASTERS

*More useful than any practical knowledge will be a capacity to keep cool in an emergency. If the emergency occurs when he is in a crowd, a picture theatre, or other such place, a Cub should be taught, as far as possible, to keep quiet, to keep alert, and to obey directions from adults at once and without panic.*

*If he is alone or with other children and one of their number is hurt, he should again know first that he must keep calm; keep his patient warm and send for adult help.*

*First-Aid is an important and difficult subject—difficult inasmuch as it requires great care and precision, exactitude, and common sense (all unnatural attributes of the ordinary boy!) The First Aid Badge is one of the most important among the Scouts' Proficiency Badges, but it is much too hard for the Cubs. The simple tests required for the Cub " First-Aider " will, however, teach the Cubs simple and practical helpfulness in very minor accidents, while Akela, by means of stories, " emergency " games, and pow-wows, should try to give the Cub that confidence that is of so much help in averting panic or muddle in unexpected situations.*

### HINTS TO CUBS

EVERY Cub will want to do his best to help somebody who is hurt, and in the next few pages you will learn how you can help in a few simple accidents.

The first thing to remember in any case of injury is to keep your head and not get excited. If the injury is slight, you may be able to deal with it, but in any case, if you are alone when something happens, do what you can as well and as quickly as you can. Cover your patient up to keep him warm; then get hold of someone else who is older and knows more about it, to take the job on, and be ready to fetch and carry for him, take a message, or do anything else which may be asked of you.

*A cut on the hand or knee.*—If anybody cuts his hand, and it is your job to render first-aid, there are two things to think about.

1. If the cut is bleeding badly, that is, if the blood is pouring out in spurts, you must try at once to stop the bleeding. Make him sit down and tell him to hold his hand well up, towards his head, while you get a clean handkerchief or a clean piece of rag (we call this a dressing). Place this on the cut and bind it firmly with another handkerchief.

2. Usually the blood will not be spurting out, but just flowing gently, and then you will have more time to prepare a dressing and also to CLEAN the cut. Whenever the skin is cut, or even scratched, an opening is made into the body and dirt gets taken in. Now " dirt " here doesn't mean what you generally call " dirt "—mud and dust; it means anything containing GERMS. Germs are living things so tiny that your eye can't see them, but if they get into a cut they may poison it so that it festers and becomes really dangerous, ending, possibly, in the loss of a finger or a hand. The worst kind of germs are those that come out of earth—such as garden mould, or mud from the road. They may cause a terrible disease called lock-jaw, so great care must be taken if anyone gets a cut while gardening, for instance. But any dust or any soiled object may and does contain germs.

So before you bandage a cut you should try to get rid of any germs which have got in, by washing them out again, with warm water if it is handy, or with cold. There are some drugs—things you buy at a chemist's—which may be put into the water in order to kill any germs you can't wash out. You will probably find some of them in the Scouts' Ambulance Box, or your mother may keep them in a cupboard at home. The good ones have very long names, such as Permanganate of Potassium crystals (that's a jaw-breaker!) Drop a few of these crystals into a basin of water to make it a beautiful purple colour. Most people keep Dettol in their homes these days and a few drops of this in water is excellent too. There may be a bottle marked Iodine Paint. This is very handy for small cuts or scratches, because you don't need any water with it. You just paint it over the cut. It stings rather—but it makes the germs curl up.

Now you want the very cleanest thing you can think of to put next to the wound. The inside part of a clean folded handkerchief would probably be the best you could do, or if you haven't go that the inside of a clean sheet of notepaper or the inside of an envelope. Having covered the cut with something of this kind, you should add padding—several handkerchiefs or pieces of rag. Then bind the whole thing up very firmly to stop the bleeding. The best thing for this is a roller bandage, of course, and you will have to be taught how to use one properly, especially how to finish it off firmly. But you could use strips of rag, or a large folded handkerchief. Make the patient keep his hand raised, or better put it in a sling, which you can make from a scarf or comforter. Remember that your help is only First-Aid so take the patient to a grown-up person who will attend to the cut more thoroughly.

*A graze.*—A graze is a bad scrape which has taken the skin off and is usually covered with dirt—grit off the road, and so on. It will not be bleeding much, as a rule. The treatment should be to wash it well with clean warm water to which permanganate, Dettol or iodine, has been added—soaking it till the dirt comes away, and clean it up with little swabs of wool for rag. When all the grit is removed cover the graze with a clean piece of rag. Bandage firmly, but not tight enough to be uncomfortable.

*Large Arm-sling.*—There are a great many ways of applying the triangular bandage; when you become a Scout you will learn these.

The large arm-sling is used to support the forearm and hand. This is how you put it on.

Open out the triangular bandage, lay it across the patient's chest so that the *point* (see diagram) comes under the elbow of

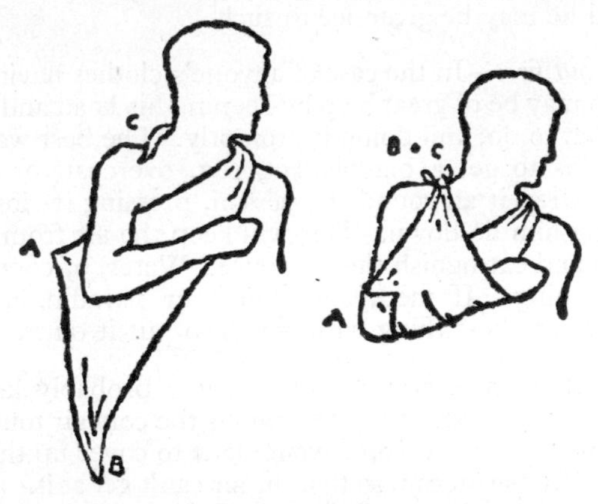


Large arm-sling.

the injured man. One of the ends will then be over the good shoulder. Take this end round the back of the neck and bring it forward over the shoulder on the injured side. Now carry the lower end up to the first and tie it in a reef knot so that the knot lies just in front of the shoulder.

(Before your knot is tied, see that your sling is drawn up so that your patient's hand is slightly higher than his elbow).

Now tidy the front of your sling by drawing any loose material towards the elbow; take hold of the point and bring it either in front or behind the elbow, and fasten it with a large safety-pin.

The points you must notice are:—

(1) The knot tying the two ends should be in front of the shoulder. If it is tied at the back of the neck, the weight of the arm will press it into the neck and cause much discomfort.

(2) The finger-tips should just show outside the bandage.

*Bleeding from the nose.*—This does not usually do much harm or prove dangerous. But it may sometimes refuse to stop, which means the patient losing a lot of blood. The old way of laying the patient down on the ground and leaving him alone isn't good, as the blood merely trickles down inside his throat. This is the way to stop it. Sit the patient on a chair, in a draught, and tell him to lean his head well back and breathe entirely through his mouth. Place a cold sponge on his nose between the eyes, and another at the back of his neck. His feet may be put in very hot water, and he may be given ice to suck.

*Putting out fire.*—In the case of anyone's clothes having caught fire, a Cub may be of great help by keeping his head and knowing exactly what to do, and doing it promptly. The best way to stop the flames is to get a big blanket, rug, overcoat, or anything thick, and wrap it all round the person, pressing it close to him and making him lie down. This will keep the air from reaching the flames and extinguish them at once. Water, of course, is the next best thing. If methylated spirit or paraffin has caught fire, sand is the best thing with which to put it out.

*Burns.*—A burn is very painful, as you probably know; but do you know that what causes the pain is the cold air touching the burned skin? So what you have to do is to cover up the burned skin as quickly as you can, so that the air can't get at it. The best thing to use is a clean handkerchief, some soft clean rags, or clean white paper; over that put some padding, and bandage up very gently.

Don't try to wash the wound. If you are indoors it may be that mother will have some baking soda. Put two teaspoonfuls of this soda into a bowl of warm water and dip your clean rag into it. Squeeze the rag out and lay it lightly over the burn. Put a pad of cotton-wool on a clean folded handkerchief on the top of the wet rag and bandage gently. If you have no bandage, wrap a towel round the part. Now you have to remember that burns, being so painful, often make a person feel queer and sick, and he can't remain standing up. Make him sit or lie down, and if he gets queer, that is very white-faced, with skin all cold and clammy, it means that he will be suffering from *shock.* I told you for your Second Star (page 137) what you should do for this, so that you will remember to wrap your patient up warmly and go, or send someone, to fetch a grown-up person as fast as you can.

*Scalds* are simply wet burns, usually caused by boiling water. Treat in the same way as for a burn, but be very, very gentle so that you don't burst any blisters which may have risen.

## Practices and Displays

A good way for Cubs to practise first-aid, and an attractive display, is to write a short, easy sketch, bringing in first-aid, and let them practise this.

For instance: Two rough little street hooligans (a popular part) are fighting. One has just knocked the other down, causing him to cut his hand on the stones and grazing his shin badly with a savage kick. A Six of Cubs come up, separate the combatants, and render first aid.

Another form of display, suitable for rallies. A Six (or more) stand facing the audience, one triangular bandage at the feet of each Cub. The Sixer stands to the right, whistle in hand, and gives orders thus: "Alert! Large arm-sling. Ready!" [Every other Cub stoops and picks up the bandage and stands fast.] Leader gives a blast on whistle, and each Cub holding a bandage turns to the right and applies it to the Cub next him. and both turn smartly to the front and stand fast. When all are ready there is a pause for the audience to see the completed sling. Then the Leader gives the command: "As you were!" and the Cubs undo the slings and lay the bandages at their feet.

## CHAPTER IX

# GARDENER

### Note to Cubmasters

*Cubmasters should remember that the hobby of gardening encourages several qualities that they would like to see in all Cubs—namely, patience or "stickability," forethought, observation, love of nature and fingercraft.*

*Also it is possible to interest Cubs from all kinds of homes, whether in town or country, in some form of gardening. The lucky ones may own gardens, but the alternative tests make it possible for Cubs without any plot of their own to know the joys of gardening at any rate in a limited sense.*

*And Cubmasters who enthuse their Packs with a gardening craze will have the satisfaction of knowing that they have started the Cubs on a hobby which is likely to become lifelong; for gardening fever is practically incurable!*

### Hints to Cubs on Gardening

Cubs who are lucky enough to have gardens of their own know that gardening is a job which is jolly interesting all the year round. In late winter and early spring the ground has to be dug, manured, and prepared for sowing vegetable or flower seeds. Then come sowing and planting—then, in summer, transplanting, weeding, and watering. In autumn there is a lot to be done in preparing for next year. Vacant ground must be dug deeply and left rough for the frost to break up. Leaves and soft rubbish must be swept up and put in an out-of-the-way corner to be dug back into the ground when it is decayed; other rubbish must be burnt and we must clear up generally, or our gardens in summer won't be worth looking at. So all gardeners have to think ahead.

Then besides planning, it is very important to " stick to it "—don't neglect your garden for a few weeks, or you will find it difficult to catch up. Weeds somehow have a way of growing faster than proper seedlings!

Another bit of advice is—look at other people's gardens when you have a chance, and listen to gardeners' talk, because you can pick up no end of tips that way.

You will get the best results if you start your gardening in the spring. If you have the choice, pick a piece of ground not shaded by trees. Dig it pretty deeply, and pick out weeds. If you can get hold of some, dig in some manure or old rotted tree leaves. Break the earth up small, and smooth it with a rake. Then you are ready to put something into the ground.

*Sowing seeds.*—All sorts of seeds can be bought in cheap packets, and often directions on the packet tell when and how the seeds should be sown. There are ANNUAL flower seeds like stock, cornflower, mignonette. There are others called BIENNIAL, which take two years before they flower. Then there are PERENNIALS, which means the plants flower every year and last several years. The best thing is to have a few of each.

When you sow your seeds, if the ground is very loose, tread it a little at first, for the seeds will grow better in fairly firm soil. If the seeds are fairly big (like sweet pea and nasturtium) you put them in one by one—just half an inch from the top of the ground. If the seeds are small—like poppy—you sprinkle them on the top of the ground, and then press the earth down, gently. Don't sow small seeds on a windy day, as they may get blown right out of your garden.

Some seeds sprout in a few days, but it depends on the weather, so don't get impatient if a week or two goes by and you don't see a sign of green. When the seedlings have grown a bit, some may have to be pulled up; this is called "thinning out," and the reason for it is that plants need lots of sunshine and air. You may have to do this a second time, since if the seedlings are crowded together, none will grow properly. Seedlings may have to be shaded from the sun when it is very hot.

*Putting in plants.*—If, instead of seeds, you decide to put in plants, always use a trowel and dig the hole big enough to allow the roots of your plants to spread out well. Cover them with fine soil and press it firmly round the roots so that the plant won't come out if pulled gently with two fingers. Keep the surface of the ground hoed so as to kill the weeds and let in the air and moisture, especially after watering.

*Staking.*—Many plants need support to prevent them being blown down by the wind. For light plants try to use twiggy sticks which will support without showing. Where a heavier stake is necessary, see that it shows as little as possible.

*Watering and weeding.*—If you think your garden needs watering, do it in the evening, and don't just sprinkle the top—the roots go down quite a long way, so a lot of water is necessary.

Pull up all weeds without mercy; it is only by experience that people learn which *are* weeds; of course everyone knows dandelion, and nettle, and weeds that are different kinds of grasses. But there are lots of others, and about the worst are bindweed and couch grass; these have horrid snaky roots which twist round other plants and stifle them.

*Pot plants.*—A pot plant needs even more care than a plant growing out of doors, and you have to know quite a few things about them. For instance, it is not easy to tell when they need water. But if you tap the side of the earthenware pot, and it rings clear, that plant is too dry; so fill up the top with water several times until the water comes through easily. If it rings dull, the plant is not very dry. If a Cub has sharp ears he can soon tell the difference. Never water with quite *cold* water out of the tap—rain water is best—and never let the pot plant stand in a saucer of water.

Sometimes ferns, and some other plants, like to be soaked in a bucket of water for an hour or two, and you can put pot plants and ferns outside on a warm rainy day. But beware of cold winds outside, and draughts in the house. Pot plants need air and sunshine, but hate draughts. Sometimes it is a good idea to sponge the leaves of the plants with tepid water to get rid of dust—but this has to be done very gently.

Good pot plants are geraniums or fuchsias, or bulbs such as daffodils or hyacinths.

*Window boxes.*—You can make these very pretty—either with bulbs in spring, or in the summer put in two or three geraniums—the pink climbing sort; or you can sow annuals. Nasturtiums grow very well in window boxes, or wallflowers, or virginian stock. Remember a good soaking now and then is better than many little sprinkles!

*Growing a bulb in water, peat moss, sand or soil.*—Get a jar with a neck smaller than the size of your bulb, so that it will not drop inside. Then fill the jar with water, choose a nice firm bulb and put it in the neck of the jar. Put it in the dark until the roots start to appear, then bring it into the light. The window-sill is a good place for it. Change the water about once a week. Do not keep the bulb too warm at first.

If you want to grow bulbs in a bowl, get a grown-up to tell you the way to do it, since it is important not to get the peat moss or soil either too wet or too dry. Remember to put your bowl in a dark and not too warm place until the bulb has grown about an inch.

*Growing mustard and cress on a flannel.*—Take a saucer or dish, and a piece of flannel just large enough to fit it. Wet the flannel thoroughly with water and sprinkle your seed all over it. See that the flannel never gets dry.

*Tools.*—A good gardener always looks after his tools. Clean them carefully after using them and put them away tidily under cover.

## CHAPTER X

# GUIDE

### Hints to Cubs

In order to earn the Guide Badge really well it is necessary for you to explore the neighbourhood of Pack Headquarters or your own home thoroughly. Don't be content with learning the address at which the Doctor lives, for instance, but make sure that you yourself can find the way there at any time of the day or night. It is no good just committing a list of names and addresses to memory so that you can say them off pat like a parrot; you yourself must know exactly where these places are and how to get to them. It is the same in regard to neighbouring towns or villages; you should know the right road to take to them, and, if possible, something about them.

### Directing Strangers

If a stranger wants to be directed he is sure to look about him for a Scout or a Cub; because he thinks a Scout or a Cub is sure to know the way; and he knows either will answer him promptly and politely, will direct him clearly, and will do it as if he liked doing it, with a smile and no idea of a reward.

If a stranger speaks to you don't look shy, or startled, or sulky. Try, rather, to look pleased and bright; and listen carefully to what he says, so that, when he has done, you won't have to look like a little idiot and say " Wot ? " If he asks you the way to some place or house, think carefully, notice where you are, try and remember just where it is; then try and remember any special landmarks he will pass on the way—such as the church, inn, station, or even pond, gate, or tree. Look at him straight and speak clearly and slowly, while you tell him exactly how to reach the place. Tell him about how long he will take to get there; and anything else you may think helpful to him. Call him " Sir " (or if it's a lady, " Ma'am " or " Miss "). If he offers you money, smile cheerfully and thank him, but say you're a

Wolf Cub, and only too glad to help, and never expect tips. When you leave him salute smartly.

You are quite likely to be asked the whereabouts of the nearest telephone-box, police station, etc. You should make a point of finding out exactly where all these places are, in order that you may tell him quite simply and clearly how to get there and how far away they are.

You should also know how to send for the police, and an ambulance, and the fire brigade, although you should never attempt to do so if there is a grown-up there to do it. The usual way to do this is by telephoning, which you have already learned to do for your second Star (see page 117).

Akela will give you the special directions needed to summon help.

### Bus Routes

People often want to know where they must stand to catch a certain bus.

If you live in the country, where buses are few, you should know where they will stop, and at what time; where they go, and how frequently they run.

If you live in the town, you should know the stopping places of at least four buses or trams, and know the route they take.

### Games and Practices

A game by which Cubs may practise the art of directing strangers, and which will at the same time prove really a game, is as follows:—

### Help the Stranger

The Pack squats round in a ring. The Cubmaster stands in the middle. " I am a poor old gentleman," he says. " I've come from London, and I don't know my way about the village, or how to reach my destination. Will someone help me ? " One of the Cubs steps forward, and salutes, saying: " Yes, sir ! "

" Thank you," says the Cubmaster. " I am now at —— and I want to get to ——" (his supposed whereabouts, and the place he wishes to get to, he whispers in the Cub's ear, or tells him out of earshot of the rest). The Cub then commences to direct the stranger clearly. The Pack listens attentively, to try and discover from his direction (1) the point at which he is supposed to be standing, (2) the destination of the stranger. As soon as the Cub has finished speaking, every Cub who knows the answer to these two questions stands up. The directing Cub then scores one point for each Cub who has understood him (showing his directions were clear), while the Cubmaster allows him two points for distinct speaking, two for politeness, and an extra one for any original piece of helpfulness the Cub has been able to show. Each Cub who knows the two correct answers scores two points. (The scoring will be made much simpler if the Cubmaster has a bag of counters or beans, and gives one for each point gained. It sounds difficult to judge whether the standing Cubs have judged rightly, but it can be done by making them answer all together (so that they cannot copy each other) and trusting each Cub to play fair and sit down again if he was wrong.)

The conversation should sound something like this:

*Cubmaster:* " I am at —— and I want to get to ——."

*Cub:* " You follow along this road, sir, for about a hundred yards. When you get to the girls' school you turn to the left, and go on down the street, passing a pond and the police-station. This brings you to the level crossing. The gates may be shut, but you can get through the little gates all right. You will then see the church in front of you. When you get there you will see a stile opposite the churchyard gate. Get over this and follow the footpath for a quarter of a mile across the fields, and you will get to the place you want. Oh, and by the way, sir " (adds the Cub, so scoring his extra point), " there's a bull in the next field, so be careful to keep to the path."

(Eight Cubs have stood up, and are eager to show their knowledge and attention.)

" Thank you, my boy " (says the old gentleman from London), " I am most grateful for your help and clear directions. Good morning."

" Good morning, sir! " replies the Cub, saluting.

" Now, you chaps," says the Cubmaster, " where did I start from?—all together."

" The station, sir! " cry the eight Cubs, in one breath.

" Right. And where am I going? "

" Willow Farm, sir! "

The directing Cub has scored thirteen points. Had he omitted to say " Sir " during the whole conversation, he would have lost one of his politeness points; and a point if he had mumbled indistinctly, or giggled, or forgotten to salute. The Cubmaster may also improve the occasion by ending up with " Thank you, little boy, and here's a sixpence for yourself"—as a test of the Cub's memory of Cub ideals. Or, "I suppose, my young friend, you are a Boy Scout?"—to test the Cub's ability to answer such a question. Or any other question that may occur to the Cubmaster's fertile imagination.

"*General Post*," using the names of neighbouring towns, villages, and localities, is a favoutite game, and is useful in impressing local names on the Cubs' minds. It will add to the excitement of the game if the various forms of postal delivery are indicated as follows:

A letter—walks.
A telegram—runs.
A parcel—crawls.
A postcard—hops.

*Questions.*—When practice is being carried on, as to names of local places, directions, whereabouts of police-station, etc., questions on local history—the Cubs sitting round on the ground in a circle—it will be found that much more interest is taken if a counter is given for every correct answer.

*Blocks.*—A good way of testing (and improving) the Cub's bump of locality and knowledge of the relation of localities to each other is to have a set of wooden blocks (like children's bricks), each initialled as follows: P.S. for police-station; M.G. motor garage; H. hospital, and so on. The Cubmaster then defines an area—the table, or a space on the ground. He places a large block as a central "landmark"—the church, or the Pack Headquarters—and leaves the Cub (or two Cubs working together) to place the blocks in their correct relation to each other and to the "landmark." (N.B.—If the Pack is also working at various models in cardboard, the Cubs might make models of various houses and shops, to be used in place of the blocks, and greatly add to the picturesqueness and fascination of the game.)

*Short Cuts.*—It is quite easy to secure a knowledge of short cuts by asking the Pack to give the quickest way between any two points in the neighbourhood. Some Cubs will favour certain short cuts as against others. It is a good plan for a Six or the Pack to go along the different short cuts mentioned and time their journeys very carefully on each so as to find out which is really the shortest.

The games suggested above are suitable for indoor training.

But most of the training for this badge should, of course, be given out of doors; the various localities being verified, and then rendered familiar to the Cubs by such games as Despatch Running, etc.

*A Knowledge of Local History.*—The history of the parish (especially in small villages) may hold but little of interest, so it is as well to seek out some building or spot of historical interest in the neighbourhood—a Gothic church, a Roman tumulus, a medieval castle or ruin, or the site of a battlefield—and weave round this the romance of the past. It will fascinate the Cub and give him a new idea. It will tend to open his eyes (so apt to be near-sighted) to a great, unknown world—the glorious past. A Gothic church will give the Cubmaster an opportunity to give a short lesson in Church architecture and its changes and phases (I have known Scouts take great interest in this). The same with a castle or ruin—here regular British history will come to the fore; with room for a sketch of life in the days when this castle was of importance. Even little country towns, if one takes the trouble to look them up in county histories, are full of romance and strange tales and have their own quaint customs and particular interest.

If a short play (or even pageant) can be made out of the local history or legends, it will be excellent for the Cubs to act this, and will be a popular item at a display or winter entertainment. Acting delights the Cub; it is full of romance; true *make-believe*, with the advantage of being organised by grown-ups, and with all sorts of fascinating costumes available! But besides the real pleasure it gives the Cub, the rehearsals and final public performance give him self-confidence; teach him to speak distinctly; train his memory, and ask of him patience, self-control, and real effort. (See also p. 235.)

## CHAPTER XI

# HANDCRAFT

### NOTE TO CUBMASTERS

*As with the Artists' Badge, effort must be taken into consideration and must count high in this Badge. It aims to develop concentration, imagination and patience as much as finger-craft or technical skills.*

*An important point is that whatever the boy makes it should be for a definite purpose: a present for somebody, something for the Group stall at a sale of work, something to use in Camp or in the Pack den, or for a Good Turn. A Cub will not be very interested in making an article if he does not know what will become of it when made.*

### HINTS TO CUBS

MAKING things is fun, but the fun soon peters out if the thing breaks or doesn't work properly, or indeed if you never finish it. Tackle simple things first and keep on keeping on until it is as good as it can be. Then you can tackle something more difficult with more chance of making a success of it.

*Materials.*—Every Cub can collect odds and ends for himself. The best way is to get two or three cardboard shoe-boxes and divide them into sections. This is done with any old piece of cardboard and a little glue. The size of the sections will depend on what you intend to put into them. Things which you can set out to collect are: match-boxes, fir-cones, clothes pegs, horse

*Things you can make.*

chestnuts, pea-nuts, match-sticks, corks, cotton reels, acorns, acorn-cups, odd beads, flat buttons, button moulds, wire, pins, and cardboard. These are placed in separate sections, and are thus to hand when required. One large box is not so good for storing purposes as several smaller ones; the things are sure to get jumbled up together and much time is wasted turning them out each time you want a pin.

*Toymaking.*—All sorts of wonderful birds can be made from fir-cones, with wire for legs and an acorn for a head. Sealing wax also makes a good head, and a piece at the end of the legs will hold the bird firm to a stand of cardboard. These birds can be used for calendars, menu-holders, pin trays, match-box holders, etc.

Thimble cases can be made from the two halves of a walnut shell fastened together with a piece of elastic and painted a bright colour.

A chair can be made from a horse chestnut, some pins, and raffia or wool to weave the back.

A candlestick from cotton reels, a meat skewer, and a thimble, is quite possible.

Three cotton reels, one small and two larger, of the variety with the round edges, can be so placed as to make an excellent doll. The small one for the head and the other two for the body; the arms and feet cut out from stiff paper or cardboard and glued on to the reels. The face marked out in ink, a button mould for the hat, and the whole painted a bright colour makes an acceptable toy. Animals may be made in the same way, with a reel for the body and legs, head and tail from cardboard.

The most jolly little models can be made from match-sticks and a little glue or seccotine. They look better if they are sand-papered before using.

Corks can be used in almost the same way as reels. They are very easily filed and sand-papered into the required shapes. Match-sticks make good legs for cork models.

Match-boxes make all kinds of furniture. Boot-buttons make handles for various pieces of furniture. Small carts can be made from match boxes. Milk tops make wheels for these carts. Match-sticks will make an axle for the wheels and two beads will keep the wheels from coming away from the cart.

*Models.*—A windmill can be made from a "Vim" tin, a skewer, a cotton reel, wire, pins, match-boxes, and paper.

Wheels can be made from a section sawn from a broom-handle.

An engine can be produced from a "Vim" tin, a cardboard

box, two pill boxes, the bottom of a date box, two pieces of flat stick, two cotton reels, and a piece of broom-handle.

The date box is again most useful in constructing a tram.

Old stockings, some wool, two white linen buttons, two boot buttons, and some pieces of bright material, make an excellent Gollywog doll.

Boot boxes make splendid foundations for cottages, theatres, stations, churches, etc.

From the little round cardboard boxes in which cheeses are packed it is possible to make a battledore, a clock, a roundabout, a drum, and a tambourine. A shuttlecock can be made from a cork and feathers.

Trees from dyed sponge, torn in pieces and seccotined on to a wooden meat skewer with a milk top as a base, will help in your jungle.

*Knitting.*—I used to knit when I was your age, although I have almost forgotten it now, mufflers and mittens and other useful things like that. There are other useful articles that you can think of for yourself, like kettle-holders. You will find it best to use thick wool or cotton, and should work with bone or wooden needles, not metal ones, unless you are going to be very ambitious and knit socks and stockings.

*Netting.*—Don't try and net too big a thing. It would take you a very long time to make a tennis-net or a hammock. A bag to hold the balls for your Six or the Pack, or a small net to use for " tenna-quoit " or " deck tennis " will be quite large enough. Great care should be taken to see that the netting is evenly done and that the cord used is strong.

*Cross-stitch.*—It is quite easy to do a cross-stitch on canvas, but you should realise that there is more in the test than this. For instance, the choice of size, shape, colours and patterns is of importance, and you should make your own choice in all these particulars. Apart from usefulness, it is the colour and the pattern that make the design.

*Rug or mat.*—Here again it is necessary to warn you against being too ambitious, and so starting off to make a large rug. That will prove a very long and tiring job. Given the right tool, a rug on canvas is easy to make so far as the actions to be done are concerned, but we have also to remember that the choice of colour and design enters into the question again. A rug made on hessian usually entails tagging pieces of cloth, etc., on to the hessian. It may be possible for you to combine with another fellow and make a rug between you of a larger size than each of you could do apart.

*Basket-making.*—Some of you will already have learnt to make baskets in school, and so you will not want to repeat what you do there. But you will find it very interesting making baskets in similar ways from rushes or twigs. This is not at all a bad thing to do during a wet day in camp, for instance. Willow, lilac and poplar twigs make good baskets. You have to be particularly careful to see that the basket is neatly finished off, and the handles put on firmly. If you make a small basket of rushes or twigs and line it with moss, you will find that it will make a very safe egg-basket. You can also line one of these baskets with moss, fill it with earth, and plant a small fern in it to take home.

*Weaving.*—Raffia is nice stuff to work with. It comes usually from palm trees that grow in Madagascar and can be dyed all kinds of bright colours. You could even dye the ordinary straw-coloured stuff for yourself with " Twink " or some other patent dye. There are lots of useful articles that can be made of raffia, mats, tea-pot stands, baskets, and so on. Weave the raffia as evenly as you can, and make your own choice of colours.

*Usefulness.*—Now you can easily see for yourselves that all these Handcraft tests give you opportunities of being useful to other people at home by helping yourself. Stick to it, therefore, and take the opportunity to think how you can make something really useful or decorative or, better still, both!

*General.*—It is no good thinking you can win this badge by using again the model you made for your Second Star, or by any potty little article you have made. It is real good stuff you will have to turn out and it will take a good deal of patience and ability on your part before you can really succeed, but stick to it and practise time and time again and you are sure to succeed in making a toy in the end in which you yourself can take a pride and feel yourself to be a real craftsman.

## CHAPTER XII

# HOUSE ORDERLY

### Note to Cubmasters

*This badge offers a fine opportunity for co-operation with the boy's Mother. She must of course be made to understand the aim of the badge and the standard to expect, taking effort and a genuine desire to help into consideration, as well as the qualifications for the badge. It will be necessary to explain to some parents that this is not an opportunity to impose unnecessary chores upon the boy, much less to use it as a threat or a bribe; whilst others should be warned that it must not be a " flash in the pan " effort simply to procure the badge.*

### Hints to Cubs

This House Orderly badge is a very useful one, as it teaches you to use your own fingers so that you can sew on buttons and do other things for yourself instead of bothering your mother or sister about it. It is by no means a girlish or kiddish thing to be able to do that. All kinds of explorers and adventurers have had to mend their own clothes during their journeys in order to keep them together. Robinson Crusoe would not have been very comfortable on his island if he had not been able to make himself clothes from skins.

Except for the first test, which you must do, there are plenty of other things to choose from. You must do six out of the eight, although of course you may take a pride in being able to do them all.

*Helping Mother.*—No one can tell a Cub how to " help Mother "—it is a lesson only love can teach. Besides, different mothers like to be helped in different ways. Each mother, when she finds her boy is wanting to Do His Best about the house, will find him a job. So learn, first, to get a real wish to *help Mother*, and then let her see this. She will do the rest.

You will already have learned a good many ways of helping

her in the house when you have been trying for the " Usefulness " part of the Two Star Test (see Bite 11), but there are one or two other ways in which you can help now that you are older and stronger.

*Making Tea.*—Anybody can make an ordinary old cup of tea, but very few people seem able to make a really good one. What you must do is to empty out the stale water from the kettle, and fill it again with fresh cold water from the tap. Put this on to boil. See that the tea-pot is clean and dry; warm it with a little hot water just before the kettle boils. Put in a teaspoonful of tea for each person and one for the pot, if it is a small number—less than a spoonful each if it is a large number. Watch your kettle carefully, and the moment it boils—really boils, bubbling hard and sending steam out of the spout—add the water quickly to the tea-pot. The best way to tell if a kettle is boiling is to hold a piece of stick or a spoon against the handle; if you feel this throbbing and vibrating like a miniature motor-car, you know at once that the water is boiling. Let the tea-pot stand for a few minutes near the fire and then pour out.

*Frying bacon or sausages.*—Bacon is usually so fat that it needs very little if any lard or dripping in the frying pan, but start cooking slowly until it has " greased " itself. Fry both sides of the rashers, turning them carefully with a fork so as not to splash boiling fat about.

Sausages will need some fat heated in the pan first, and they must be well pricked with a fork before you put them in the frying pan, or they will explode.

*Frying eggs.*—Break your egg carefully into a cup. When the fat in the pan is boiling hard, slip the egg in gently, so that it does not break. Keep the boiling grease well round it with a knife, and if it sticks raise it with a knife, and let the grease get under. Don't put too much fat in the pan; just enough to cover the bottom when it melts.

To poach an egg you break it into a cup, and then slip it very carefully into boiling water, take it out, strain the water off, and put it on toast. A drop or two of lemon added to the water will make the egg set firmer.

*Preparing, boiling, and frying potatoes.*—The proper way to prepare potatoes is as follows. Wash the potatoes clean. Then scrape new potatoes and peel old potatoes, taking out the eyes with the point of a knife. Put each potato as you finish it into a bowl of clean water, where you can keep them till wanted. To boil potatoes: put new potatoes into *cold* water, with a little salt; old potatoes should be put into *boiling* water, with salt; boil until they feel tender, when you prick them with a fork. Strain the water off, and stand the saucepan, with the lid half on, at the side of the stove for a few minutes. This dries the potatoes and makes them mealy. Don't forget though that potatoes boiled in their jackets are better for you than if you peel them, but be sure to scrub them hard before you cook them. To fry potatoes: peel your potatoes and cut them into very thin slices. Dry well on a clean cloth as potatoes are always wet when cut. Heat some fat in a frying-pan and wait till the bubbling stops and you see a thin blue smoke. Put the potatoes in at once. Be very careful not to let them burn. Keep turning them over until they are golden brown and nice and crisp. Cold, cooked potatoes can also be fried. Cut them into thick slices and cook the same way.

*Washing up.*—Washing up sounds simple and dull. But there is a *right way* of doing even dull things. You should have a clean basin or sink full of very hot clean water, with a little soap or washing-soda in it, a mop, and clean dish-cloth. Always begin by washing the cleanest things, spoons and forks, small plates, teacups, etc., then plates and knives, and lastly greasy dishes. Glasses should be washed in cold water and polished with a dry cloth.

*Cleaning windows.*—If the windows are very dirty get some whitening, and smear it well all over them with a wet cloth. When this is dry, rub off with a dry cloth, and polish with a leather. Another way is to wipe the windows well with a wet leather, and rub up with a dry leather. Don't clean windows while the sun is shining on them, as you can't see if you have cleaned off all the smears or not.

*Cleaning silver and brass.*—Put a very little cleaning polish or powder on a soft rag and smear it thoroughly all over the object to be cleaned. Then take another soft cloth and polish it till it is really bright and shiny. The less polish you use the better, as it sometimes leaves white marks in the cracks. Elbow grease is by far the best!

*Sweeping a room.*—Your mother will very likely have a carpet sweeper or a vacuum cleaner of some kind. If not, this is what you must do. Wash some tea-leaves well until no brown colour comes out. Squeeze them out and have them ready on a plate. Or you can soak a sheet of newspaper in water, squeeze it out and tear it into small pieces. Move the furniture out of the way and scatter the tea-leaves or paper over the floor, and sweep from the corners and sides to the centre of the room. The damp tea-leaves will collect the dust as you sweep and prevent its flying over the room. When you have all the dust swept into the middle of the floor it is quite easy to collect the heap into a dustpan with a small brush. Look out you leave no tea-leaves or paper behind.

*Dusting a room.*—Use a duster, not a dusting brush which only sweeps the dust somewhere else. Pick up the dust into the duster as you go and shake it out of the window constantly. Be very careful to go into every corner and dust the legs of the tables and chairs as well as the tops. Dust all the ornaments and frames and what-nots as well as the furniture.

But however well you have swept and dusted a room, it is not really " done " unless you leave it tidy. There is probably a right place for everything and that is where it must be put. It makes all the difference to the look of a room if everything is shipshape, rugs straight, cushions plumped up, tablecloth squared off and so on.

*Laying a table.*—Try to think ahead of what everybody will need for the meal, and see it is in the right place on the table before you begin. Notice how your Mother lays out the cutlery and the crockery, the glasses and the salt, pepper and mustard, and see if you can't do it exactly the same next time. A vase of flowers might be the finishing touch, but it's not so important as having the right number of knives, forks and spoons for everybody.

*Making a bed.*—This is one of the things you must learn, and the best way is to help somebody who knows how, for a start. You'll soon learn the knack of it, but be careful about tucking in the corners properly, and of course the sheets and blankets must be absolutely smooth.

*Needle and button.*—The needle to be threaded is not a darning needle with a whopping big eye, but the kind of needle that is used to sew a button on a shirt. This needs a good eye on your part, and a steady hand, and, hey presto! the thing is done. But you will find you will want practice, so as to be sure of it. White thread should be used, because then you can see if you have kept it clean! The button should be sewn on properly so that it has a neck, can go through a button-hole, and stand hard wear.

The job should be done as neatly as possible, so that the cloth on which the button is sewn is left neat and clean and tidy. After this in camp you will be able to sew on your own missing buttons, and in your home, too, I hope.

*Darning.*—We don't expect you to be able to do " invisible mending," but you should be able to darn a hole in your jersey and stockings neatly. Naturally you will choose wool of the same colour for the job, and will work as carefully as you can in the way you have been shown. There is no good rushing a job like this. " Softlee, softlee catchee monkey," as I am always telling the Scouts. It would be great, though, if you could look after and mend your Cub uniform all by yourself, instead of having to get someone else to do it for you.

*Mending a tear.*—This is perhaps the most useful thing we can learn. Being healthy and active animals, we are always tearing our clothes on bushes and trees and so on, and making nuisances of ourselves by asking other people to mend them for us. Let us do our own mending in future. If we start off with this intention we shall soon find that we have to be neat and careful about it, otherwise the tear will break out again, and the rent will be worse than it was before.

*Washing and Ironing.*—Any Cub likes to feel that he is a handy-man, and now I am going to tell you how to do the simple but necessary job of washing and ironing your scarf.

Fetch a basin and fill it with water as hot as you can put your hands into comfortably; then if you have any soap flakes, throw in a handful (Cub size) and whisk it into a lather with your fingers. Take your scarf; open it out, and put it into the water. When it is well soaked, rub the material between your fists in the soapy water, until you have been all over the scarf. If you have no soap flakes, rub it with a cake of common (not scented) soap.

Bring it out of the water every now and then and hold it up to be sure that you have not missed any part, and have got out all the dirty marks. When it is clean, take it out of the water and squeeze it as free from soap as possible.

Empty the basin and fill it again with clean cold water. Rinse your scarf in this, shaking it about well to get out all the soap. This done, gather up the scarf and twist it between both hands to get it as dry as possible. (Of course if you have a wringer you would put it through that.)

Peg out the scarf on a line, preferably out of doors, and leave it to dry.

Now we come to the ironing. You may begin your preparations for ironing as soon as your scarf is dry enough. It should feel very damp, but not wet.

If you have an ironing board, get it ready. If you have not, spread a piece of blanket over one end of a table and cover the blanket with an old clean piece of sheet or a clean towel. Perhaps you are lucky enough to have an electric iron; if so I do not need to telll you how to heat it—but remember, whatever you do, you must switch off the current once your iron is *really* hot. It will keep hot long enough to iron a scarf, and if you do not switch it off then, you are not only wasting electricity but you may go away when you have finished and forget that you have left it on. Many bad burns have come about in this way.

If you have ordinary irons, use two irons if possible (the second will be heating while you are using the first). Put them on the stove, or over a lighted gas ring. Don't forget to have an iron holder or an old duster handy, for the handle of the iron will be very hot when you lift it off. While your iron is heating, fetch the scarf and spread it over the ironing board or table. Put the iron stand, or a large flat iron weight, at one side of the table ready for the iron to stand on, for you must not leave the hot iron on the sheet or you will burn it. Now test your iron by holding it very carefully an inch away from your cheek. If you can feel the heat, it should be ready. You can now start ironing with an electric iron, but with an ordinary iron, you must either put on an ironing shoe, or else you should rub the iron hard over a piece of clean cloth or white paper to remove any dirt that may be on the bottom of the iron. You are now ready. Put your iron on one point of the scarf and run it with long even strokes up and down and across, steadying the material with your left hand. You will have to put the iron down now and then to rearrange the material, but do not forget to *put it on the stand* as I have told you.

When the scarf is free from creases, you may hang it up again for a little while to air it and ensure that it is quite dry before you put it on.

### Tests

A test and proof of whether the Cub is a good House Orderly will be the state of his Den at the Pack Headquarters. It should be a marvel of cleanliness and neatness. It should be the envy and despair of Scoutmasters—who will begin to wish the Scouts had a House Orderly Badge, to teach them all this, and give them a real keenness about orderly work.

Best of all, if Mother, when she is called on by the Cubmaster, can say there is nothing in the world like the Cub Pack for making boys helpful and useful and polite.

These tests go on all the time, without examinations. But there will, of course, have to be examinations as well. So, Cubs, see that the examiner really *enjoys* the cup of tea; it will put him in a good temper to pass your brasswork, your windows and even your potatoes!

There is scarcely need to suggest any games by which Cubs may practise all this. One hears of children " playing at house." But Cubs don't need to *play* at it—they are going to do it really. And it should prove more fascinating than any game.

## CHAPTER XIII

# OBSERVER

### Note to Cubmasters

*The choice of the birds and animals and flowers and trees to be studied is left to the discretion of the Cubmaster, and the wishes of the Cub, those most common in the locality being most suitable for observation. Instruction concerning these cannot, therefore, be included in this book. But there are many excellent works, published at low prices, in which all necessary information will be found. It may be pointed out that, although books are necessary for obtaining accurate and detailed knowledge, the subject should be studied as much as possible direct from Nature. The Cubs will find " stalking " the birds and beasts very fascinating—but it will take patience and self-control. Although Cubs should be allowed to seek and take interest in the birds' nests, and be able to recognise their eggs, " nesting " and making collections of eggs should not be permitted. It is, very often, actually cruel when done by small boys; and, anyhow birds'-nesting gives rise to so much cruelty and destruction that it is better to teach Cubs to leave it alone altogether, and to take every opportunity of impressing on their minds and imaginations the cruelty of robbing birds of their nests, eggs and, especially, young* (*see also page* 73). *Substitute for the desire to possess eggs themselves the desire to watch over and protect a brood so that it goes forth to be useful to one's fellow-men either by its singing or by grub-killing.*

### Useful Books

" *The Observer's Book of British Birds* ";
" *The Observer's Book of Wild Flowers* ";
" *The Observer's Book of Trees and Shrubs* ".
(*Messrs. Warne.*)

### Stalking

Something has already been said on the subject of stalking in Bite 8, but it is of extreme importance that a would-be Observer should know how to stalk, or else there will be no animals or birds for him to see; they will all be frightened away.

The main thing to remember is to move very quietly and smoothly, and to be able to " freeze," or remain perfectly still, at any moment. Learn to walk so that the whole of your foot rests equally on the ground, point your toes straight forward, as then they will not meet so many obstacles, and keep the arms and body as still as possible as you move. The Deer Stalking Game, mentioned on p. 205, will help you to move quietly, and there are other indoor stalking games which will give you a lot of practice in preparation for real stalking out of doors. As well as keeping your body balanced (and the Star Tests help here), you have to keep your eyes and ears well open, so as to see and hear anything at once. When you spot an animal or bird out in the open, stand stock-still for a moment and then move cautiously towards it, crouching low down as you go, until you come near enough to observe it carefully. Make a mental note of its size, colours, actions, noise, etc. It is useless to make notes on paper on the spot as the noise and movement you make will frighten it away. These notes should be made as soon as possible afterwards.

You will quickly find that most of your real observing will have to be done alone. It is a mistake to sit still in one place, you will be able to see more if you move about quietly. Very soon you will find how fascinating real observing is, and will be able to fill in many a happy afternoon for yourself.

The best thing that an Observer can do is to keep a diary or Nature Log in which he jots down all that he observes of any interest about Nature when he is out in the open. On wet days, when he has nothing else to do, he can illustrate it with sketches, photographs, or pictures of animals, birds, etc., cut out of the papers. He will then have a complete and lasting record of what he has seen. It is possible for a whole Six, or even the whole Pack, to keep a Log of this kind to which every Cub contributes from time to time.

## Exploring

*Tracking by ground signs.*—There are many ways of exploring. One is tracking by *ground signs*. But while an ordinary boy would just look out for

an ——→

a Cub keeps his eyes open, and his mind on the alert, and notices lots of little things, which tell him which way anyone in front has gone. But I have found that Tenderpads often make little mistakes, which mean that they " lose the scent " altogether, or waste a lot of time. Even quite good Cubs make mistakes because they forget to be very much on the alert, or are in such a hurry that they overlook things, and end in wasting more time than if they had gone a little slower.

A game which Cubs can play is "*Follow the Trail.*" A party of cowboys are to start off for a long journey across the prairie. They are expecting a party of their mates to follow them in a week's time. So they agree to make Scout signs and leave messages all the way. The Cubs having divided into two parties, one starts away across the fields and woods—preferably along a path or track. They make arrows pointing in the direction they are following, either on the ground or on fences or stones. They hide messages, written on paper or on white stones or pieces of wood, saying how they are getting on; where water may be found or warning their pals of various dangers. "Don't follow this road," (X) is also made when necessary. Meanwhile the second party of Cubs start (having given the cowboys ten minutes' start) *not* as the expected friends, but as a party of Indians, who have picked up the trail and are hot on the track of the "palefaces." They follow, destroying all the cowboys' tracks and signs, and reading their messages. Indian scouts may be sent on, singly (fast runners) to reconnoitre, and report on the number and deportment of the cowboys. But the Indian scout does this at his own peril. If he is *seen* by the palefaces he becomes their prisoner, and must go on with them. (Any cowboy seeing an enemy Scout gives the Cub's cry, whereupon the Indian *must* play fair and surrender). The palefaces eventually run short of provisions, at the end of half a mile (or more) and are obliged to halt. Believing Indians to be following them, they take cover. The Indians, finding that the trail has come to an end, search for the cowboys (*seeing* and calling out the name being equal to killing), but any paleface who manages to creep out of his cover and *touch* an Indian before he is seen himself kills him (puts him out of action). The game is won by the party having the largest number of survivors when the Cubmaster blows a whistle.

*Landmarks.*—Finding the way by landmarks is very different from finding your way by ground signs. Instead of looking on the ground you've got to look about you. A landmark is something in the landscape which always remains there, which everybody knows, and which can easily be seen, such as hills and knolls, large ponds, lonely trees or rocks. Churches and large buildings may also be called landmarks, and are very useful for finding your way. You should get to know all the landmarks round your home, for two reasons: (1) so as to be able to help strangers to find their way; (2) so that if you lose your way when you are out you may be able to tell where you are. Perhaps you will find yourself in a wood, and you won't know a bit which way to start back. Well, if you climb a tree, and see away to the left a silver line that is the river shining in the sun, you will say, " Now, if the river is on my left I must go in *this* direction, and I shall be going home. I see the mill on the river bank, so I must be about five miles from home." Or perhaps you see a church tower, or a big hill that rises up behind your home. That is what finding your way by landmarks means. When you are near your home it is easy, but when you are in a strange place this is very important. When you go to camp, the first thing you should do is to notice the landmarks all round, and then you will know how to find your way back to camp, if you are sent on an errand. A Cub shouldn't have to *ask his way*.

*Compass Direction.*—Of course you know how important a compass is for guiding a ship in the open sea; there are no landmarks there to help. But perhaps you think a compass is not much good on land. In England you find sign-posts and heaps of landmarks—churches, ruins, hills, and woods. But in other countries it is different. In the Australian Bush, for instance, where the grass you have to ride through is higher than a man's head, and there are often no roads, and only faint tracks—let alone milestones—a compass is very useful. Perhaps there will be no landmark at all, except a distant hill, and that may be hidden in a mist, or by the falling dusk. Strangers sometimes ride for hours and hours, thinking they are going straight ahead, and really they are riding through the long grass in a circle, and arrive back, hours later, at the very place they started from! If they went by the compass that would not happen to them. (You will find the way to read the compass in Bite 11.)

But there are other ways of knowing where is the North, South, East, and West, besides looking at the compass. When you become Scouts you will know how to find the North by your watch and the sun. And how to tell the direction by the stars. But here are a few very simple ways any Cub can use. Remember, first, that if you can tell *one* direction—say the East—you can tell the others easily. If you know which is the east, stretch out your right hand, straight from your side, pointing at it. Then you will be facing due North, and the South will be at your back, and your left hand will be pointing West. The same follows, of course, whichever point you know. If it's the West you know for certain, stretch your left hand to it; or if it's the South, turn your back to it. This will always bring your face to the North.

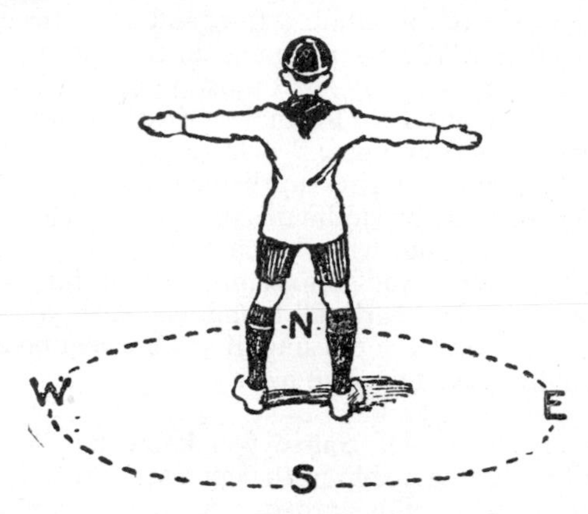


Now, of course, the best way to tell the direction is by the sun. You all know that the sun rises in the East, and moves over to the West and sets there. Well, if the sun is very low—just risen—you know that's the East. Or if it has been risen some hours, you think of the way it moves round, in a great arch, and you can judge (roughly) whereabouts it rose, and that will be the East. If it is sunset time, of course that's easy—you can tell the West at once.

But there is a great, steady compass that always stands ready for you, and doesn't shift about, like the sun. Every village has one and towns have heaps of them. Once you see one you can always tell the compass direction at once. Do you know what it is? Why, the church. Nearly all churches point East. That is, the altar lies at the East end. Do you know why churches look eastwards? Because the Holy Land lies away to the East; the land where Jesus Christ was born and lived and died. That is why we always look East in our churches.

So remember that the church is a compass, and if you point with your right hand in the same way as the church, you will usually be facing North. But when you look at the church to see the compass direction, remember that someone once said—that all church spires are fingers pointing to Heaven. And, after all, that's the most important direction in life!

## Games to Play

1. *Kim's Game.*

Kim's Game is not hard, and only takes practice to get good at. You can play it with your Six. Collect on a tray (or on a circle on the floor) a number of articles—buttons, knives, pencil, pen, match, nib, inkpot, match-box, etc.—not more than twelve things. Get your Six to sit round where they can see the tray and let them look at it for one minute—or until you have counted fifty. Cover up the tray and make a list of all the articles on a piece of paper.

When you are given your look at the tray, notice at once which are the objects you would be likely to forget, and stick them in your memory, specially, leaving the easy ones to look after themselves. For instance, the Scout knife and the ink-pot will stand out in your memory by themselves, while the linen button, the nib, and the match-box would slip out very easily.

The same thing applies to any other game of observation and memory.

2. *Deer stalking.*—The Cubmaster acts as deer, not hiding but standing, and occasionally moving. The whole Pack go out to find the deer; each tries in his own way to get up to it unseen. Directly the deer sees a Cub he directs him to stand up as having failed.

After a certain time the Cubmaster calls " Time " and all stand up at the spot which they have reached, and the nearest to the deer wins.

The same game may be played to test the Cubs in stepping lightly.

The umpire is blindfolded. The practice is best carried out where there are dry twigs, stones, gravel, etc., lying about

Each Cub starts in turn to stalk the blind enemy, beginning at a point 100 yards away, and he must do it fairly fast—say, in one minute and a half. The Cub who succeeds in getting nearest to the umpire before being heard and stopped, wins.

3. *The " Naval Raid " Game.*—An open door represents the harbour entrance, two blindfolded Cubs, one on each side, the British cruisers.

The other Cubs—the enemy vessels—try to enter the harbour one by one through the door so quietly as not to be caught by the sentinels.

4. *Practice in Ambushing.*—The Pack splits up into two parties, one of which goes out in advance and hides in bushes, etc., by the roadside. The other party follows, and calls out those Cubs whom they can see *without leaving the road.* They continue as long as desired; one party alternately hiding and seeking. At first, time should be given for the hiders to arrange themselves; later they should be able to do so quickly.

Opportunity can always be taken when someone drops out for the rest of the party to get under cover as quickly as possible, so that when he returns the party has disappeared as if by magic. This always causes fun with the Cubs.

5. When the Cubs are proficient in ambushing, they can split up into three Sixes. One Six forms an exploring party, the others represent " natives."

The exploring party goes out in proper form, and at every building, village, or clump of trees, halts and sends out scouts, just as a real explorer would. One of the " native " Sixes will have hidden themselves, and act sometimes as friendly, sometimes as hostile tribes.

While one " native " patrol is doing the business, the other can be going further on and getting ready.

If properly arranged this game is capable of producing much grand fun; and at the same time quite a lot of different Cub activities can be taught with it.

6. *Hopping.*—A " river " is marked on the ground, with stepping-stones, and a ford; the Cub has to hop across from one end to the other. He must not rest at all on either bank, but keep hopping all the time.

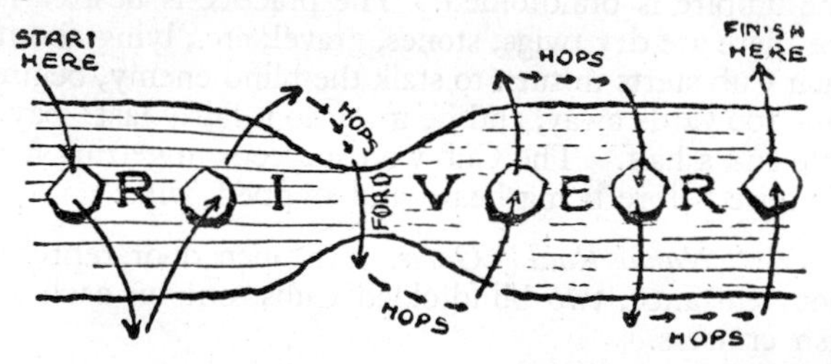

These various games will give you practice in stalking (see p. 200) and in keeping your wits about you as well as your eyes and ears so that you will gradually become a better Observer and quickly be able to recognise different animals and birds and to discover different flowers, trees, and shrubs. Whichever of these three subjects you select for your Badge you must try and study it for yourself and not just depend on books or on what is told you. An observer is one who finds everything out for himself even if it does take a great deal of time and patience, but discovering things for yourself is really great fun.

## CHAPTER XIV

# SIGNALLER

BEFORE beginning to learn to signal you should think carefully what signalling means. It means that you are sending a message to someone who is out of reach of your voice. It is very difficult to give a really clear message, with details, to someone without being able to speak to them. So your job is to signal it very clearly and correctly, making it as easy as possible for the other person to understand you.

So, from the beginning, do your best to signal well; don't think you can send a letter any old way, just because you are only practising.

Here are some notes on signalling in Semaphore and Morse, but you will not be expected to learn them both.

### SEMAPHORE

Before you begin to bother about that letter or word you are sending, learn to hold yourself and your arms correctly.

1. Stand firmly, your feet a little apart, and facing the receiver squarely.

2. If using flags grasp the sticks firmly, right down by the flags, your first finger pointing along the flag, and the stick running up your arm.

3. Always keep your arms quite stiff; don't let them be bent, or the sticks wobble.

4. Know the seven different positions at which the flags can be used singly, and be able to make the movements quite correctly and briskly.

5. In practising the movements always go round like a clock, that is, beginning with your right hand.

Now you know *the way to signal*, so it is time for you to learn the alphabet in Semaphore. This will mean really doing your best and giving all your mind.

The first circle—A to G—you make all with your right hand as far as D (which is straight up over your head), and the rest with your left. Get to know these seven letters perfectly well in and out or any way before you learn to make any others. You can even make easy words with them, like BAG, FAG, FED, CAGE, DEAF. Make these and get other Cubs to read them, and ask them to make some for you to read, so that you will get used to seeing them the other way round. When you are quite sure of these letters carry on.

H in Semaphore

The second circle—H to N—you will find takes both arms—the right one as if you were making A, the left one brought across your chest. You then go on moving the left arm round, while you keep the right arm *quite still*. You will thus be making H, I, K, L, M, N. (You notice J is left out in this circle—it comes later.) Practise these just as you did A—G, and then go on to the next.

The third circle—O to S—here your right arm sticks at the B position, while the left goes round. You go on, like this, always moving your right arm slowly (like the little hand of a clock) and the left one fast (like the big hand). It is very simple until you get to U in the fourth circle. After U difficulties begin as the letters no longer go straight round the circle. You will have to learn each one separately and go on practising until you really do know them.

There are some special signs, too, for the general answer, for numbers, letters and the " erase " which you must learn. There are special names for the letters, too, which signallers use.

Once you know the alphabet and how to make the letters, all you need is practice. You are only expected to send short, simple words slowly but correctly.

A silly thing Cubs often do when they are signalling, and which makes it impossible for anyone to read their messages, is to waggle their arms about while they think how to send the next letter. Keep *quite still* at one letter until you have remembered how to make the next, and then make it calmly, but briskly. The other fellow won't mind waiting while you think, but he can't tell what on earth you mean if you wave your arms about like a windmill!

When you have got as far as sending words, there is this to remember. At the end of every word bring your flags down sharply to the *ready* position—that is crossed in front of you. But don't come down to the *ready* position after each letter in the word—keep still and pause for a moment at the letter made, before going on.

### Morse

You will find signalling in the Morse Code rather more difficult than in Semaphore. But it has many advantages. For instance, later on you may be able to signal Morse in many ways: with flags, with the telegraph key, with light (heliograph or electric light), etc. If you are good at winking it is even possible to " talk " in Morse with your eyes! So, you see, to learn Morse you need not think of the flags at first, as you do in Semaphore. It is time enough for Morse flags when you become a Scout. Now I am going to explain Morse to you as clearly as I can—but it will take all your attention, and an awful lot of " best."

In the Morse Code letters are formed by dots and dashes. Written they look like this · — (A), — · · · (B), and so on The question is, how can you show the difference between a dot and a dash? Well, it is all a matter of long and short pauses. Whatever way you are sending remember that a dash takes three times as long to make as a dot. You can see that easily if you look at the Morse signs written. Here's a dot . and here is a dash —, just three times as long. But before I tell you any more, you must learn the alphabet in Morse. What I have already told you is only to get it well into your head that whatever way you are sending, and at whatever speed, *a dash is always three times the length of a dot.* If you don't remember that, no one will ever be able to read your messages, whatever way you send.

The simplest way to learn the alphabet is as follows:—

| *Dots—* | | *Dashes—* | |
|---|---|---|---|
| . | E | | |
| . . | I | — | T |
| . . . | S | — — | M |
| . . . . | H | — — — | O |

*Opposites—*

| | | | |
|---|---|---|---|
| A | . — | — . | N |
| B | — . . . | . . . — | V |
| D | — . . | . . — | U |
| F | . . — . | . — . . | L |
| G | — — . | . — — | W |
| Q | — — . — | — . — — | Y |

*Sandwiches—*

| | | | |
|---|---|---|---|
| K | — . — | R | . — . |
| P | . — — . | X | — . . — |

*Letters with no Opposites—*

C — . — . J . — — — Z — — . .

Now that you can make a letter, try a word. And remember that *at the end of each letter* you must make a pause as long as a dash. Here is a word in Morse: " Dash, dot, dash, dot (pause), dot, dot, dash (pause), dash, dot, dot, dot." That spells " Cub." Go on practising words till you are *quite used* to sending and reading, and practise winking with your eyes (calling the right eye " dash " and the left " dot "), or just saying words to yourself in " dot, dash " language as you go to school or lie in bed. Another important thing to remember, whatever way you are sending is to go right ahead *continuously*, from start to finish, in making a letter. If you stop in the middle, the person who is reading will think you meant to make two letters. Like this: if you were sending C (which is — . — .), and you made half

(— .) and then paused, and then sent the second half (— .), they would think you meant to send N, N.

Again there are some special signs which you must learn if you are going to send Morse messages successfully.

You can write Morse as it is written in this book, making a small space between each letter and a thin line between each word, like this:

— . .  — — — / — . — —  — — —  . . —  . — . /
— . . .  .  . . .  — /

### Codes

This sort of writing can be read by any Signaller of course, but there are many codes which no-one can read except the person who knows the " key."

For your Signaller's Badge you will have to send and receive messages from a friend in code which you can choose for yourself.

ENO SI SIHT

Of course you can read that? RO TAHT?

They are simply written backwards and are so easy that anybody could read them. Yours must be harder.

If your name is John, your secret alphabet might start with a J instead of A, and you must work out a key for yourself and your friend:

A B C D E F G H I J K L M N O P Q R S T U V W X Y Z
J K L M N O P Q R S T U V W X Y Z A B C D E F G H I

Your signature, still assuming that you are John, will look like SXQW, and nobody could understand that unless they knew the key.

Here's another simple form of code which you can puzzle out for yourself:

GEOEO EDELE UECEK!

Now you work out a different sort of code for yourself and you'll have a lot of fun.

## CHAPTER XV

# SPORTSMAN

### Note to Cubmasters

[*See also Note on Games in Part III.*]

*In deciding what qualifies a Cub for his Sportsman's Badge, the most important factor is his personal behaviour during games.*

*Anybody who has had much to do with boys (and even older lads) must have noticed the terrible habit of some of arguing and cavilling while playing team games. It ends in destroying the spirit of play and even in " rows." This tendency should be treated very severely by Cubmasters; and also the tendencies not always to play quite fair and to show bad temper when beaten. It is these last two faults that really give rise to all the arguments. After two or three definite warnings the Cub should be " ordered off." He will very soon learn the proper spirit of play. A proper severity about arguing, bad temper, etc., will promote discipline, instant obedience, and self-control.*

*Another matter to which Cubmasters should pay attention is the lack of self-control and pluck among many of the boys when they get hurt in games. Cubmasters should expect and encourage a show of the Spartan spirit. Stoicism will be quite a new idea to the Cubs—but an excellent one! " Death agonies " on the field, and going off in tears, should not be allowed. Starting early to inculate the Spartan spirit into the boys, as it is possible to do with Cubs, should make all the difference.*

*The Cubs should know that if a boy faints or is taken ill (as they sometimes are on occasions like Rallies) they should not get excited, but carry on as usual, and leave the Cubmaster as free as possible to look after the boy.*

*Any grievous demonstrations of agony on the part of a boy who has got a hack on the shin or such other injury incidental to the game should be suppressed by chaff provided, of course, the injury is quite slight.*

*We have an excellent opportunity through this badge of training manliness, so let us make the best possible use of it.*

## Hints to Cubs

### Self-Care

If you want to be a good footballer or hockey-player, or team-player of any sort, you will have to look after yourself quite a lot all day, and not just when you are playing on the field. If you have not seen to it that you have a good wind you will find yourself puffing and blowing like an old cab-horse, while the " enemy " dashes off towards your goal with the ball. If you have not done your best to make yourself strong and healthy, you will find that your legs ache, you get tired out, and, in fact, that you're no good at all, compared with boys who have been more sensible and looked after themselves.

And what is it that causes you to be short-winded, small, weak, easily tired, and so on?

Here are the commonest causes; eating unwholesome food, and bolting it in a hurry; not taking regular exercise; a lazy way of walking and sitting; doing silly things, like eating green apples; going to bed late; and sleeping with closed windows.

Once you know what makes you a bad team-player it is not so very hard to remedy it. You will find all about how to make yourself strong, healthy and big in Bites 10 and 13. Follow out the instructions you find there—remember to breathe deeply; eat good food and chew it well, instead of making a little pig of yourself with bull's-eyes and toffee; go to bed early and get up early, and sleep with the windows open. If you do your best at all this, you will find you can play games ten times as well.

### Team Playing

Football, Hockey, and Rounders are the chief games by means of which Cubs will try to obtain their Sportsman's badge.

So, first of all a few hints on Football, and on the chief branch played by Cubs: " Soccer."

The first thing is to learn to kick properly. A good player never kicks with the end of his toe unless he is taking a place-kick; always with the *instep!* If you naturally kick with your right foot, learn to kick with your left also; this is quite easy *if you always try to do so whenever the ball comes to your left foot.*

Next, you must learn to shoot. *Never shoot* (*i.e.* aim at goal) *with the toe-end* even from a place-kick! Remember that unless you take the free-kicks for your team you never have the chance of placing the ball just as you like it, and then taking a run for your shot!

So don't waste time doing that when you are "shooting-in," but always practise shooting while you are running, and always *with the ball on the move.* A good tip is to imagine the word "Low" ringing in your ears just as you are about to shoot, for it is harder for many boys to keep the ball down below the cross-bar than to send it between the uprights.

*Dribbling.*—Whatever position you play you ought to learn how to "dribble"; if you are a forward you must learn to dribble *well.* Don't kick the ball past your opponent and run! That is the "kick and rush" game; and even a fast sprinter is easily held if he can't do anything else. The GREAT RULE is *Try to keep the ball as close as possible to your toe* while you are running; if an opponent comes in your way it is then quite easy to touch the ball slightly to one side and continue to run.

*Choosing your position.*—If you have the opportunity of choosing your position in a team, these hints will help you to make the best choice; but always remember that an occasional game in a totally different position makes you a better all-round footballer, and through it you may discover that you are really better in a new position.

A *Forward* must be able (1) to dribble well; (2) to shoot hard and true; he is generally light in weight.

A *Half-back* should be (1) a good tackler, good at "getting in the way"—of an opponent, of course; (2) a fairly good dribbler; (3) able to use his brains when on the field, so as to pass to his forwards properly; (4) long-winded.

If you think you are not specially suited for any of the other lines, try half-back.

A *Full-back* should be (1) a good and fearless tackler; (2) a strong kick. He is generally, but not always, a heavy boy for his age. If you are rather tall, try your hand as *Goalkeeper*; you are bound to improve with practice, and can use your hands as well as your feet.

*Combination.*—You are not much use in a team if you cannot pass properly. Whatever your position, remember that you are not the only player on you side, but are, so to speak, part of a machine, and when the ball leaves you, see that it goes to one of your own side; a selfish player is always a hindrance to his own team and an advantage to his opponents. If you are a good dribbler you will be a useful forward UNLESS you always try to get the ball past a defender by dribbling and never by passing to an "unmarked" man on your own side; for if your opponent knows that you *always* dribble and never pass he will go straight in and tackle you, but if he knows that you are just as likely to pass as to dribble, it makes him hesitate, and you are very much more likely to beat him.

### SPORTSMANSHIP

*Captain.*—Always do cheerfully and immediately whatever your captain tells you to do. Never "grouse" at him or about him; and if he blows you up for not playing as he expects you to, remember that it is part of his duty to do so, just as much as it is for him to say "Bad luck!" or "Jolly good shot!" if you are playing well. The captain who never says a word to you when you continually make a hash of good and easy things may be an awfully nice chap, but he is a poor captain.

*Temper.*—A sportsman always keeps his temper under the most exciting and provoking circumstances. Our British games are good for you, not only physically but morally, for *if you play them in a clean sportsmanlike manner* they develop self-control. However great the odds against you, never give up until the game is ended, as there is a chance of pulling it out of the fire until the last minute has gone. *In all games*—not only in football—you must learn not to be upset or bad-tempered if you lose. Try your best throughout the game, but never say or even allow yourself to think "The other side won, but we were the better team!" This does sometimes happen, as there is a certain amount of luck in all games, but a good sportsman takes losses without grousing or worrying, and, when beaten, is always ready to give the victor the credit due to him.

If you are the captain see that your team gives the opponents a hearty cheer at the end of the match, and if you are not captain and your team does not do this, just suggest it to him; perhaps he has not thought of it.

*Referee (or Umpire).*—Never criticise the referee's decisions. Every referee makes mistakes; in fact, every human being does; why, even a Cub makes mistakes sometimes! So if you feel a grudge against a referee, try to referee one or two games yourself, and you will soon sympathise with him in his task.

## Rounders

With regard to sportsmanship the hints given for Football hold good.

Here is a plan of a Rounders field.

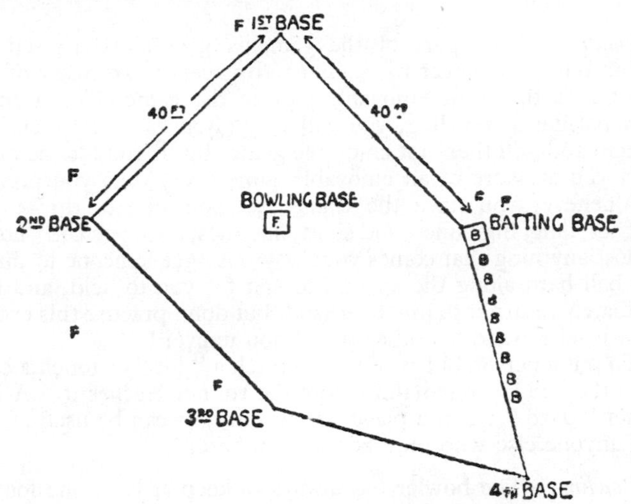


*B stands for the members of the Batting side.*
*F stands for the members of the Fielding side.*

There are generally nine players in each team. The bases have to be well marked and you have to run round the outside of the marker.

*Batting.*—The members of the team who are waiting to bat stand in a line between the fourth base and the batting base. When it is your turn to bat, you must hold on to the rounder stick very tightly because if you let go just as you were giving a mighty swipe it might hurt one of the fielders very severely.

Then watch the ball all the time it is coming towards you, keep your eye on it and think of nothing except hitting it.

It is generally rather dangerous to hit the ball high up into the air as you will be caught unless you are quite sure you can hit it right away beyond the fielders.

If you should hit it behind the batting base you won't be allowed to run past the first base. You have got the choice of three balls, but must run at the third. When you get to a base you have to touch it or you may be put out. Only one person can be in a base at a time.

A rounder is scored whenever a player manages to reach the fourth base without being put out or the ball getting back to the bowler's hands.

*Fielding.*—This part of the game is generally despised by young boys, but never by really good players. To many of the latter it is the most enjoyable part of the game; if you enjoy only batting or bowling, you will very often have bad luck in a match, and will then not enjoy the game; but if you like fielding, then you are sure of an enjoyable game every time you play.

Whenever you have the chance get someone to throw you catches, long, high ones, and short, hot ones, until you can "hold" almost anything that comes your way; also get someone to throw the ball hard along the ground to you for you to field, and immediately return it to him overhand (but don't practise this except on a level ground, as other turf is too uneven!)

To put a person out you have to catch a " hit " or touch a base with the ball in your hand before the runner reaches it. A ball is not " dead " when a player is put out, but can be used to put out anyone else who may be out of a base.

*Bowling.*—The bowler has always to keep at least one foot in his base. A " no ball " is one higher than the shoulder or lower than the knee, and if you bowl three of them, one after the other, your opponents count half a rounder.

(There are several varieties of Rounders—the American " Baseball " is one of them, so get to know of them and try them in your Pack.)

### Hockey

Here, again, the words on Sportsmanship are the same as those given under " Football." The general idea of the play is very similar to football, using the stick much as a cricket bat. For this reason most good footballers with a little practice soon become at least useful hockey players. As at football kicking a ball about is bound to improve your play, so at hockey your stick-work will improve if you practise running with the ball close to your stick. *Don't knock the ball ahead and run after it* when you are dribbling! That is the same as " kick and rush " in football. It will improve your dribbling if you practise *tapping* the ball across your body to your left side and returning it to your right with your stick reversed, repeating the process several times. This develops your control of the ball.

Practise " bullying " smartly; there is an art in it, and a good man can win a " bully " almost every time he meets an ordinary " bullier."

## CRICKET

This gives you an idea where the Fielders may be placed on a Cricket Field. You will spot at once that there are seventeen of them on this field, when you know very well that there are only eleven in a Team. But all these places could not be filled at once. It is for the Captain to decide how he can best use his men.

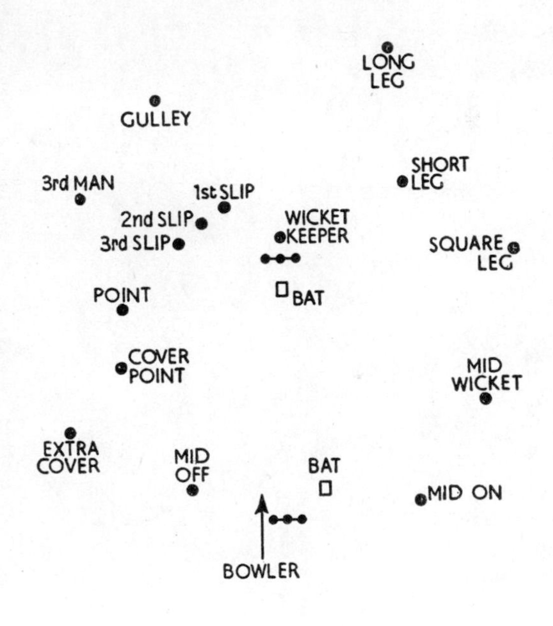

### Rules

All these games have rules or laws which every Player must know and understand and, of course, obey. A game wouldn't be any fun without them.

Any good player will explain them to you, and you will have to explain to the Examiner, in turn, things like the off-side rule in football, what constitutes a foul, what l.b.w. means, and the number of players and where they play in the field.

One law to remember in every game is the Wolf Cub Law, for a true sportsman knows the importance of "not giving in to himself."

## CHAPTER XVI

# SWIMMER

### Note to Cubmasters

*For your own protection as well as for that of your boys you must have a Life Saving Picket of two good swimmers always on duty while bathing is going on—undressed, with overcoats on, in a boat or on the shore, ready at any moment to go to the rescue of anybody who may get into dfficulties.*

*Bathing should not be permitted at all unless you know the place is perfectly safe.*

*Many lives have been saved through these precautions being the rule with the Boy Scouts.*

(See Rule 331 of *Policy, Organisation and Rules.*)

*A few remarks explaining the reason for the choice of the various tests may be useful.*

*Swimming.—Twenty-five yards is chosen as the distance, because if a boy can swim ten yards properly a few days' practice will enable him to swim twenty-five yards and more. If he can only struggle across ten yards of water he can't* swim!

*Floating.—Very easy and quite useful. A great help in giving balance in the water. Practising for this test will help the Cub no end towards the actual swimming test; but as floating is rather dull the boys often neglect it, and struggle at swimming before they have learnt balance in the water.*

*Swimming on back.—This is not so very difficult after the Cub has learnt to float; adds interest and variety to his swimming and is important in view of Rescue work when he becomes a Scout.*

*Duck's Diving.—This is not really difficult, like diving from the side of the bath. When a Cub has learnt to dive he will have conquered all " funk " of the water, and the absurd fear of* going under *which so many boys keep for years.*

*Honey Pot.—This requires no skill—only a little " spunk,' which many Cubs (and Scouts) lack in the water. If a Cub hasn't enough grit to " honey pot," he doesn't deserve a swimmer's badge!*

*There is a huge moral discipline in these tests. A funky little Cub will have advanced a big step and conquered himself in a large measure when he has dared to perform a " honey pot " or learnt to dive!*

## Hints to Cubs

The first thing to learn is to have confidence—not to be afraid of the water. Don't imagine you're going to drown if you happen to go under—it takes a lot to drown anybody! When you learn to dive you will find the hard thing to do is to sink and *keep under*—and that you are always popping up like an indiarubber ball. If you happen to swallow a little water, never mind—it's not poison. Don't *cling* to people who are teaching you to swim, as if you were a little drowning rat. Pretend you're a *fish.* Once you are " at home " in the water, half the battle is won.

*Floating.*—The next thing to learn is balance in the water—how to *keep* up. So start by learning to float. To do this just let yourself lie comfortably in the water—as if you were in bed—with your head right back till your ears are under. Your toes should just peep out of the water. Don't stiffen yourself as if you were a little bit of board; balance yourself comfortably, and keep your head well back—it's much harder to float if you keep your ears out. Practise floating, because in your test you will have to keep it up for a whole minute in the sea or for half a minute in fresh water.

*Swimming.*—Don't start trying to swim till you can float. Once you know how to keep up and balance you will not find swimming hard, if you really try and remember the few hints I am going to give you now.

1. Don't struggle and work hard, and swim at a great pace as if you were trying to win a race. That won't keep you up. Take long, slow, gentle strokes, shooting your arms out in front of you evenly, then bring them outwards as if you were pushing the water away with your open hands. This movement will bring your elbows back to your sides. Then shoot your arms forward, and so on. Some boys find it easier at first to swim like a dog. I learnt that way, and it is very usual among Australian boys.

2. Don't kick with your legs just any old how. Remember the way you have seen a *frog* swim, and do just exactly what he does

with his legs. And keep your legs down, well under the water. Your feet should make no splash above the surface.

3. Don't hold your breath and look as if you were going to burst at any moment. *No one* could swim like that. And don't puff and blow like an old broken-winded horse, just breathe slowly and evenly, always keeping your lungs full, as this makes you buoyant, like an air-ball. A good swimmer can talk or sing or whistle while he swims.

4. Don't use water wings. They stop you learning to *keep up* by your own effort, and they make your balance wrong. You are much more likely to tip up or topple over suddenly and get an unexpected ducking than if you learn without them.

5. Don't try and keep up long at first. Two good strokes and then a toe on the bottom and another try is better than ten hurried, struggling strokes ending, as likely as not, in a ducking and much spluttering! Practise your arm strokes smoothly and slowly, keeping one toe on the bottom till you feel confident enough to raise it, and try and swim a few strokes.

If you follow these rules carefully and someone helps you a little at first, by holding you up and giving you confidence, it ought not to be long before you can swim. But remember it means sticking to it *and* Doing Your Best.

*Duck's Diving.*—This is really quite easy, though it may sound hard. It is not difficult, like diving from a board as a Scout has to do. It is called " Duck's diving," because you have to do exactly what a duck does when it dives. So, if you get a chance, watch the ducks, and then you will know just how to do it. In case you haven't any ducks handy to learn from, here are a few hints.

1. To begin with, don't be in a funk. Believe me, it's awfully nice under the water, especially if you keep your eyes open, when everything looks a beautiful pale green and full of thousands of bubbles. Make up your mind to like it, and try to feel like a duck or a fish.

2. Stand in water up to your arm-pits. Take a big breath, tuck your head down, chin on chest, shove your head into the water, at the same moment kicking up your legs (they should really come up out of the water behind you). Make an effort to get to the bottom with your hands: touch it if you can. Then point your hands up, give a kick with your legs, and there you are up again. Remember your head is *bound* to come up, and your feet

are bound to reach the bottom again firmly, so there is nothing to be afraid of. Be sure and keep your eyes open, it makes all the difference.

" *Honey Pot.*"—If you find diving beats you—and it won't if you follow what I've told you and Do Your Best—you can try a " honey pot " to pass your test. This anyone can do, because it is not a matter of skill, but simply of pluck—and no Cub is going to own he hasn't got pluck! All you have to do is to take a big jump off the side, bend up your knees and clasp your arms round them. See how far you can get and how big a splash you can make! If you take a good long run along a spring-board (or even from the side) you will be able to get a long way. But of course a simple " honey pot " from the side of the bath or out of a boat will pass you in the test. A Cub who passes this test proves he is no funk, but a sportsman, and deserves the Swimmer's Badge.

Just a few words of advice about your bathing.

Remember to obey your Cubmaster implicitly, as to when and where you bathe.

Don't swim out of your depth in the sea unless you are with your Cubmaster, or a Scout who can swim well.

Don't stay in until you are cold and blue and shivering, as it may give you cramp.

Don't bathe after a meal for at least an hour and a half or two hours, otherwise you are very likely to get cramp in the stomach or limbs. This doubles you up and you cannot swim. Lots of boys get drowned every year for not following this advice.

Never try to duck or splash other Cubs while they are learning to swim or float, as it may spoil their confidence in the water. Remember how you would hate it if they did it to you!

Remember that you are bathing in order to learn to swim, or to improve your swimming, and don't be tempted to play about all the time with the younger Cubs who are not trying to earn their Swimmer's Badge.

## PART III

# OBJECTS AND METHODS OF WOLF CUB TRAINING

### Hints for Cubmasters

DON'T be frightened by the length of these Hints; they are only intended to be suggestive or helpful to beginners.

### Object of the Wolf Cub Training

Our object in taking up the training of the Wolf Cubs is not merely to devise a pleasant pastime for the Cubmasters or for the boys, but to improve the efficiency of the future citizens of the British Commonwealth and Empire.

The past training of these has not proved adequate for the requirements of to-day, and if the training is not good enough for to-day, much less is it good enough for to-morrow, and it is to to-morrow that we must look forward.

*Character* is acknowledged to be of greater importance than mere book instruction for citizen efficiency. And yet no practical scheme exists for its inclusion in education to even an equivalent extent.

Efficiency has been defined as " being gaugable by the amount of supervision that a man needs " (Robert E. Meadows). But this, of course, applies only to the extent of moral efficiency, whereas physical efficiency is also of the highest value in completing the citizen efficiency of a man.

*Physical health* and how to develop it should be as much a part of education as scholarly, scientific, or technical attainments.

The thousands of hours and the tens of thousands of pounds that are lost annually through strikes or lock-outs are as nothing compared with the tens of thousands of hours and the hundreds of thousands of pounds that are lost through preventable physical, inefficiency and ill-health.

Our training of the Cubs therefore is directed to these two main ends as shown diagrammatically at the beginning of Part II.

It is done at the most important time of their lives, when they are most mouldable both in body and in mind to receive the right directions.

With a foundation laid thus early we may hope that the subsequent structure may be all the more satisfactory, especially since it forms part of a progressive system to be continued and maintained during the period of his Boy Scout training, so that when he comes to years of discretion, health-athleticism, coupled with character, will be the habit of the majority rather than the accomplishment of the few.

The Wolf Cub Pack is designed to be a Junior Branch of the Scout Movement in order to meet the eagerness of a large number of small boys who want to be Scouts and who are as yet too young.

It doesn't do to put them to the same tasks and tests as the older boys, especially in the company of the older boys, as they are likely to overdo themselves in the effort to keep up to the mark. At the same time the older boys on their part do not care to mix with " kids " in their pursuits. It is for every reason better to keep the two apart.

Cub training is different from but a step towards that of the Scouts.

No boy's character is firmly set at eleven or twelve years of age, and Cubmasters must realise that unless the work of the Pack really leads to that of the Troop they are, to a large extent, failing their boys. It is *possible* for a boy to lose, in a very short time, much of the good he has gained by being a Cub if the work is not carried on until he is old enough to choose good from evil.

A normal Wolf Cub Pack is not a separate organisation, but part of a Scout Group. The Cubmaster should work in close co-operation with the Scouters, the Scouts, the Senior Scouts, and the Rover Scouts. He should make it plain to every new boy and to every new boy's parents that the Pack is only an " ante-room " to the Scouts, and he should always keep the ideal of a " better Scout " before the Cubs.

At the head of the Group there is the Group Scoutmaster who exercises general supervision over all sections of the Group but delegates the detailed responsibility for the management of each section to the Scouter in charge of it. The Cubmaster is thus responsible to the Group Scoutmaster for the conduct and management of the Pack. He will be a member of the Group Council, consisting of all the warranted Scouters of the Group, whose task is to direct the general policy of the Group as a whole.

The Cub Law and Promise are naturally more simple than those of the Scout—it would not be right to ask the younger boys to undertake duties and promises which they could neither grasp nor carry out. Cubmasters should of course teach their boys in a simple and practical manner and in consultation with their Chaplain what is meant by their Promise of "Duty to God" (see also Religious Policy quoted on page 244), and should give what other religious and moral instruction they think necessary to prepare the Cub for becoming a good Scout.

*Method.*—Our method of training is to educate from within rather than to instruct from without; to offer games and activities which, while being attractive to the small boy, will seriously educate him morally, mentally, and physically.

Our aim, as Fisher wrote, is to promote "not so much the acquisition of knowledge as the desire and capacity for acquiring knowledge."

In other words, the Cubmaster's job is to enthuse the boy in the right direction. By acting on this principle he will save himself considerable trouble in reaching his goal and in producing a smart Pack of keen and capable boys.

It is the means by which the modern schoolmaster scores over his more old-fashioned brother, since he develops a boy to be efficient rather than scholarly, to have character rather than erudition—and that is what counts towards success in life.

By "efficiency" I don't mean mere money-making skill, but a general intelligence and capability to live a free, prosperous and happy life.

To preach "don't" is to incite the doing of wrong. Rather infuse the right spirit; as powder is to the shot so is spirit to action.

Direct moral instruction—like drill—produces a pleasing veneer, but unless there is properly seasoned character below this will not stand wear.

Lord Morley has said: "It is well known to the wise, but an everlasting puzzle to the foolish, that direct inculcation of morals should invariably prove so powerless an instrument, so futile a method."

Wise old Plato long ago gave us the right lead in education, and one which only now is beginning to be followed, when he said that there was innate good in every child, and the aim of education should be to develop these natural " instincts of virtue " through suitable practices. Here is no mention of reading, writing, and 'rithmetic as essentials, but of enlarging the natural instincts, *i.e.*, character by practices, not merely by precepts.

The average boy (if there is such a thing as an average boy) does not want to sit down and passively receive theoretical instruction. He wants to be up and actually doing things in practice, and this is a good lever to work upon if only the teacher will recognise it as the instrument ready to his hand.

Your first step then is to study the boy himself; to recognise his likes and dislikes, his good qualities and his bad, and to direct his training on these.

### The Attitude of the Cubmaster

There are two fundamental points to be considered in dealing with the Cubs. The first is that the only man who can hope for real success as a trainer of Cubs is the one who can be their " elder brother." The " commanding officer " is no good, and the " schoolmaster " is doomed to failure (though probably in neither case would the man recognise it himself, or admit it). This fact is being proved daily by the successful results obtained by our Cubmasters, many of whom, of course, are ladies.

By the term " elder brother " I mean one who can place himself on terms of comradeship with his boys, entering into their games and laughter himself, thereby winning their confidence and putting himself into that position which is essential for teaching, namely—where, by his own example, he leads them in the right direction instead of being a finger-post, often too high above their heads, merely pointing the way.

But do not misunderstand me and imagine that I ask the Cubmaster to be " soft " and " namby pamby." Far otherwise; comradeship necessitates firmness and straightness if it is to be of lasting value.

### The Make-up of the Cub

The second item to recognise, although it is of first importance, is that the boy of eight to ten is in every way quite different from the boy of eleven to fifteen. I don't mean that the change comes about with a bang in the tenth year, but the younger boy is growing relatively, in mind and body, more rapidly than the elder one, and the transition gradually comes about approximately at those ages in the average boy.

*Boyhood's Phases:*

6 to 8—Dramatic instinct and make believe.

8 to 11—Self-assertive individuality and rivalry.

11 to 15—Hero worship and co-operative loyalty.

It may be taken for granted that boys of Cub age have the following propensities, namely—to lie, to be selfish, to be cruel, and to be bombastic or pharisaical; but it must be at once recognised that these attributes are not born of malicious design, they are rather the natural outcome of the peculiar attitude of mind at that age. It has to be recognised that while the elder boy—he of Scout age—is full of hero-worship and eagerness to work in a gang under a good leader and in competition with other gangs, especially in chivalrous service, the younger boy, just emerging from the chrysalis of childhood, is more of an individual, feeling his feet, as it were, more self-centred, for the first time finding himself able to do things, anxious to do things himself and to make things, and the moment that he achieves a step of any kind he is prone to "show off."

He is only just out of the age of toys, and is still very much in the land of make-believe. He is eager to have, but not to give. He is at the most mouldable period of his life.

Thus there are many seeds of evil beginning to sprout into pliant tendrils ready to trail off in wrong directions, but easily taken in hand and trained aright.

The question which troubles many of us is, how can this best be done?

It is evident that the Cubmaster must be quick to recognise the evil points where they show themselves. The very usual process on the part of parents who have forgotten their childhood is at once to repress such propensities in the rare cases where they have been smart enough to recognise them; but repression is the very worst possible line to take. It is the cutting of shoots which makes them branch out into more devious growths; it tends to make the boy to lie more cunningly, to secrete his selfishness, and to put a better gloss on his hypocrisy.

The qualities shown at these three stages may be summarised as follows:—

| Up to 8 years. | 8 to 11. | Over 11. |
|---|---|---|
| DRAMATIC. | PERSONAL RIVALRY. | CO-OPERATION. |
| Dawning constructiveness | Individuality | Constructiveness |
| Make-believe | Constructiveness | Inventiveness |
| Fairy stories, etc. | Inquisitiveness | Team games |
| Extravagant humour | Eagerness for new experiences | Games with rules |
| | Absorption in new games | Discipline |
| | Collecting stamps, scraps, etc. | Hero-worship |
| | Romping, rowdy games | Romance |
| | Restlessness, mental | Adventure |
| | Restlessness, physical | Active virtues |
| | Cruelty | Sensitiveness |
| | Thoughtlessness | Dawning conscience etc. |
| | Fondness of showing off | Sense of pathos |
| | Brave deed stories | Sense of humour |
| | | Sense of sympathy |

Little boys are apt to bombast and hence to lie without any really vicious intent, but it is well to cure this habit in its early stages lest worse befall.

To cure lying it is well, when you nail a lie, not to abuse the boy for it, but merely to show that you are not taken in by it. Contempt will conquer some boys, and ridicule is pretty certain to cure others. Whenever he tries to lie again, some mild chaff to show him that the first lie is not forgotten will probably have a very wholesome effect. But, on the other hand, you have to be at pains to show that past misdeeds are not continually remembered against him, but that you trust him and have faith in him to conquer these signs of weakness.

Selflessness can be taught in a practical way by getting boys to give things away to others.

A youngster cannot naturally keep still for ten minutes—much less for hours as is sometimes expected of him in school.

We have to remember that he is suffering from the "growing itch," both mentally and physically. The best cure is to change the subject, let him out for a run, or for a war dance.

For his athletics do not be content to let him merely run about doing things, but help him with advice and, if you are not too fat, with example, how

| | |
|---|---|
| To run | To vault |
| To jump | To bowl |
| To throw | To catch, etc. |

These are really better for him physically and mentally than even Swedish Drill, as they are direct preparation for practical work in games, etc., while they are equally good in developing his organs and muscle by natural process.

The relation between Cubmaster and Cub has its analogy in the care of wolf cubs by the mother wolf, as described by W. J. Long in his book, *Northern Trails*, a book, by the way, from which many charming stories of wolf cubs in the jungle can be extracted for Wolf Cubs in the Den.

Of the mother wolf he writes:

" In the bright afternoons and long summer twilights she led the cubs forth on short journeys to hunt for themselves. No big caribou or cunning fox cub, as one might suppose, but ' rats and mice and such small deer ' were the limit of the mother's ambition for her little ones. . . . It was astonishing how quickly the cubs learned that game is not to be picked up tamely like huckleberries, and changed their style of hunting—creeping, instead of trotting openly so that even a porcupine must notice them, hiding behind rocks and bushes till the precise moment came, and then leaping with the swoop of a goshawk on a ptarmigan.

" A wolf that cannot catch a grasshopper has no business hunting rabbits—this seemed to be the unconscious motive that led the old mother, every sunny afternoon, to ignore the thickets where game was hiding plentifully, and take her cubs to the dry sunny plains on the edge of the Caribou Barrens.

" There for hours at a time they hunted elusive grasshoppers, rushing helter-skelter over the dry moss, leaping up to strike at the flying game with their paws like a kitten, or snapping wildly to catch it in their mouths and coming down with a back-breaking wriggle to keep themselves from tumbling over on their heads.

" Then on again, with a droll expression and noses sharpened like exclamation points, to find another grasshopper.

" Small business indeed and often ludicrous this playing at grasshopper hunting."

So it seems to us; so also perhaps to the wise old mother who knew all the ways of game, from crickets to caribou and from ground sparrows to wild geese.

But *play is the first great educator*—that is as true of animals as of men—and to the cubs their rough helter-skelter after hoppers was as exciting as a stag hunt to the pack, as full of surprises as the wild chase through the soft snow after a litter of lynx kittens.

And though they knew it not, they were learning things every hour of the sunny playful afternoons that they would remember and find useful all the days of their life.

And so it is with our Wolf Cubs. We teach them small things in play which will eventually fit them for doing big things in earnest.

The great principle for dealing with the Wolf Cub Pack, and one by which the youngsters can be attracted and their failings remedied is by making the Cubs into a happy family—not a family but a HAPPY family.

Boys want noise: let them have it. When they play let them play heartily, if the Cubmaster has the sense to organise his programme that way.

*Laughter essential.*—We have advocated in the Scout training the development of the Scout Smile as a necessary adjunct; with the Cubs the smile should be a laugh. Laughter counteracts most of the evils of the very young and makes for cheery companionship and open-mindedness. *The boy who laughs much lies little.*

## How to Run a Pack

Having considered the make-up of the younger boy and the spirit in which to deal with him—and this is a step of first importance towards success in training him—let me offer a few suggestions on the organisation and training of a Pack.

Be content to begin with only a few boys. One is too often tempted to make a start with a large Pack. To do so is to make a mistake.

You want first of all to establish the right tone on a small scale; to have a handful of yeast to leaven the lump when you get it.

Even then do not go for too big a Pack. I have found by experience that eighteen is as many as I can deal with in giving individual training. Allowing for your being much more capable, I suggest that twenty-four is as large a Pack as any man can adequately train.

Of course you can easily *drill* a hundred and twenty-four, but that is not *training* them.

### ORGANISATION

*The Six System.*—Scout Troops are divided into Patrols—Cub Packs into Sixes.

A Six consists of six boys under the charge of a Sixer who is helped by a Second. These leaders should only be given actual responsibility in leading and in teaching under the Cubmaster's direct supervision. A Sixer is *not* a "junior Patrol Leader" and should not be looked upon as capable of taking charge of or of training his Six.

Most Cubmasters consider that a Sixer should be a Two-Star Cub before he is actually invested with his second armlet, and that a Second should, at least, have won his First Star.

Cubmasters are advised to run a Sixers' Council and a Sixers' Instruction Meeting. A Sixers' Council consists of the Cubmaster, the Assistant Cubmaster, the Sixers, and sometimes the Seconds. It is a body which holds regular but very informal meetings at which the plans of the Pack are discussed, and the Cubmaster has an opportunity of correcting, or praising, and of advising his leaders.

The Instruction Meeting generally follows immediately after the Sixers' Council Meeting—the two taking about three-quarters of an hour in all. At this, old work is revised and new work done. Most Cubs having very short and faulty memories, a Cubmaster who wants to have good helpers—because that is what Sixers really are—must give them some such time to themselves.

*Meetings.*—Meet as often as you can on fixed days and at fixed hours. Punctuality on the part of the boys should be a test not so much of their obedience as their eagerness to be there for fear of missing a good thing. Punctuality on your own part is even more necessary.

Have your programme of doings prepared beforehand.

There must be no pausing to think what you will do next, and the boys should learn anything but idling.

Have no onlookers or boys awaiting their turn. Every Cub should be busy all the time, at work or play. Remember the young mind at that age cannot stick at a thing for long. Frequent change with variety and contrast should distinguish your programme. Play is the most important thing of life to a boy, so have plenty of games.

Insist on smartness in little things—by praise and not by punishment—in such details of dress, neatness of scarves, and especially alertness of carriage and readiness in saluting.

Keep right away from any form of military drill. " Forming fours," except when playing O'Grady, should be " taboo " at a Pack Meeting. The circle is the Cub formation—not the rank, and you can get a circle easily enough if your Cubs understand the call " Pack! Pack! Pack! ! "

Meetings should start and end with the Grand Howl, and the following outline programme is just an example of what has been found to work successfully:—

| | |
|---|---|
| Start. | Grand Howl. Flag break. |
| 5 minutes. | Inspection of uniform, etc. Collection of subscriptions. |
| 10 „ | Mentally and physically active game, e.g., a round game for the Pack, or relay races. |
| 15 „ | Six work under Sixers, Old Wolves supervising. |
| 10 „ | Quieter games, or play-acting, or a jungle dance. |
| 10 „ | Instruction under Old Wolves. |
| 5 „ | Quiet game. |
| 5 „ | Yarn. |
| End. | Any ceremonies. Grand Howl. Flag down. Pack Prayers. |

*Ceremonies.*—The two most important Cub ceremonies are the Investiture and the Going-Up. These should *never* be performed in any haphazard fashion. Outline schemes for them will be found in Bites 6 and 15. A Cubmaster can make any small Pack variations that may appeal to him and to his Cubs, provided that the main outline is adhered to, and that every care is taken to keep the ceremonies within the understanding of the Cubs. Over-elaboration generally means fidgeting. Simplicity and solemnity should be the keynotes of all Cub ceremonies.

*Parents.*—A great help to success is to be in touch with the parents of your Cubs, to consult their ideas, and most especially to interest them by explaining your reason for the different steps you are taking. You should visit them at least once a year, invite them to Pack functions and camps, and get their help with the boy's Cub work at home.

*Records.*—Every Pack should have its own properly kept Register—showing the Cub history of each member—and a simple Log Book will be interesting reading in the future. Each Sixer can have his own Six Book in which to enter the attendance and the subscriptions of his Six, but one of the Old Wolves will need to " keep an eye on it " for him.

*Accounts.*—Cubmasters must see that Pack Accounts are kept, and, where boys' subscriptions are concerned, the boys have the right to inspect the accounts. It is as well to put someone definitely in charge of this side of Pack organisation, and to co-ordinate matters with the other sections of the Group. If any outside subscriptions are received, a Committee must be formed —probably in conjunction with the Group—to deal with these.

### Training

*Story-telling.*—The Cubmaster can command rapt attention at any time by telling his Cubs a story, and through it he can convey the lesson he wants to inculcate. It is a gilding to the pill which never fails—if the teller is any good at all.

The story must be told in an easy, unstilted way and with some dramatic accompaniment—the high voice of the old woman, the whining voice of the jackal, the snarling voice of the tiger, and hand action to illustrate the creeping of the snake, or the fists of the fighter shot out. But be careful not to overdo this so that the Cubs rivet their attention on your actions instead of your words.

Above all, don't let the run of the story be interrupted when all are agog to hear the climax—no questions to or from the audience—carry them along with you to the big sigh of excited repletion at the end.

Occasionally it may be a good plan even to *read* a good yarn. If this is properly done, the Cubs can be got to appreciate the value of good books. Telling a yarn is, however, always better than reading one.

You will find Gearing's *It's Time for a Story* (B.S.A. 5/-) very helpful.

*Play-acting.*—Another valuable and ever popular form of character education is that of dressing-up and play-acting.

Sometimes this is useful in connection with the stories told. I need scarcely try to count up the various points of development which underlie it, such as self-expression, concentration of mind, voice development, imagination, pathos, humour, poise, discipline, historical or moral instruction, loss of self-consciousness, and so on. The Cubmaster will recognise these for himself the moment that he realises what a mine of help acting provides for him, and how the Cubs, being at a dramatic and make-believe age, will meet his efforts half-way. Charades and impromptu plays are just as good in their way as more highly designed and rehearsed shows.

*Games.*—In Part I, I have merely indicated in each of the steps of training an example or two of games and practices, but this is not in any way intended as a full or complete list. I leave that to the ingenuity of the Cubmaster.

But it should be understood that in this direction lies a great means to success, especially if games can be thought of in relation to their moral and physical benefits to the boys and grouped accordingly on some such principle as this:—

*For discipline and Co-operation.*—Team games such as:—

| | |
|---|---|
| Rounders | Basket Ball |
| Football | Hockey |

*Concentration of mind and effort.*—Ball-catching, Marbles, Stepping-stones, Skipping.

*Observation.*—Kim's Game, Thimble-hunting, Tracking, Leaf-hunting.

*Construction.*—Kite-flying, Model aeroplanes, Six models.

*Finger-craft.*—Knots, Paper-gliders, Combination pictures (for screens, scrap-books), Homecraft.

*Physical.*—Climbing, Hop, step and jump, Ball throwing, somersaults, relay races of all kinds.

*Eyesight.*—Far and Near, Patterns, How many? And so on.

When used with such ends in view games are, as education for young boys, equal to hours spent in schooling.

*Pack Holidays and Cub Camps.*—This is a most valuable opportunity in the study of Cubs, for in a few days you will learn more about them than in many months of ordinary meetings, and you can influence them in matters of character, cleanliness, and health in such a way as may form lasting habits.

It must not be forgotten, however, that Pack holidays and camp are amongst the most serious responsibilities that a Cubmaster can undertake. It is no light thing to take young children from their homes and to make yourself entirely responsible for them for the time they are with you.

Camp is not essential for Cubs as it is for Scouts and it is far better not to attempt camp at all unless you have all the facilities and experience which are necessary. It can also be said that Pack Holidays are not essential. But there are many advantages, some of which are mentioned above. In any case it is advisable only to take part of the Pack—the older and more responsible boys. Pack Holidays and camp should not last too long. It is an enormous strain on those in a position of responsibility, and by carrying it on too long you may even dull the keenness of the boys. A week is the outside period, and a long week-end, say from Friday night to Tuesday or Wednesday morning, is quite sufficient. Again, it is not advisable to take Cubs too far from home. A short distance is a big enough adventure for them and if you are far from their homes you may be faced by really serious difficulties in case of illness or any kind of accident.

In Pack Holidays, when the Cubs sleep in a building, conditions are easier than when they are under canvas, but there must be at least *two* warranted Scouters, one of whom must be a C.M., D.C.M., or A.D.C. Wolf Cubs. More help is needed when Cubs are under canvas and so it is laid down that there should be at least one adult for every six Cubs in camp, excluding the Scouter in charge. A minimum of three adults is always desirable and they must be warranted in the same way as they have to be for Pack Holidays. In this way one Old Wolf can take the general responsibility, another can attend to the cooking and the third will see to the amusement of the Cubs.

Mixed camps of Cubs and Scouts are not approved and are undoubtedly bad for all concerned.

You will find two books in the *Scouter* Series: *Camping for Cubs* and *Pack Holidays* a great help in advising you what to do and what to avoid.

Remember you are making yourself responsible for the safety, comfort and health of your Cubs and that you must not let them suffer by reason of your inexperience. Learn how things ought to be done; plan everything beforehand; arrange every detail; leave nothing to chance; and as far as is humanly possible provide against accident or emergency. A good Pack Holiday or camp *may* be of lasting value to your Cubs. A bad one *will* be a lasting reproach to you, your Pack and probably to the whole Movement. It is better to train your boys by methods possibly less attractive and slower than to risk doing them harm.

Finally, don't attempt to run either until you have had some experience and understanding of the difficulties and responsibilities. You must have the necessary knowledge and practical experience before you take your own boys.

### Summing Up

The idea is through:—

*Handicrafts*, to develop application, constructiveness, etc.

*Nature study*, to develop observation, religion, kindness to animals.

*Games*, to develop laughter, good nature, and comradeship.

*Athletics*, to utilise individual emulation for physical development.

*Team Games*, to develop unselfishness, discipline, esprit de corps.

In conclusion, let me say the scheme which I have suggested has purposely been left sketchy in many of its details. It is merely an outline on which a Cubmaster can build his own course of training.

The essential is that the aim and spirit as here indicated should be thoroughly grasped. I do not want Cubmasters to feel themselves otherwise fettered by traditions, rules and syllabuses.

Their own experience and imagination, their own boyishness and sympathy with boy nature will be their best guide.

A point is not to introduce the Boy Scout training directly into that of the Cubs. It is not adapted to them, and it would tend to rob the Cub of his ambition ultimately to be promoted to the higher grade of Scout.

I hope, therefore, that this Handbook will be found to be of use to Cubmasters, not only by suggesting lines of activity and the reasons for them, but also by showing to them that the difficulties which may at first strike them as being mountains are, when properly negotiated and contested, merely mole-hills, and that the work involved is as fascinating to the instructor as it is valuable to the young lives in his charge and to the future citizenhood of the British Commonwealth and Empire.

# APPENDIX

*All Commissioners, Secretaries of Local Associations, Cubmasters, and other Scouters must possess a copy of " Policy, Organisation, and Rules of the Boy Scouts Association " (Price 2/-, from Imperial Headquarters, 25, Buckingham Palace Road, London, S.W.1), which embodies all the Rules for Wolf Cubs. A copy of this pamphlet is issued free to every Group from time to time.*

*The following general instructions are based on the Rules:—*

## The Scout Group

A COMPLETE Scout Group consists of a Wolf Cub Pack, a Scout Troop, and a Rover Scout Crew, with the addition, if desired, of a Senior Scout Troop, but may at any given time consist of one or more sections only. Each Group should have a Group Scoutmaster.

## The Cubmaster

A Cubmaster is a person who holds a Cubmaster's warrant, issued by the Boy Scouts Association, and who is in charge or in joint charge of the Pack of the registered Group indicated on his warrant.

When a Cubmaster ceases to have charge, or joint charge, of a Pack, his warrant lapses, and should be returned to Imperial Headquarters through the proper channels.

The qualifications for Cubmaster are as follows:—

(*a*) A general knowledge of the *Wolf Cub's Handbook*, of *Scouting or Boys*, and of *Policy, Organisation, and Rules of the Boy Scouts Association.*

(*b*) A full appreciation of the religious and moral aim underlying the scheme of Scouting.

(*c*) Personal standing and character such as will ensure a good moral influence over the boys, and sufficient steadfastness of purpose to carry out the work with energy and perseverance.

(*d*) Age not less than twenty.

(*e*) Ability to obtain the use of some sort of club-room for Club meetings.

(*f*) Three month's probationary service with a Pack.

Cubmasters are recommended by the Local Association, and must be approved by the District Commissioner before receiving a warrant from the Chief Scout. Ladies are eligible for this rank.

Where a Pack is attached to a Group, though the Group Scoutmaster will exercise general supervision, he will delegate the fullest amount of responsibility in the actual management of the Pack to the Cubmaster.

*Assistant Cubmasters.*—The qualifications are the same as for Cubmaster except for the provision of a room and that an age of 18 years only is required. Ladies are also eligible for this rank

UNIFORM

*Male Cubmaster's Uniform.*

Hat. Khaki (four dents), flat brim, leather band round crown, and lace worn at back of head and tied in front on the brim of the hat.

Scarf. Of the Group colour worn with a woggle (other than Gilwell pattern).

Shirt. Dark blue, khaki, green or grey, with two patch pockets (buttoned), and shoulder straps optional; or a jersey or sweater of the same colours.

Shorts. Dark blue, khaki or grey.

Belt. Brown leather or web.

Stockings. Any plain colour; worn turned down below knee with green tabbed garter showing on outside.

Boots or shoes. Brown or black.

Shoulder badge. Indicating the Group; worn on right shoulder or on both, according to the custom of the Group.

County and other emblem. If and as authorised under Rules 342-345.

A shoulder knot, if any, worn by a Scouter in accordance with Part VIII (P.O.R.) is of the colour appropriate to his rank as therein specified.

If desired on appropriate occasions, a khaki uniform coat or tunic with khaki shirt and collar, may be worn.

With a uniform coat or tunic a green tie must, or with an ordinary jacket may, be worn instead of a scarf.

Trousers, or breeches with stockings, are permissible.

A walking stick or thumbstick may be carried on appropriate occasions.

*Lady Cubmaster's Uniform.*

The following uniform is worn by Lady Cubmasters and Assistant Cubmasters:

Beret of Scout green colour or Scoutmaster's hat (four dents): Any one of the following in khaki, green, blue or grey (1) coat, with or without belt of same material, skirt and shirt of same colour, *or* (2) shirt or jersey, and skirt with Scout belt, *or* (3) one-piece frock with Scout belt; scarf of Group colour or green tie; brown, khaki, or black stockings; brown or black shoes or boots; shoulder badge indicating Group on right shoulder or on both, according to custom of Group; county and other emblem, if and as authorised; stick or thumb-stick, plain overcoat or mackintosh, lanyard, haversack or rucsack and knife are optional.

*Cubmaster's Badge.*—A Wolf head, in circle of green enamel, worn on the front of the hat or, on the beret, over the left eye-brow. Tenderfoot or Wolf-head pin when in mufti.

Assistant Cubmasters wear similar badges in red enamel. The Tenderfoot Badge must be worn on the left breast of shirt, jersey or tunic, provided the wearer has taken the Scout Promise.

This ruling came into force on July 1st, 1947. Those holding warrants before that date may, if they so desire, continue to wear the Wolf's head badge as stated in P.O.R. Rule 304.

*Cub Instructors.*—Scouts or Guides of 15 or over acting as regular instructors to Wolf Cub Packs are entitled to wear a wolf's head in green, on a khaki ground, on the left breast. The badge is granted on the recommendation of the Cubmaster.

Girls of 16 and over who are not Guides, with the approval of the G.S.M. and D.C., may, after a probation period of six months, be invested as Scouts, and wear a C.I. badge on a green beret and appropriate Cub Scouter's uniform.

## Starting a Pack

A person possessing the qualifications described on page 239 and desiring to form a Pack of Wolf Cubs should communicate with the Secretary of the Local Scout Association. (If any difficulty is found in ascertaining the address of the Local Secretary, the Secretary at Imperial Headquarters will furnish this.)

If a Scout Group already exists, the Group Scoutmaster should be asked to apply for the approval of the District Commissioner and of the Local Association to the formation of a Pack within it.

(Fuller information will be found in a pamphlet entitled " How to Start a Wolf Cub Pack," obtainable free of charge from Imperial Headquarters.)

## Warrants

A Cubmaster is not eligible for a warrant signed by the Chief Scout until he has served three months with a Pack. At the end of this time he should apply for a warrant through his Local Secretary, but in all cases both the Secretary and the District Commissioner should be kept fully informed of what is being done from the very beginning.

## Training

The newcomer to the ranks of the Old Wolves has to-day tremendous opportunities for learning the job. Training facilities have developed to a point where a very great deal of practical help and guidance is available to all, and it is expected that Scouters will avail themselves of the opportunities. Perhaps the best training of all is to work as an assistant to an experienced Akela and the newcomer to Cubbing should always seek the advice and the practical help of those working nearby who have been in the game for some years. This is part of the scheme of pre-Warrant training, which is now a necessary qualification for a Warrant.

Beyond that nearly all counties now offer frequent Preliminary Courses which, apart from being very good fun, do set the new Scouter on the well-tried road that experience has shown needs to be followed if Cubbing is to be interpreted on the basis of this Handbook. Then there is the Wood Badge, one of the goals at which every Scouter should aim. Fullest information about Training Courses can always be obtained by writing to the Camp Chief at Gilwell Park and it is hoped and, indeed, expected that in accepting a Warrant you are resolved to seize every chance for equipping yourself better to do the job.

### Correspondence

All correspondence with Imperial Headquarters (regarding warrants, badges, or any other matter) should be carried on through the District Commissioner, and not directly by the Cubmaster. [Orders for equipment may, however, be addressed direct to the Quartermaster at Imperial Headquarters.]

### Packs

The Cubmaster should have at least one Assistant Cubmaster to ensure continuity. If the Pack consists of more than three Sixes, an additional Assistant Cubmaster is desirable. Except in special circumstances, a Pack should not consist of more than 36 boys.

A Group Committee must be formed to assist the Group with finance, with propaganda, in obtaining club-rooms, camping grounds, etc., and to be responsible for Group property. Separate Pack Sub-Committees are sometimes formed as a part of the Group Committee.

### Sixes

Sixes consist of five Cubs and a Sixer. They are named after the colours of wolves (i.e., grey, white, black, brown, tawny, and red), and the Cubs are marked as belonging to the different Sixes by wearing a small triangular piece of cloth of Six colour, sewn firmly at the top of the left arm, just below shoulder, with point upwards. Sixers are marked by two armlets of yellow braid, ½ inch wide, and 1 inch apart, worn above the left elbow. Seconds wear one armlet.

### Uniform

The officially recognised Wolf Cub uniform is as follows:—

*Cap.*—Green with yellow piping, with cloth Wolf's head badge in front.

*Scarf.*—Of the Group colour, worn with a woggle other than Gilwell pattern.

*Jersey.*—Dark blue, khaki, green, or grey; sleeves down or rolled up at the discretion of the Cubmaster.

*Shorts.*—Dark blue, khaki, or grey.

*Stockings.*—Any plain colour; worn turned down below the knee, with green tabbed garter showing on the outside.

*Boots or Shoes.*—Brown or black.

*Shoulder Patch.*—Small, triangular piece of cloth of Six colour, sewn firmly at the top of the left sleeve, just below shoulder, point upwards.

*Shoulder Badge.*—Indicating Group, worn on right shoulder or on both, according to the custom of the Group.

*County or other Emblem.*—If and as authorised.

*Great-coats, Haversacks, or Mackintoshes.*—(Optional).

(Nothing but the above may be worn visibly.)

### Examiners

The First and Second Stars are granted to Cubs on the recommendation of the Cubmaster. The Proficiency Badges can only be granted when the Cubs have been passed in the tests by at least one qualified and independent examiner, approved by the Local Association.

### Badges

*The Wolf Cub Badge*, which is granted by the Local Association on the recommendation of the Cubmaster, must be worn, in cloth form, by all grades of Wolf Cubs in uniform on the front of the cap and on the left breast of the jersey. It is also issued in the form of a brass button-hole badge which should be worn in mufti.

Only such Proficiency Badges as are described in Part II, Chapter I, of this Handbook are open to Wolf Cubs. Badges of rank and Proficiency Badges and Decorations are the registered designs of the Association, and are copyright. They can only be obtained from Imperial Headquarters through the Local Association.

*Service Stars.*—Cubs may wear a six-pointed metal badge with yellow cloth background on the left breast above the Wolf Cub Badge to show length of service. When drafted up into the Scouts, Cubs wear this star on the left breast.

### Religious Policy

The following policy has received the approval of the heads of the leading religious bodies in the United Kingdom:—

(1) It is expected that every *Scout* shall belong to some religious body and attend its services.

(2) If at any time a *Scout* does not belong to a religious body, the Scouter must endeavour to put him in touch with one, which should, if possible, be that to which his parents belong or into which he may in the past have been baptized or otherwise admitted; the approval of the parents of the *Scout* must be obtained.

(3) If a Group is composed of members of one particular form of religion, it is the duty of the G.S.M. to encourage the attendance of all members of the Group at such religious instruction and observances as the Sponsoring Authority may consider desirable. See also Rule 180 (2).

(4) If a Group is composed of members of various forms of religion they should be encouraged to attend the services of their own form of religion, and Group Church Parades should not be held. In camp any form of daily prayer or divine service should be of the simplest character, attendance being voluntary.

(5) Where it is not permissible under a rule of the religion of any *Scout* to attend religious observances other than those of his own form of religion, the Scouters of the Group must see that such a rule is strictly observed while the *Scout* is under their control.

The Sponsoring Authority is responsible in certain cases under Rule 10 (2) for the religious training of the *Scouts*; and in all cases must undertake the general support and encouragement of the Group and endeavour to maintain its continuity. In no case is the Sponsoring Authority, as such, concerned in matters of *Scout* training, for which the G.S.M. is responsible to the L.A. and D.C.

### Pack Holidays and Camps

When a Pack proposes to camp outside its own District, at least 21 days' notice must be given by the Scouter in charge to his District Commissioner, who will inform the Secretary of the County in which the camp is to be held (who will inform the Commissioner of the District to be visited).

In the case of a Cubmaster or Assistant Cubmaster wishing to take Cubs to camp for the first time, or after an adverse report has been received on a previous camp, the preliminary permission of the District Commissioner should be sought at least three months before the proposed commencement of the camp, and before any intimation of the camp has been given to either Cubs or parents. The D.C. in any case must not give permission unless he is satisfied that the C.M. or A.C.M. has acquired the necessary knowledge and practical experience. In the same way, when giving permission for Pack Holidays the D.C. must be satisfied with the leadership and accommodation. In both cases the special Camping Permit (Wolf Cubs) must be used.

No Cubs may go on Pack Holidays or to camp without the previous permission of the District Commissioner.

Save in exceptional circumstances, and with the specific consent of the District Commissioner, Cubs and Scouts may not camp together.

On Pack Holidays Cubs must sleep in a Group Headquarters, Church Hall or other suitable building. When camping, some form of clean, permanent shelter, or a weather-proof marquee, large enough to accommodate all the Cubs in camp in case of wet weather, must be available. If a marquee is used as a permanent shelter it must be additional to the tents in which the Cubs sleep.

Enough sleeping bags or blankets must be provided to enable each Cub to make up a separate bed.

Camp raiding is strictly prohibited.

### PUBLICATIONS

The *Scout* (price 6d.) has Wolf Cub pages every week. *The Scouter*, a monthly magazine for Scouters, contains material for Cubmasters, and all official notifications (10s. 6d. per annum, by post from Imperial Headquarters, or from any newsagent).

# BIBLIOGRAPHY

How to Run a Pack, by " Gilcraft " (Pearson, 5/-).

Wolf Cubs, by " Gilcraft " (Pearson, 6/-).

Games for Cubs, " New Gilcraft Series—No. 4." (Pearson, 8/6).

It's Time for Another Story, by J. B. Gearing (B.S.A. 5/-).

Pack Holidays and Cub Camping (Scouter Series Nos. 14 & 15, 1/- each).

Duty to God in the Wolf Cub Pack, by Hazel Addis (B.S.A. 5/-).

Jungle Dances and their Variations (B.S.A. 6d.).

Jungle Animals and Totem Poles (B.S.A. 6d.).

Cubbing: a Word to Parents (B.S.A. 2/6d. per doz.).

How to Start a Pack (B.S.A. 6d. each).

## BOY SCOUTS, ORGANISATION CHART

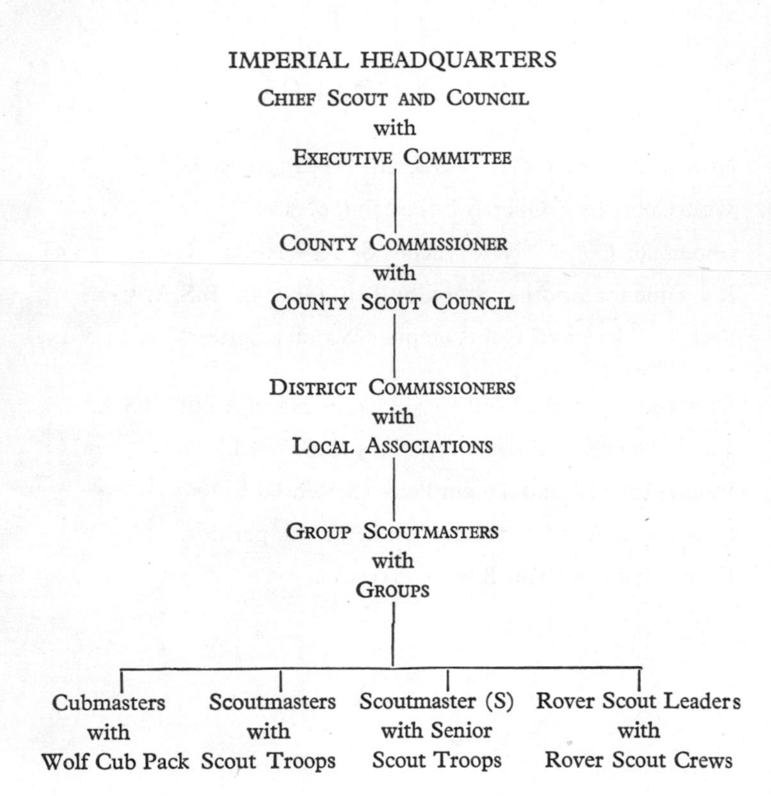

# INDEX